FRED BASSET YEARBOOK 2009

Summersdale Publishers Ltd
46 West Street
Chichester
West Sussex
PO19 1RP
UK

www.summersdale.com

Printed and bound in Malta

Drawings by Alex Graham and Michael Martin

ISBN: 978-1-84024-778-7

Substantial discounts on bulk quantities of Summersdale books are available to corporations, professional associations and other organisations.
For details telephone Summersdale Publishers on (+44-1243-771107), fax (+44-1243-786300) or email (nicky@summersdale.com).

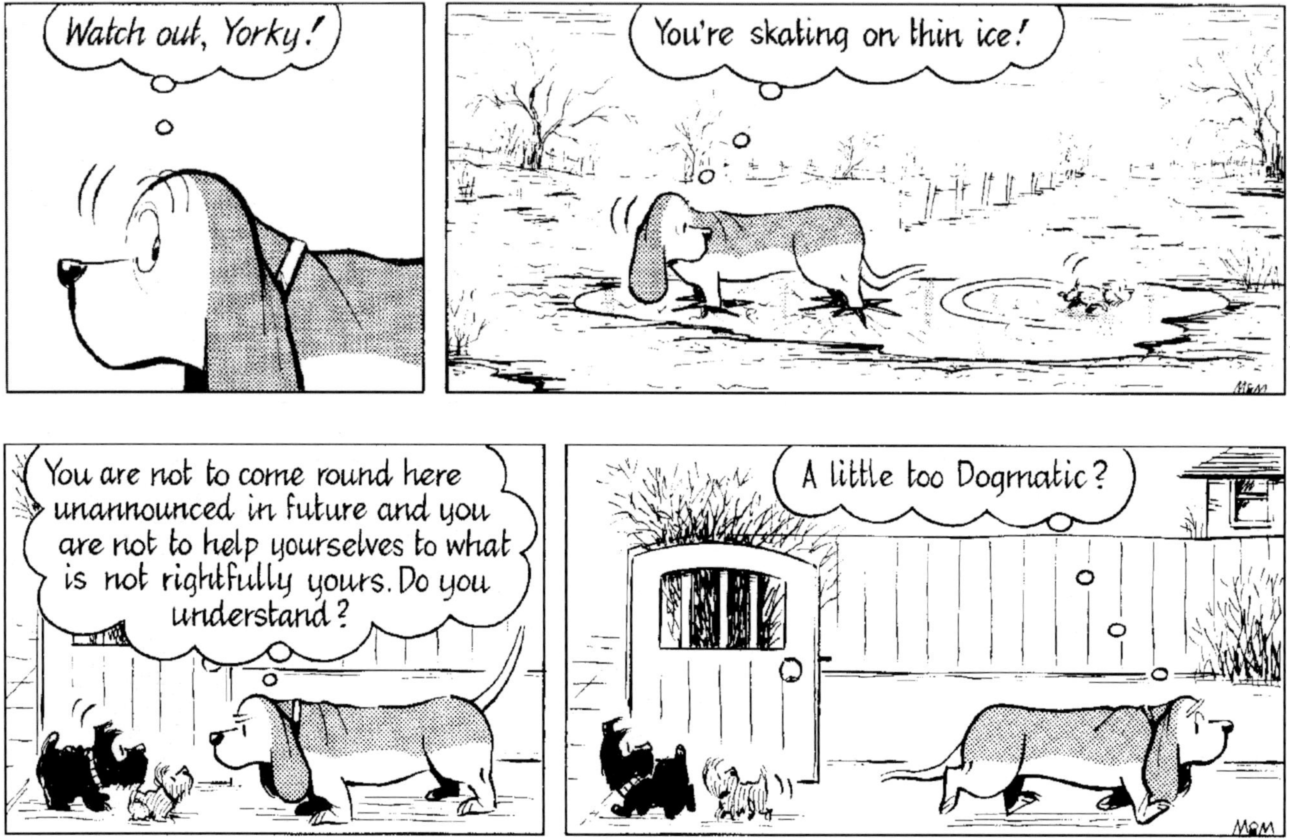
Watch out, Yorky!
You're skating on thin ice!
You are not to come round here unannounced in future and you are not to help yourselves to what is not rightfully yours. Do you understand?
A little too Dogmatic?

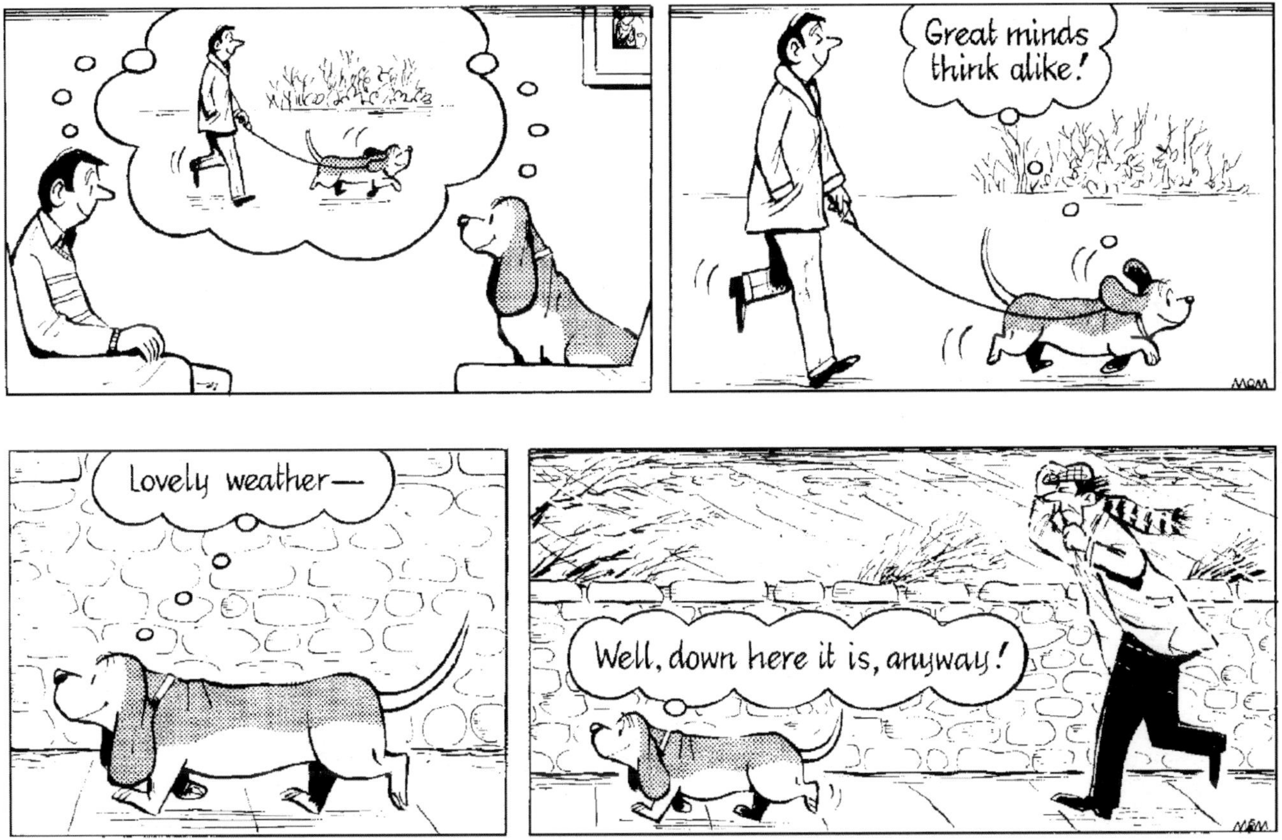
Great minds think alike!
lovely weather—
Well, down here it is, anyway!

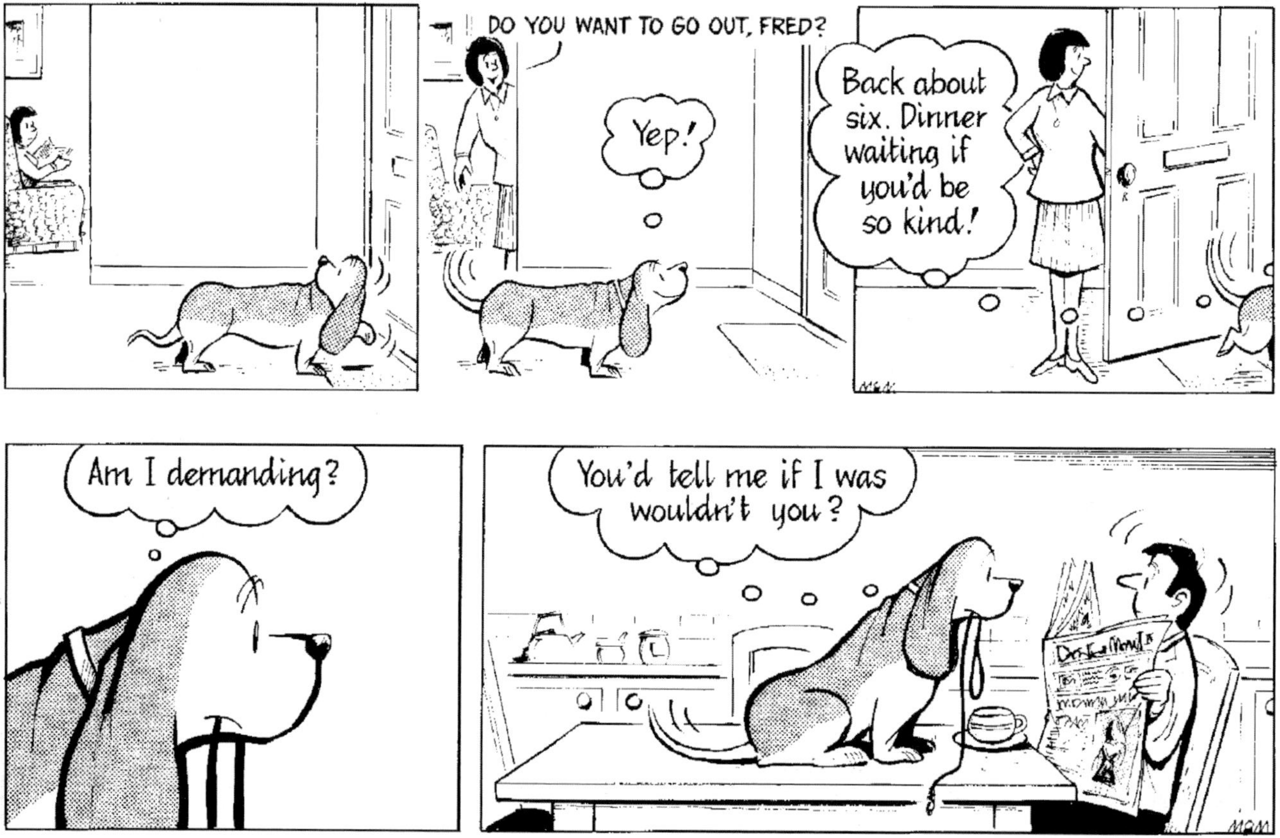
DO YOU WANT TO GO OUT, FRED?
Yep!
Back about six. Dinner waiting if you'd be so kind!
Am I demanding?
You'd tell me if I was wouldn't you?

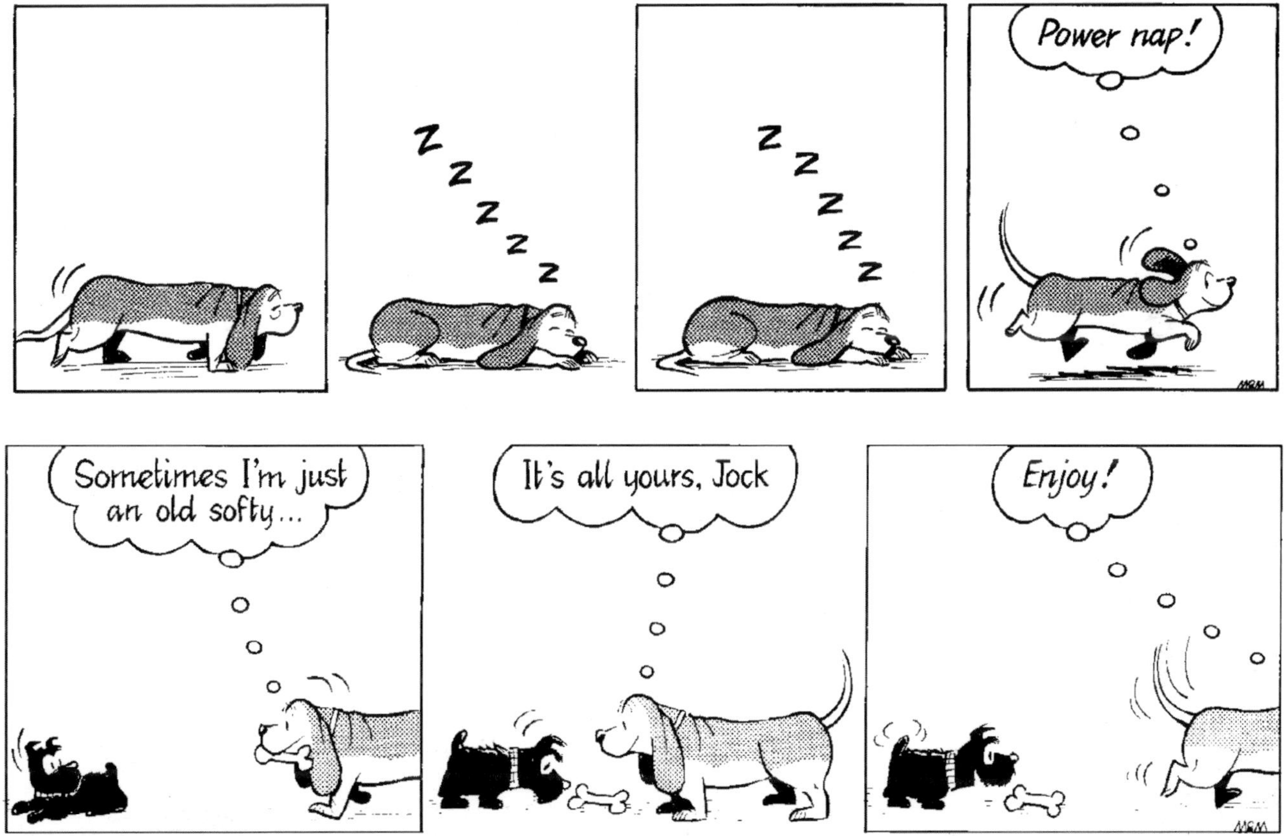
Power nap!
Sometimes I'm just an old softy...
It's all yours, Jock
Enjoy!

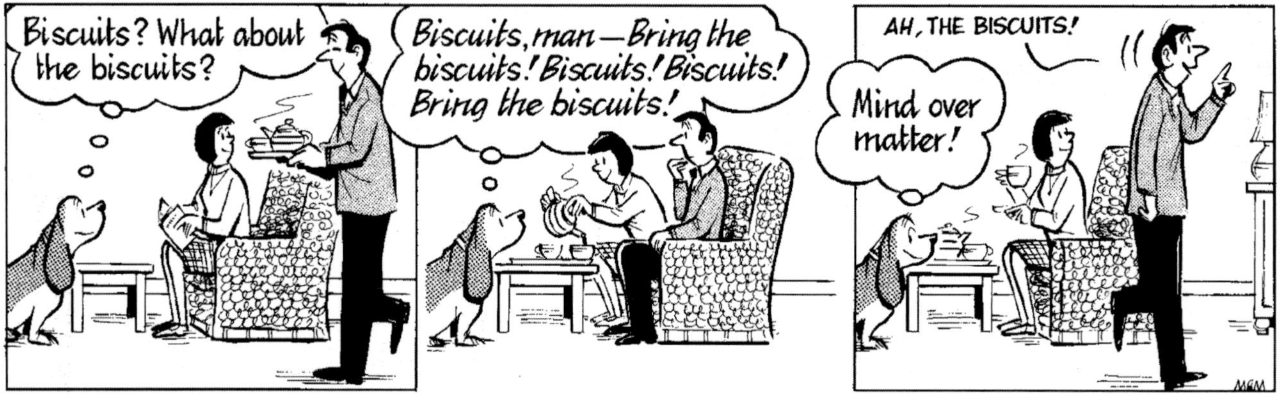
Biscuits? What about the biscuits?
Biscuits, man—Bring the biscuits! Biscuits! Biscuits! Bring the biscuits!
AH, THE BISCUITS!
Mind over matter!

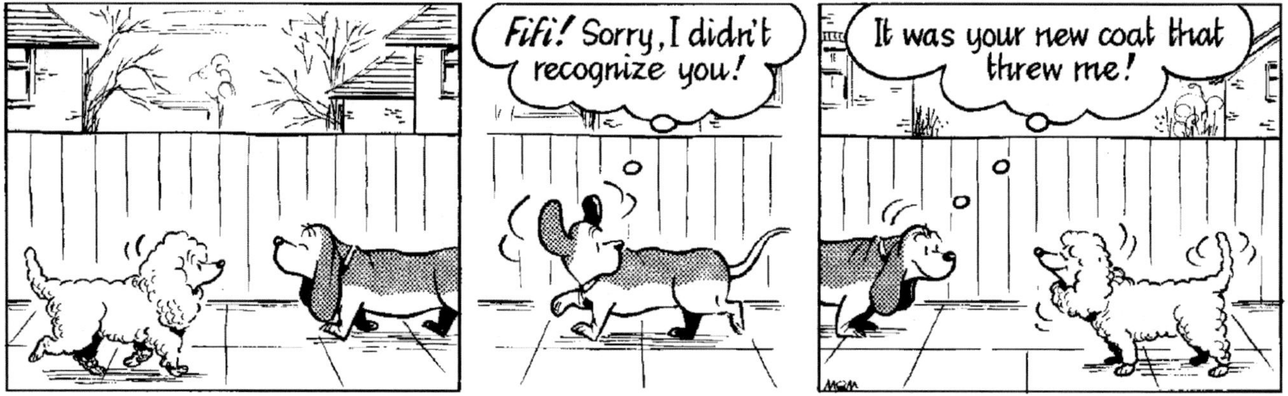
Fifi! Sorry, I didn't recognize you!
It was your new coat that threw me!

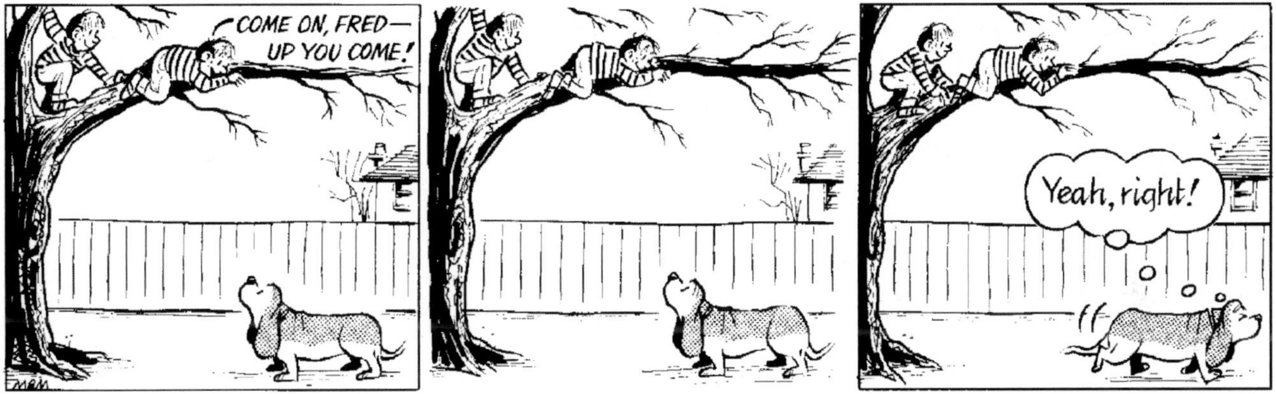
COME ON, FRED—
UP YOU COME!
Yeah, right!

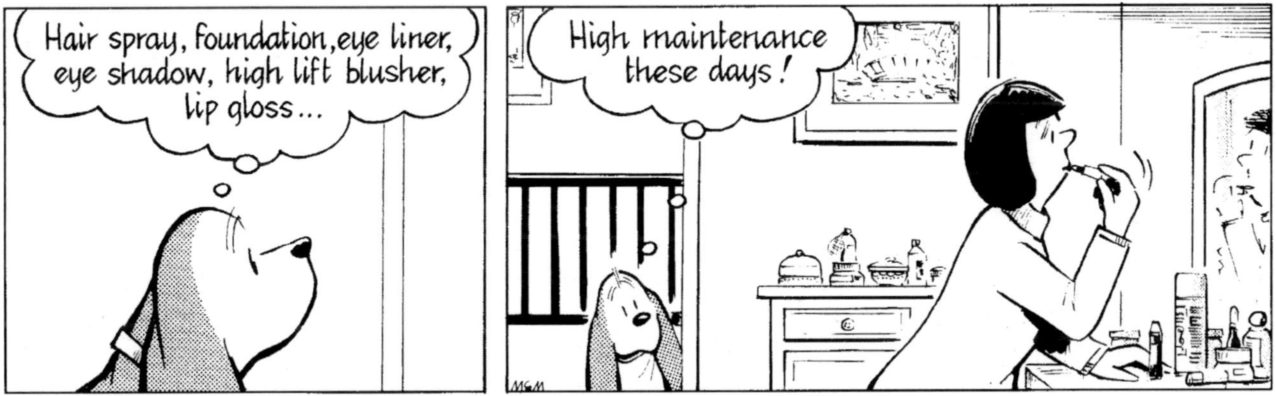
Hair spray, foundation, eye liner, eye shadow, high lift blusher, lip gloss...
High maintenance these days!

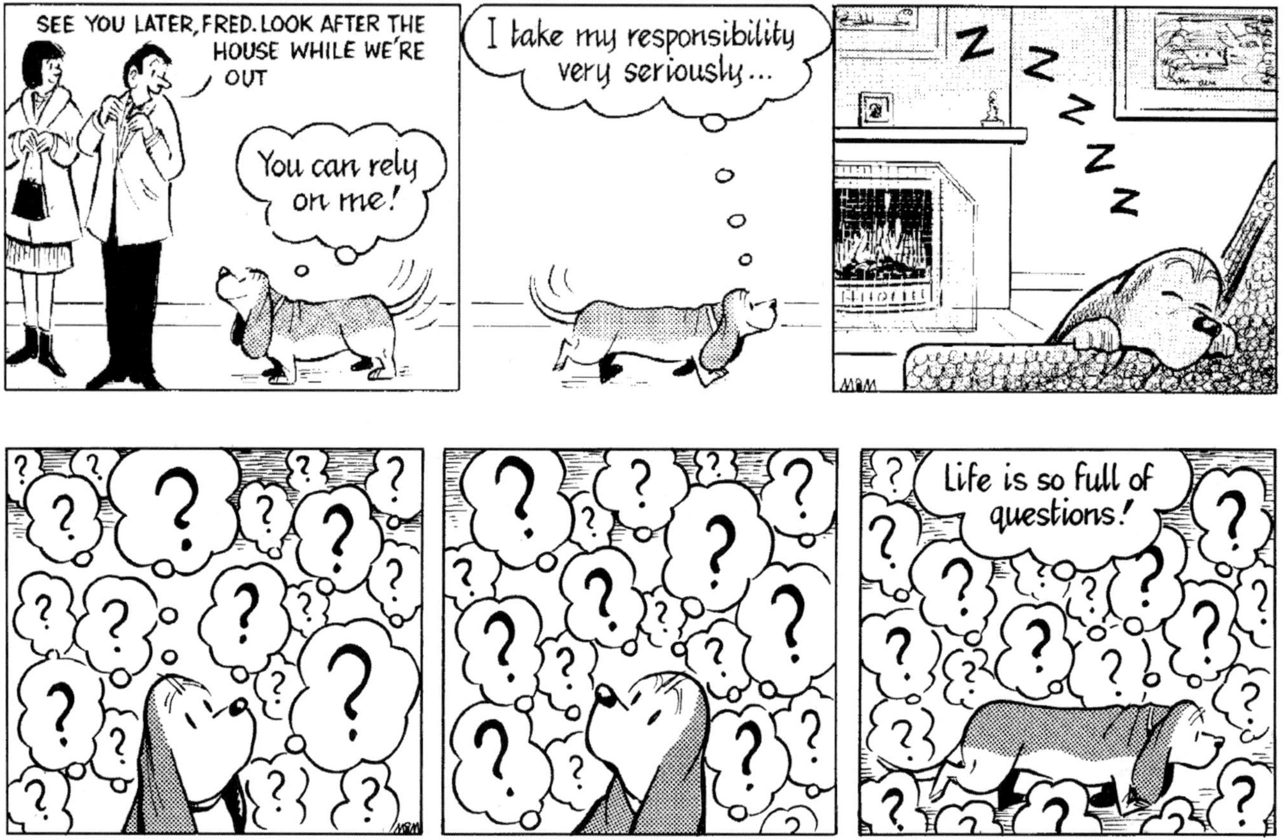
SEE YOU LATER, FRED. LOOK AFTER THE HOUSE WHILE WE'RE OUT
You can rely on me!
I take my responsibility very seriously...
Z Z Z Z Z
Life is so full of questions!

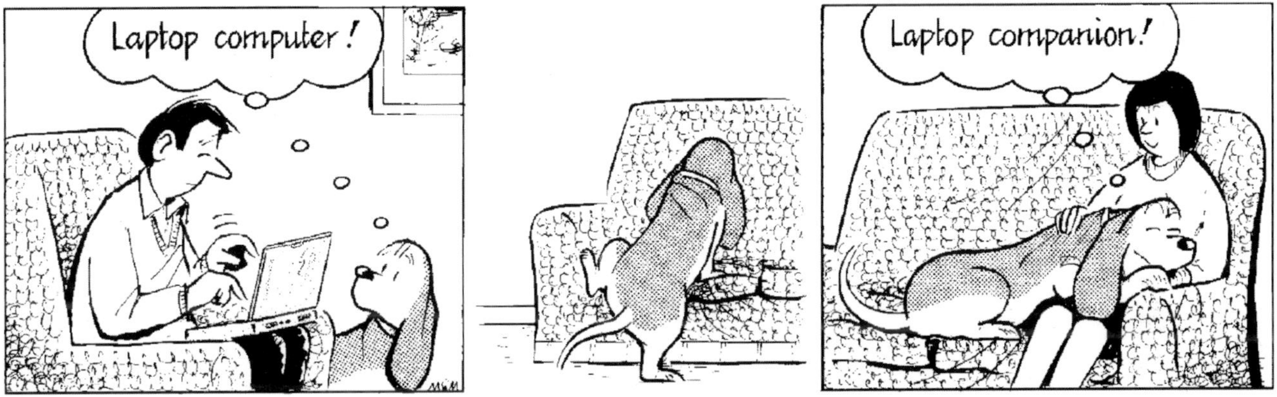
Laptop computer!
Laptop companion!

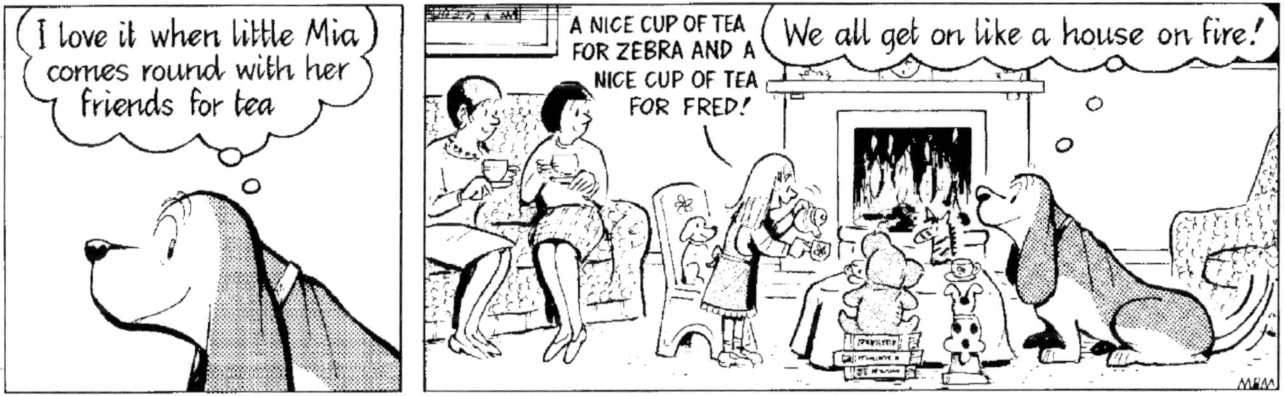
I love it when little Mia comes round with her friends for tea
A NICE CUP OF TEA FOR ZEBRA AND A NICE CUP OF TEA FOR FRED!
We all get on like a house on fire!

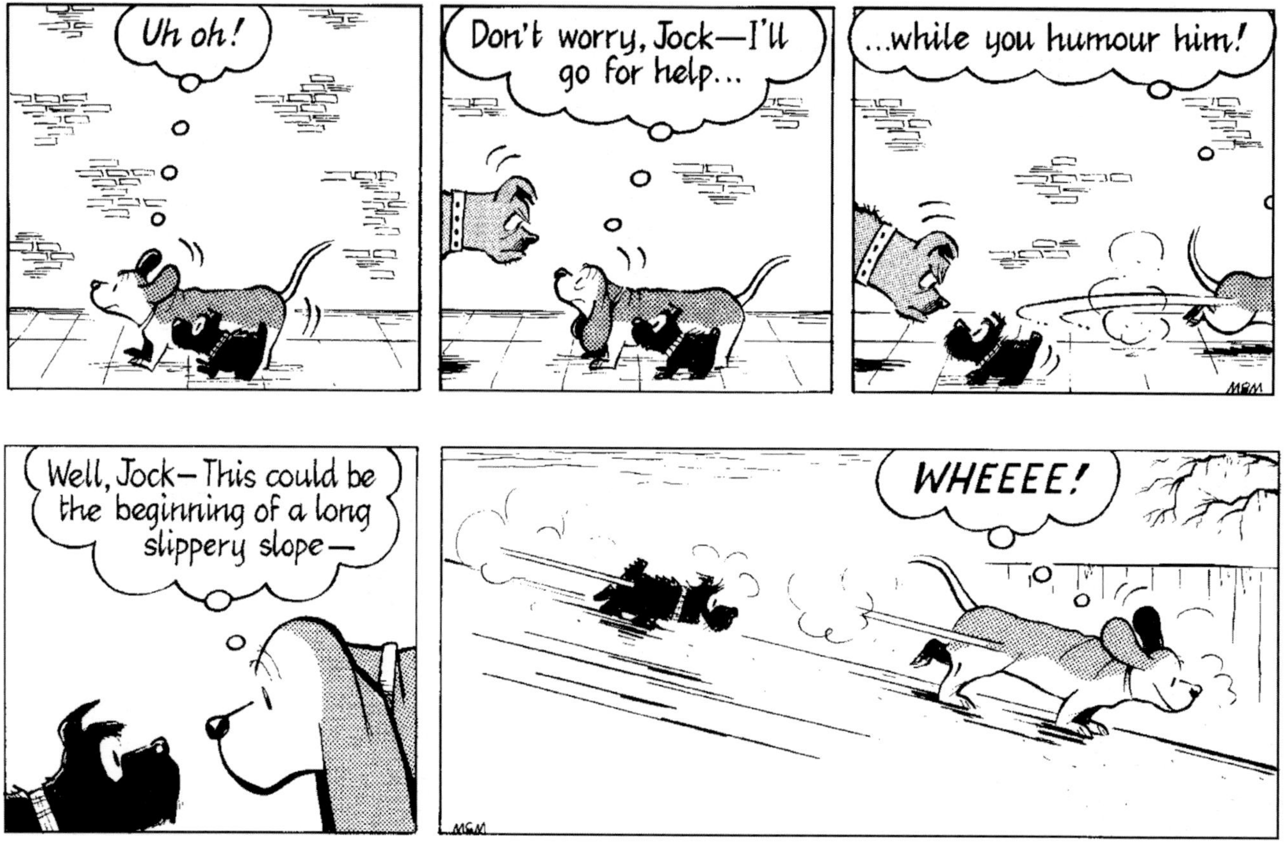
Uh oh!
Don't worry, Jock—I'll go for help...
...while you humour him!
MGM
Well, Jock—This could be the beginning of a long slippery slope—
WHEEEE!
MGM

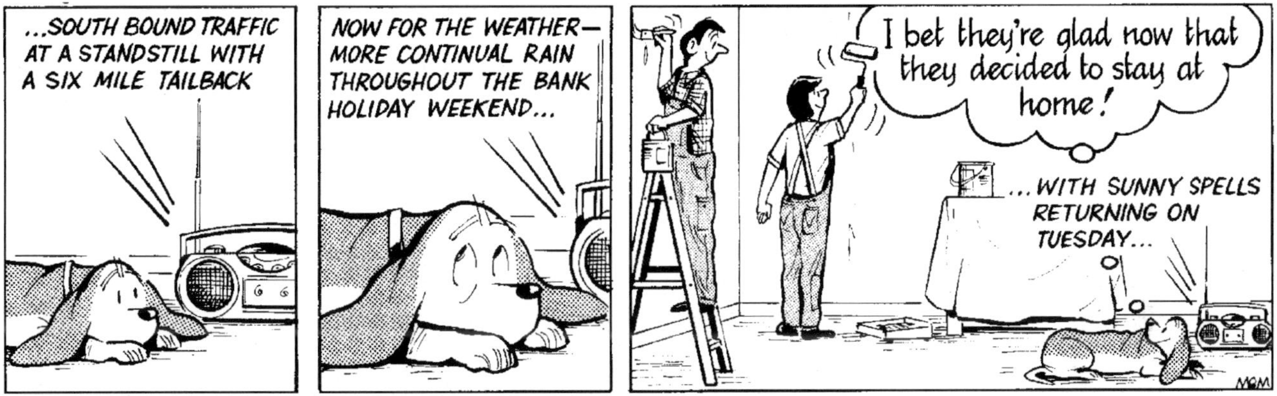
...SOUTH BOUND TRAFFIC AT A STANDSTILL WITH A SIX MILE TAILBACK
NOW FOR THE WEATHER—MORE CONTINUAL RAIN THROUGHOUT THE BANK HOLIDAY WEEKEND...
I bet they're glad now that they decided to stay at home!
...WITH SUNNY SPELLS RETURNING ON TUESDAY...
M&M

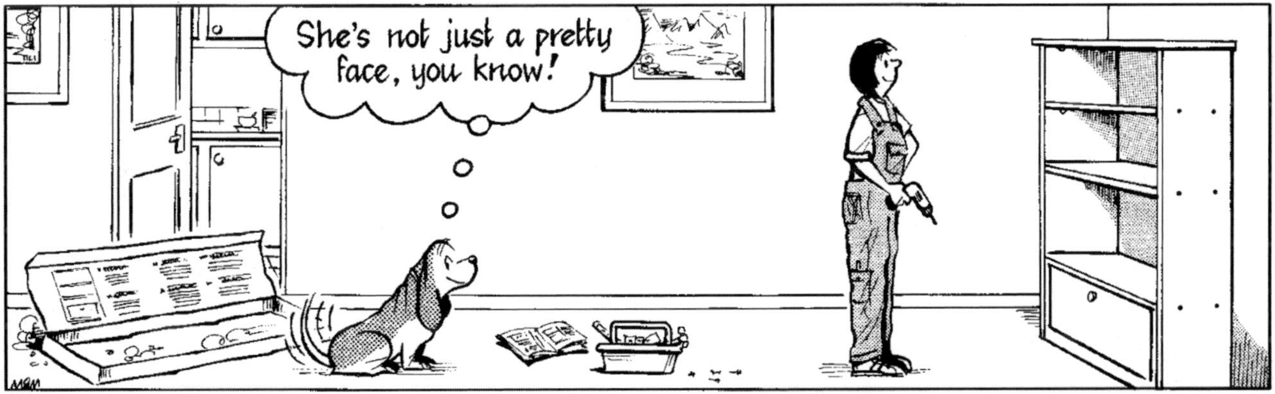
She's not just a pretty face, you know!
M&M

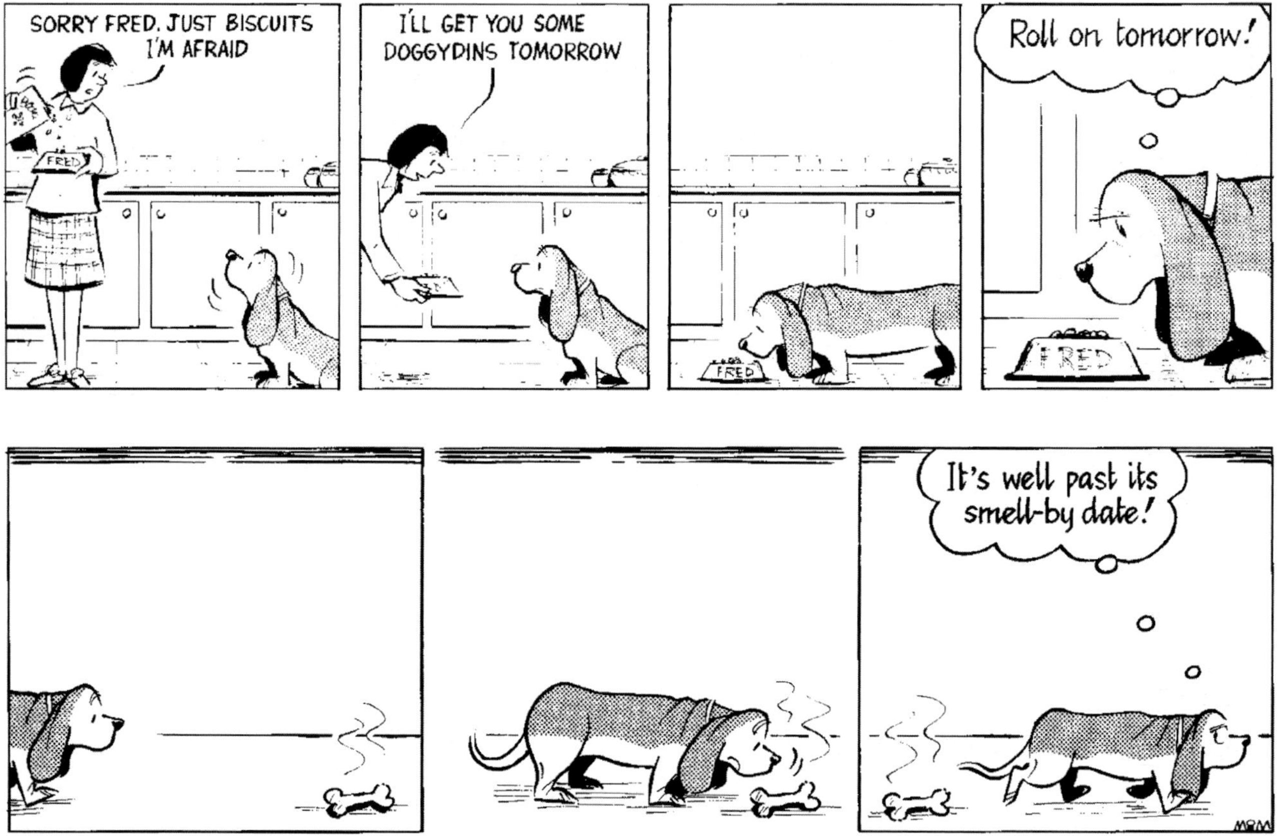
SORRY FRED. JUST BISCUITS I'M AFRAID
FRED
I'LL GET YOU SOME DOGGYDINS TOMORROW
FRED
Roll on tomorrow!
FRED
It's well past its smell-by date!
MGM

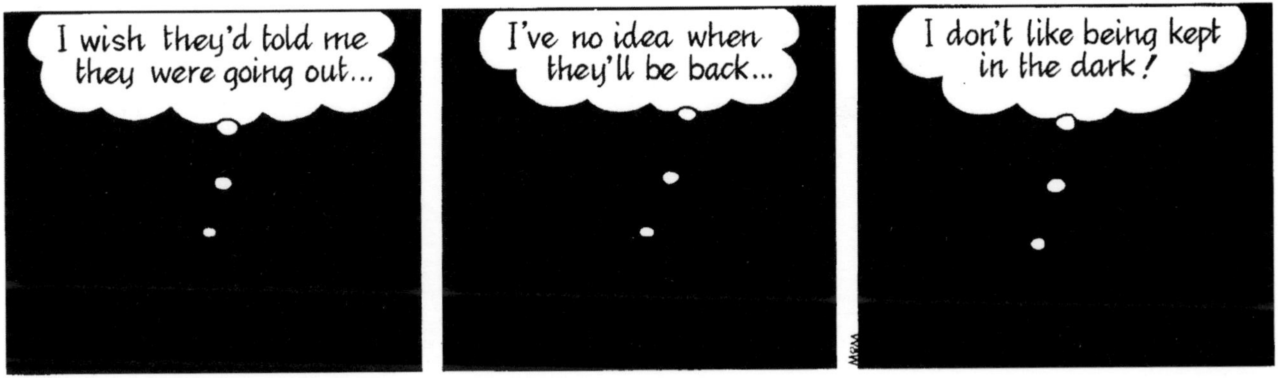
I wish they'd told me they were going out...
I've no idea when they'll be back...
I don't like being kept in the dark!

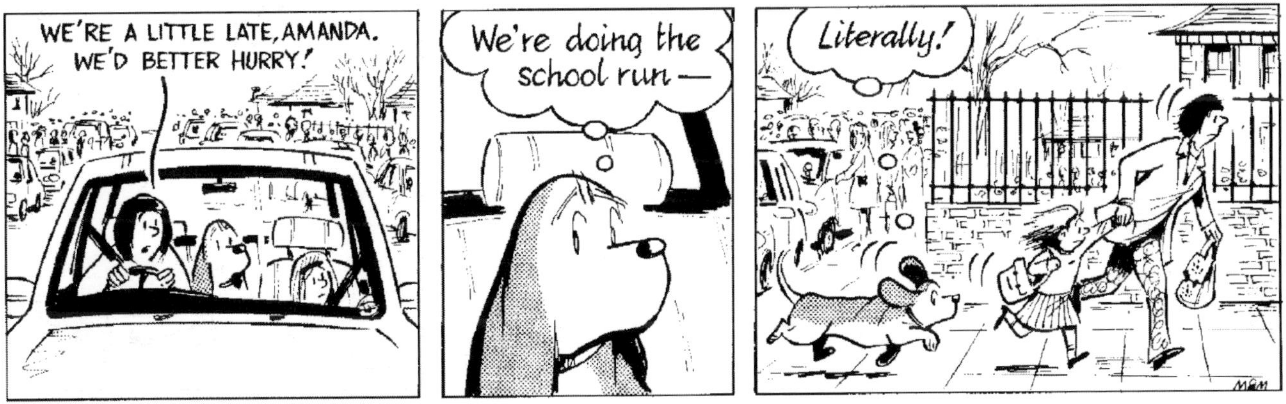
WE'RE A LITTLE LATE, AMANDA. WE'D BETTER HURRY!
We're doing the school run —
Literally!

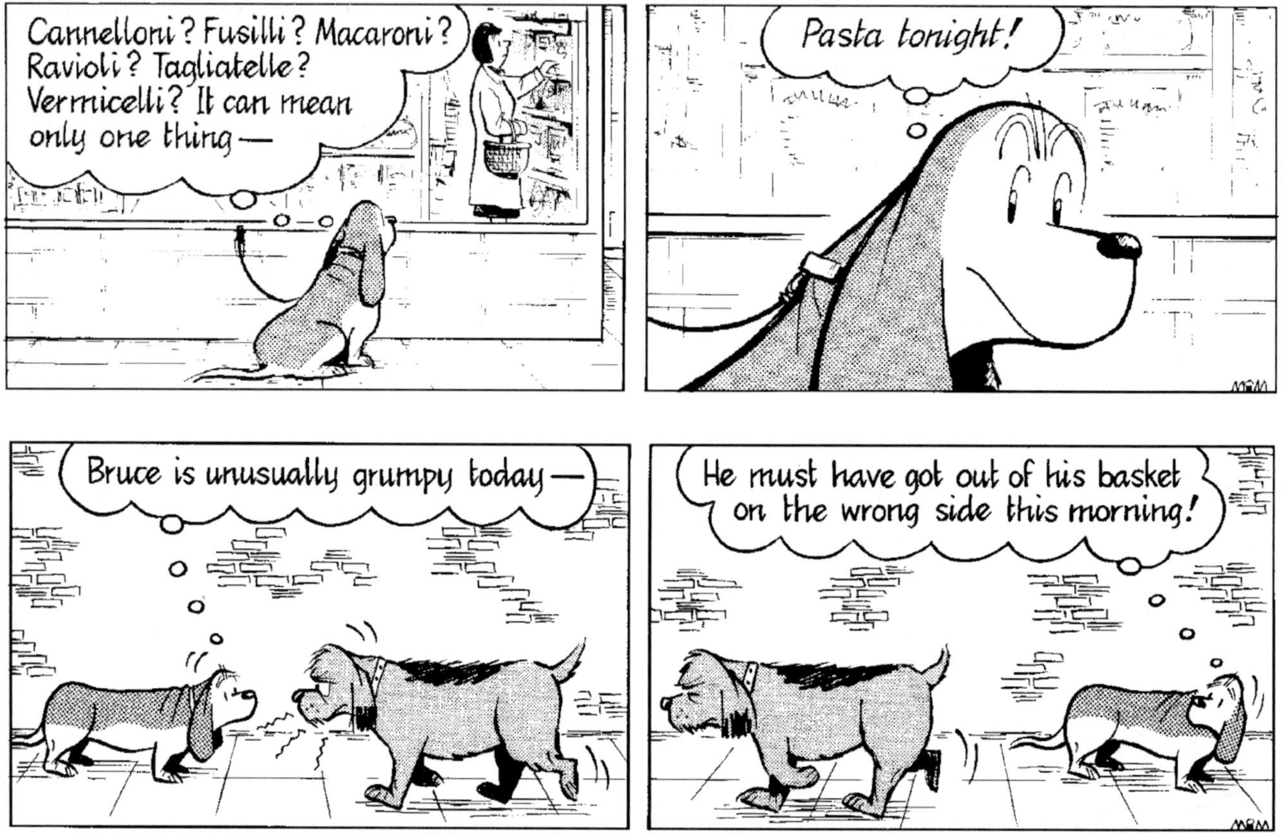
Cannelloni? Fusilli? Macaroni? Ravioli? Tagliatelle? Vermicelli? It can mean only one thing—
Pasta tonight!
MBM
Bruce is unusually grumpy today—
He must have got out of his basket on the wrong side this morning!
MBM

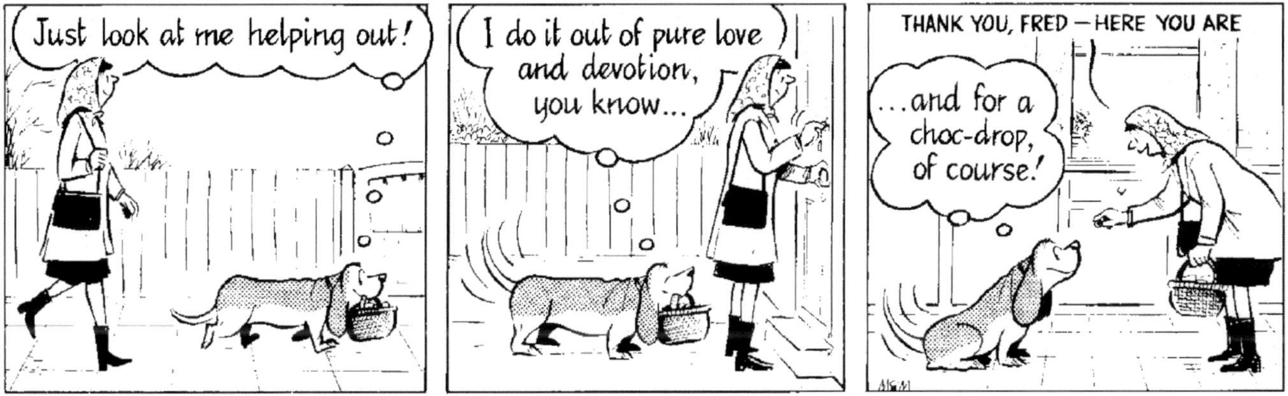
Just look at me helping out!
I do it out of pure love and devotion, you know...
THANK YOU, FRED — HERE YOU ARE
...and for a choc-drop, of course!

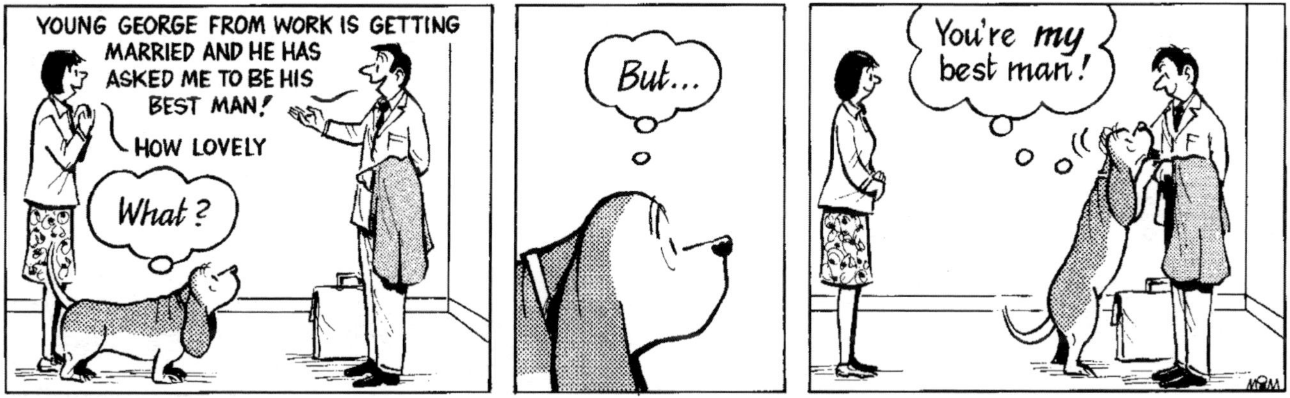
YOUNG GEORGE FROM WORK IS GETTING MARRIED AND HE HAS ASKED ME TO BE HIS BEST MAN!
HOW LOVELY
What?
But...
You're *my* best man!

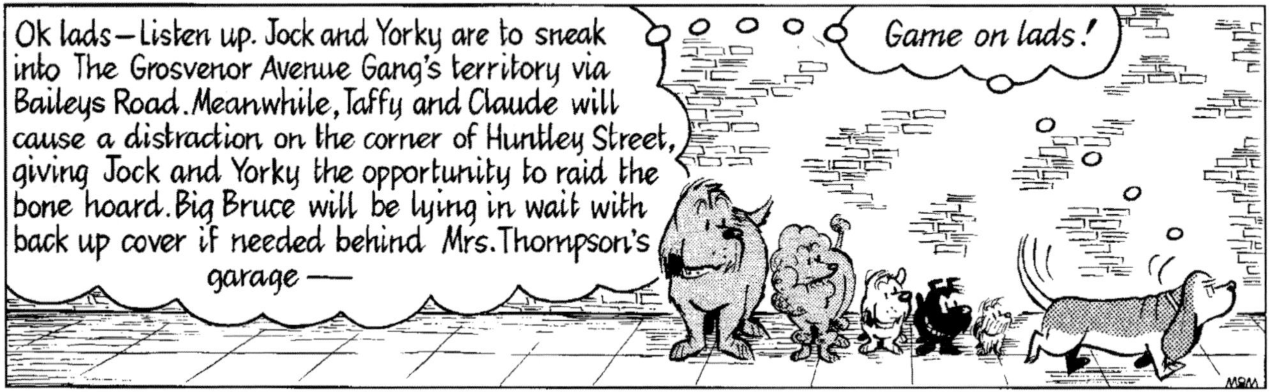
Ok lads—Listen up. Jock and Yorky are to sneak into The Grosvenor Avenue Gang's territory via Baileys Road. Meanwhile, Taffy and Claude will cause a distraction on the corner of Huntley Street, giving Jock and Yorky the opportunity to raid the bone hoard. Big Bruce will be lying in wait with back up cover if needed behind Mrs. Thompson's garage —
Game on lads!

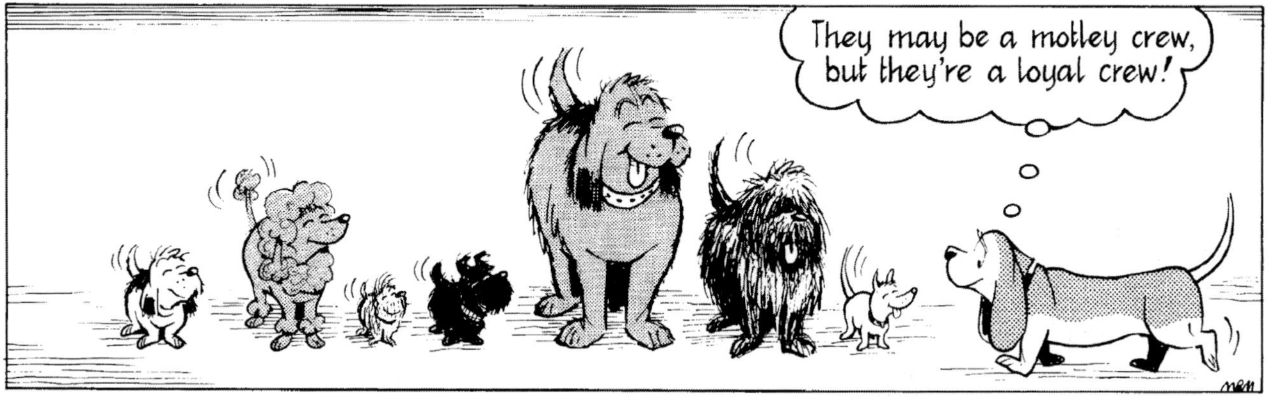
They may be a motley crew, but they're a loyal crew!

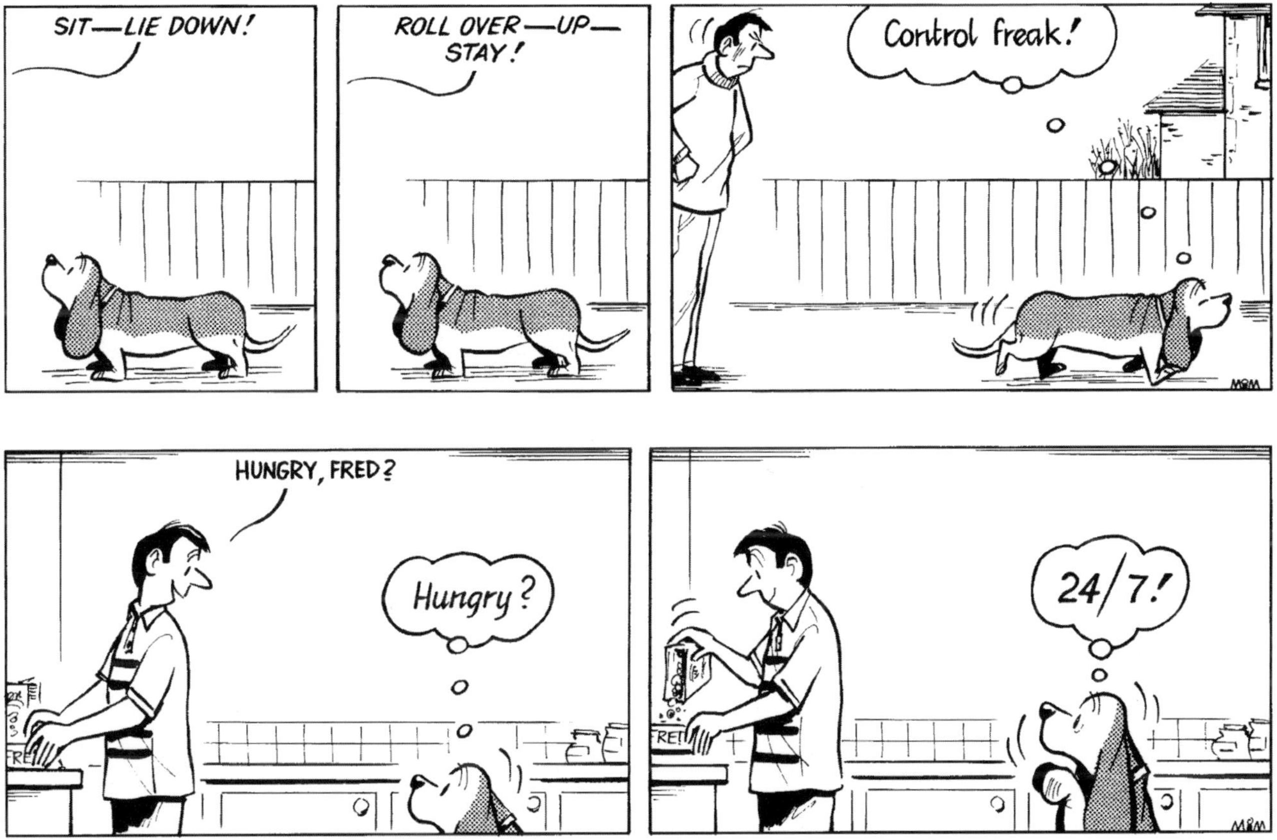
SIT—LIE DOWN!
ROLL OVER—UP—STAY!
Control freak!
M&M
HUNGRY, FRED?
Hungry?
24/7!
M&M

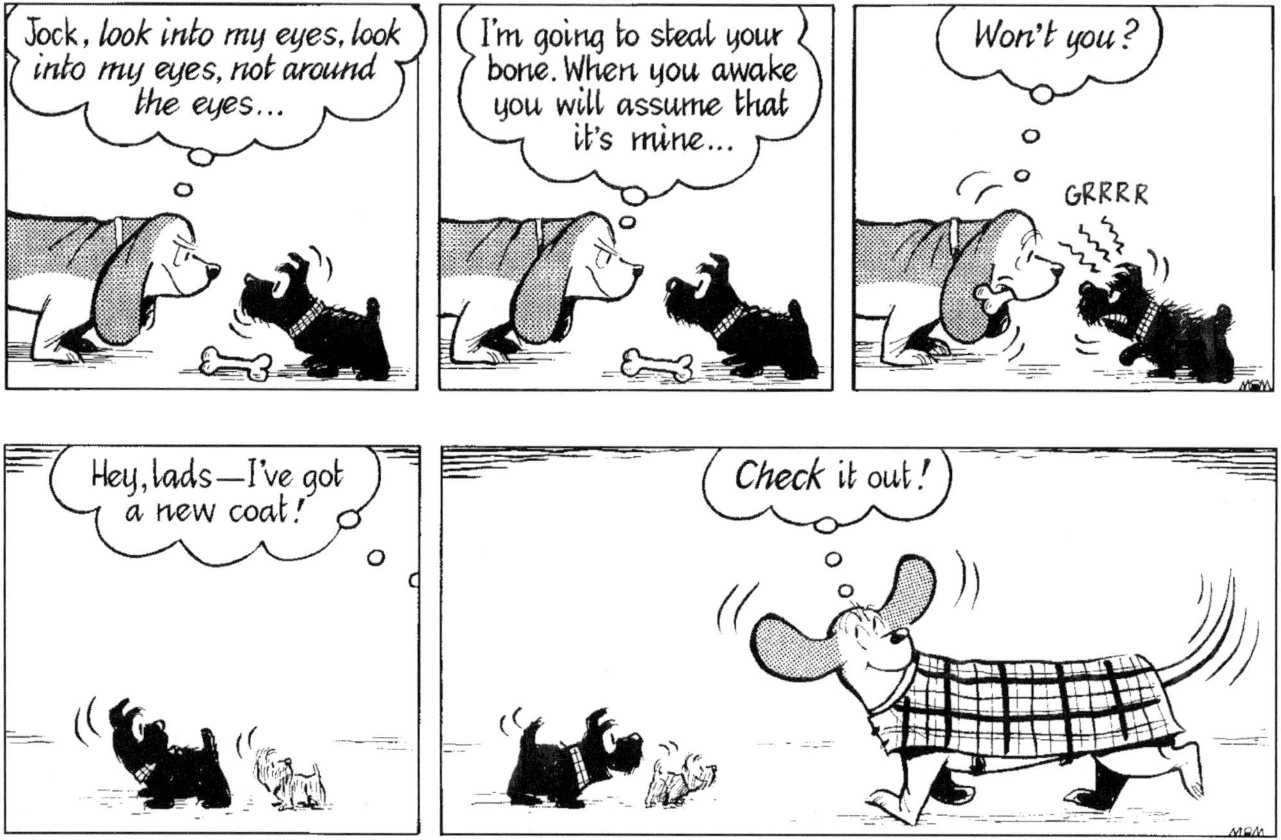
Jock, look into my eyes, look into my eyes, not around the eyes...
I'm going to steal your bone. When you awake you will assume that it's mine...
Won't you?
GRRRR
MGM
Hey, lads—I've got a new coat!
Check it out!
MGM

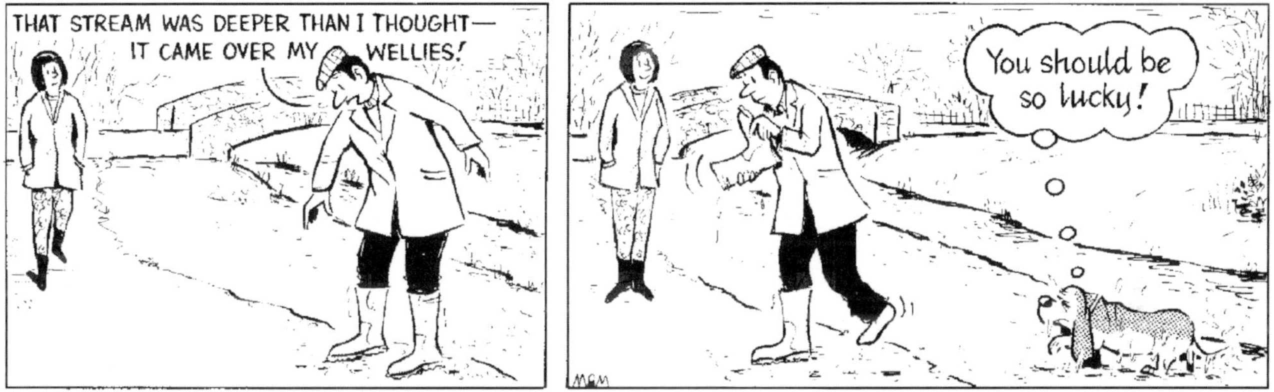
THAT STREAM WAS DEEPER THAN I THOUGHT—
IT CAME OVER MY WELLIES!
You should be so lucky!
MGM

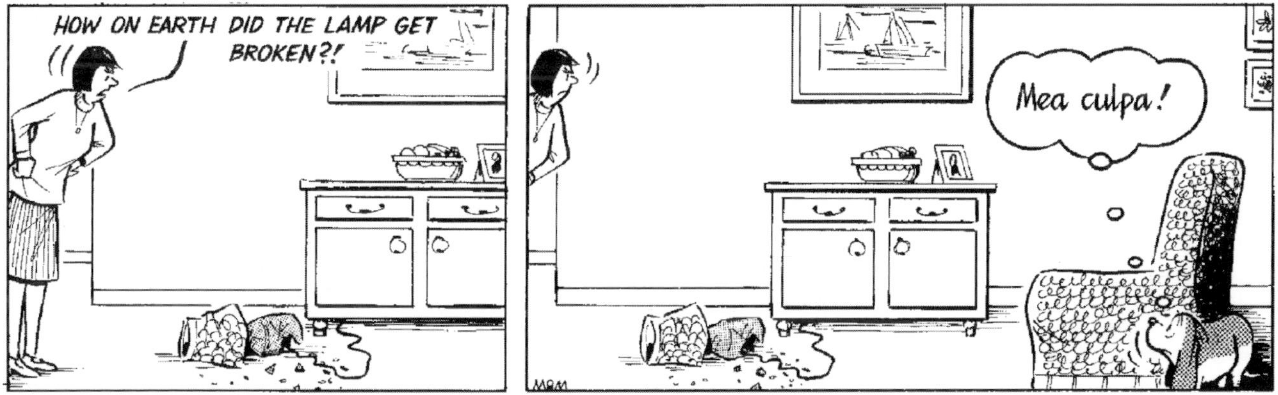
HOW ON EARTH DID THE LAMP GET BROKEN?!
Mea culpa!
MGM

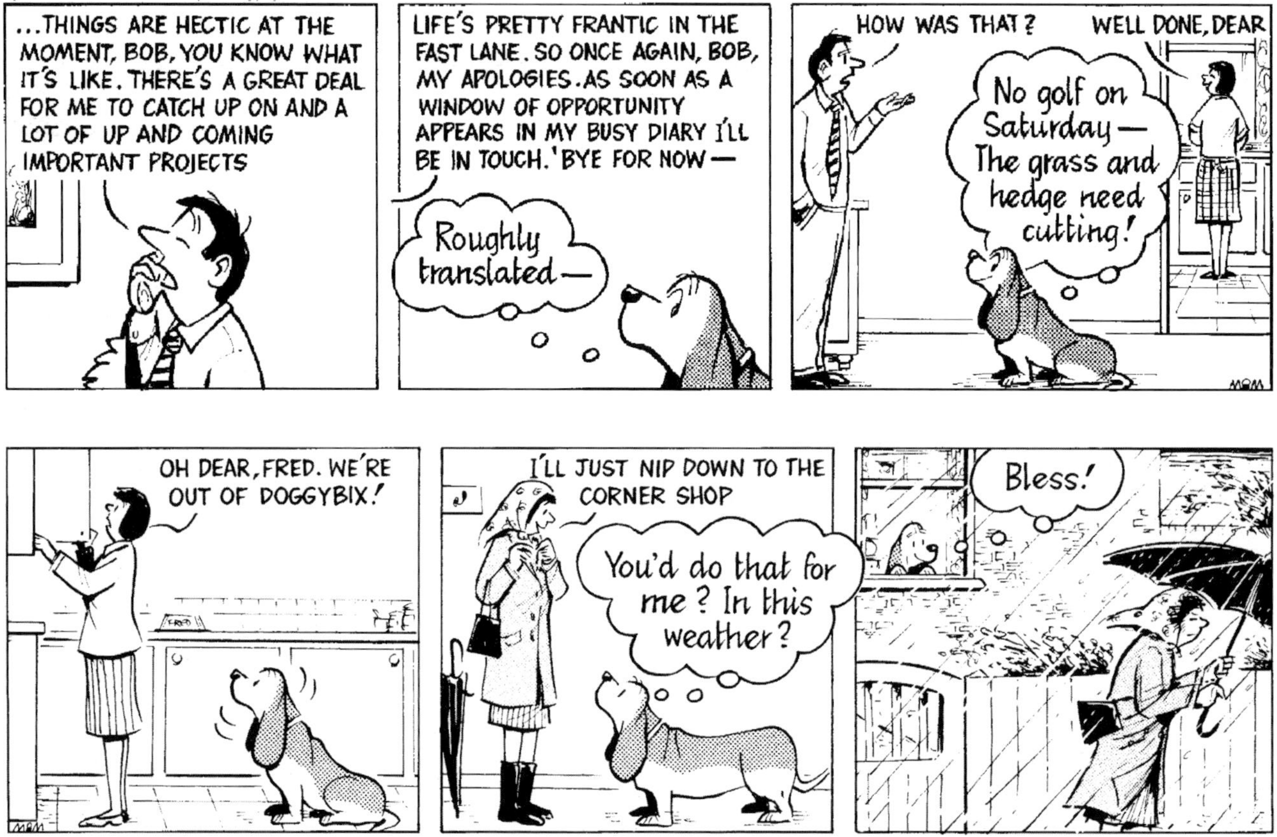
...THINGS ARE HECTIC AT THE MOMENT, BOB, YOU KNOW WHAT IT'S LIKE. THERE'S A GREAT DEAL FOR ME TO CATCH UP ON AND A LOT OF UP AND COMING IMPORTANT PROJECTS
LIFE'S PRETTY FRANTIC IN THE FAST LANE. SO ONCE AGAIN, BOB, MY APOLOGIES. AS SOON AS A WINDOW OF OPPORTUNITY APPEARS IN MY BUSY DIARY I'LL BE IN TOUCH. 'BYE FOR NOW —
Roughly translated —
HOW WAS THAT?
WELL DONE, DEAR
No golf on Saturday — The grass and hedge need cutting!
OH DEAR, FRED. WE'RE OUT OF DOGGYBIX!
FRED
I'LL JUST NIP DOWN TO THE CORNER SHOP
You'd do that for me? In this weather?
Bless!

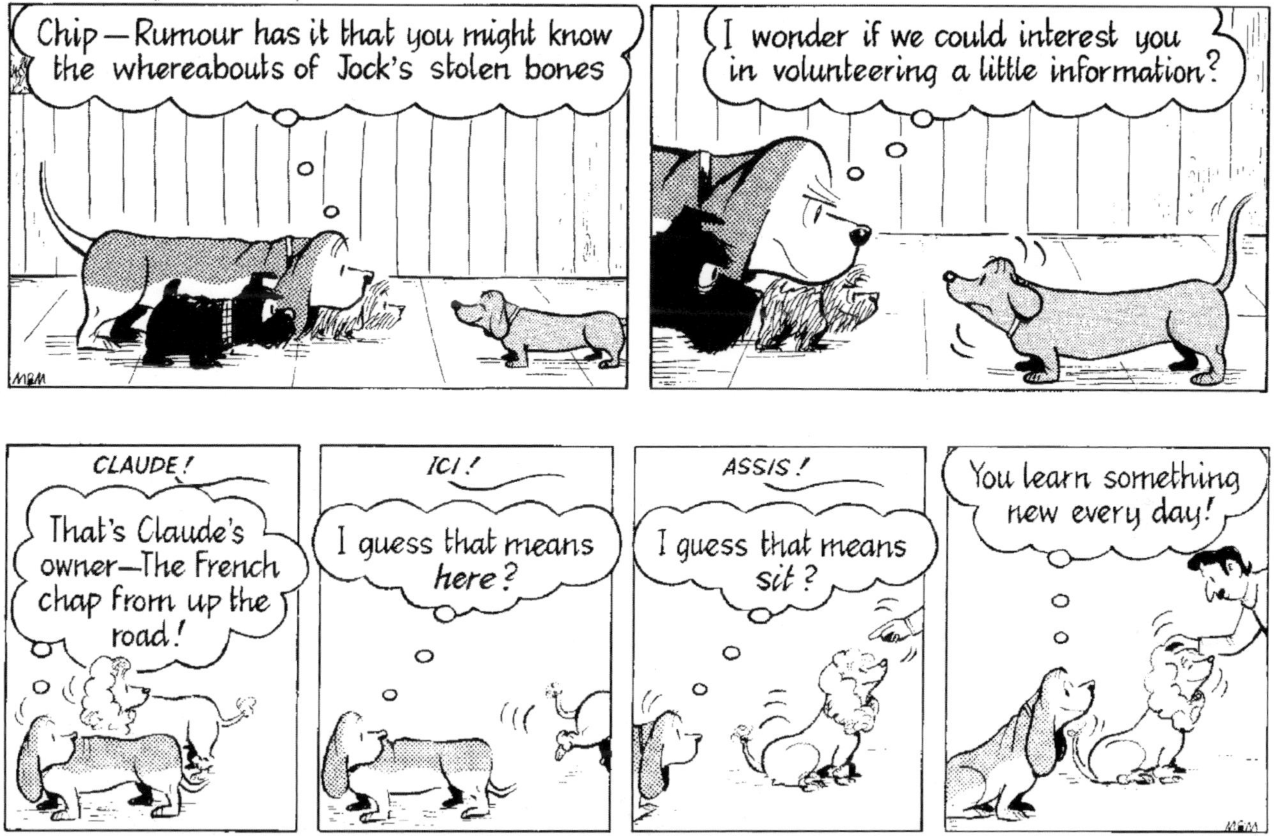
Chip—Rumour has it that you might know the whereabouts of Jock's stolen bones
I wonder if we could interest you in volunteering a little information?
CLAUDE!
That's Claude's owner—The French chap from up the road!
ICI!
I guess that means *here*?
ASSIS!
I guess that means *sit*?
You learn something new every day!

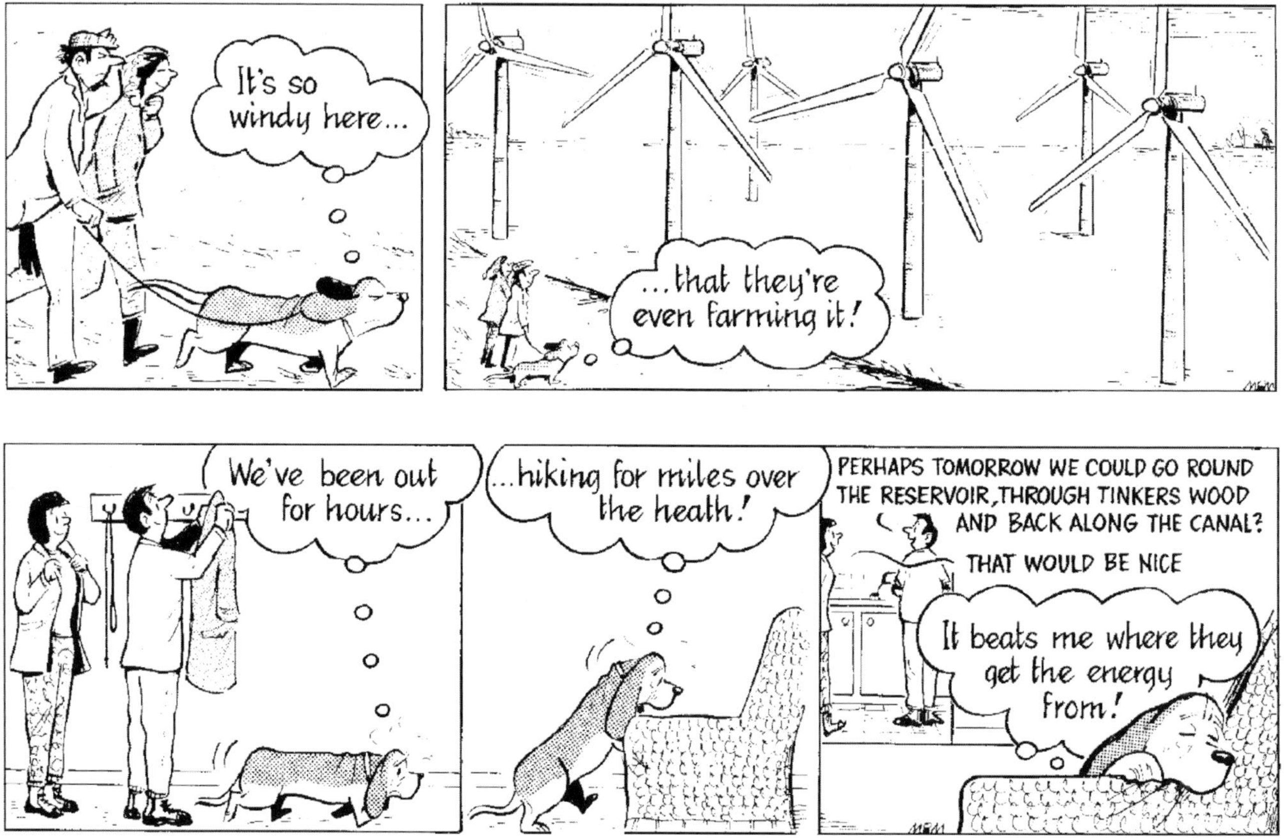
It's so windy here...
...that they're even farming it!
MGM
We've been out for hours...
...hiking for miles over the heath!
PERHAPS TOMORROW WE COULD GO ROUND THE RESERVOIR, THROUGH TINKERS WOOD AND BACK ALONG THE CANAL?
THAT WOULD BE NICE
It beats me where they get the energy from!
MGM

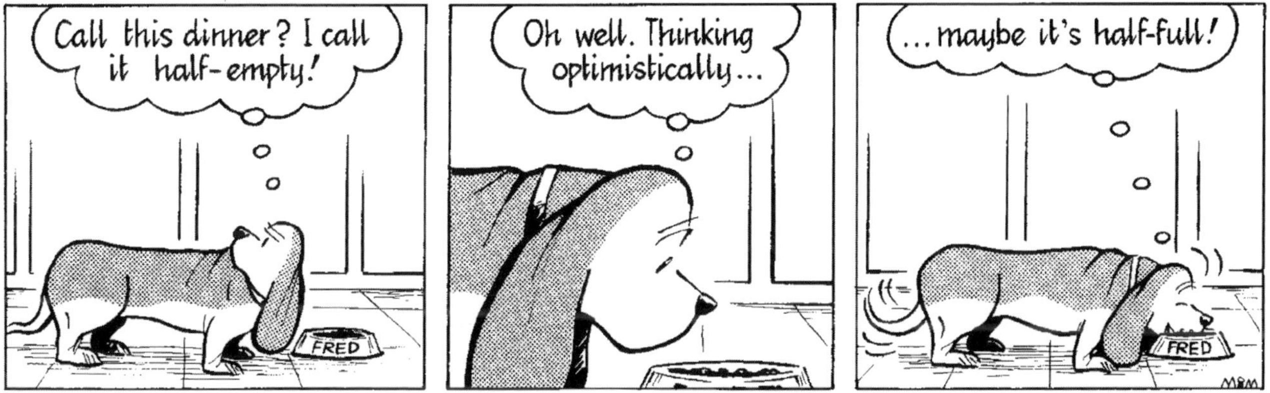
Call this dinner? I call it half-empty!
FRED
Oh well. Thinking optimistically...
...maybe it's half-full!
FRED

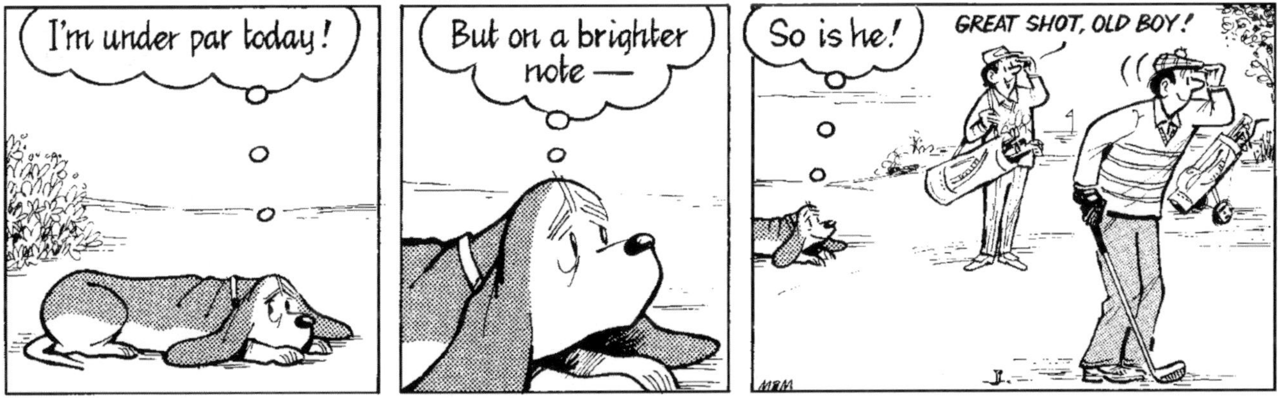
I'm under par today!
But on a brighter note —
So is he!
GREAT SHOT, OLD BOY!

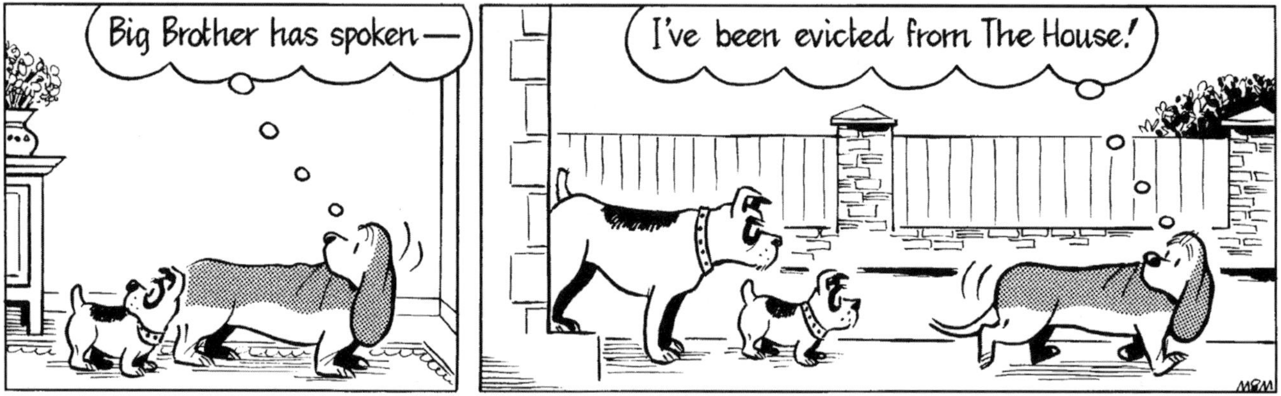
Big Brother has spoken —
I've been evicted from The House!

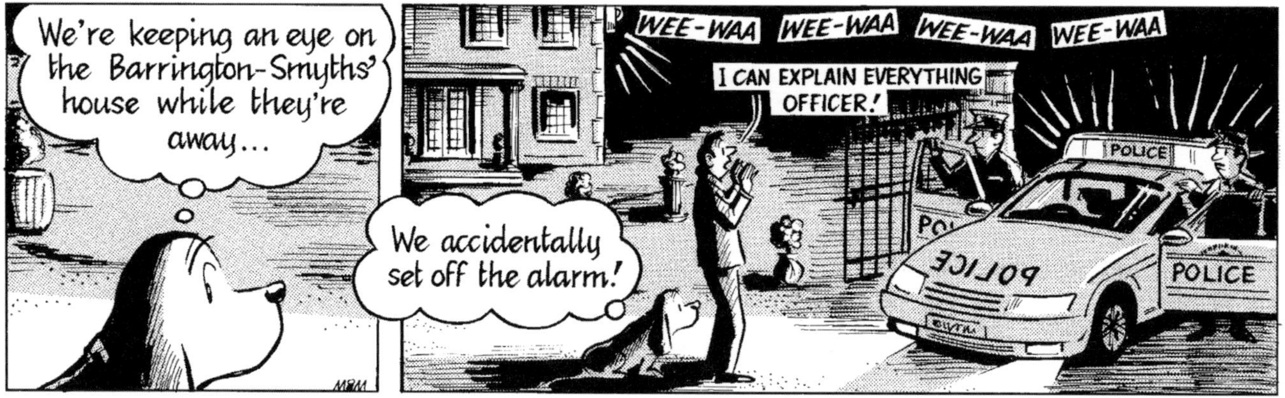
We're keeping an eye on the Barrington-Smyths' house while they're away...
We accidentally set off the alarm!
WEE-WAA
WEE-WAA
WEE-WAA
WEE-WAA
I CAN EXPLAIN EVERYTHING OFFICER!
POLICE
POLICE

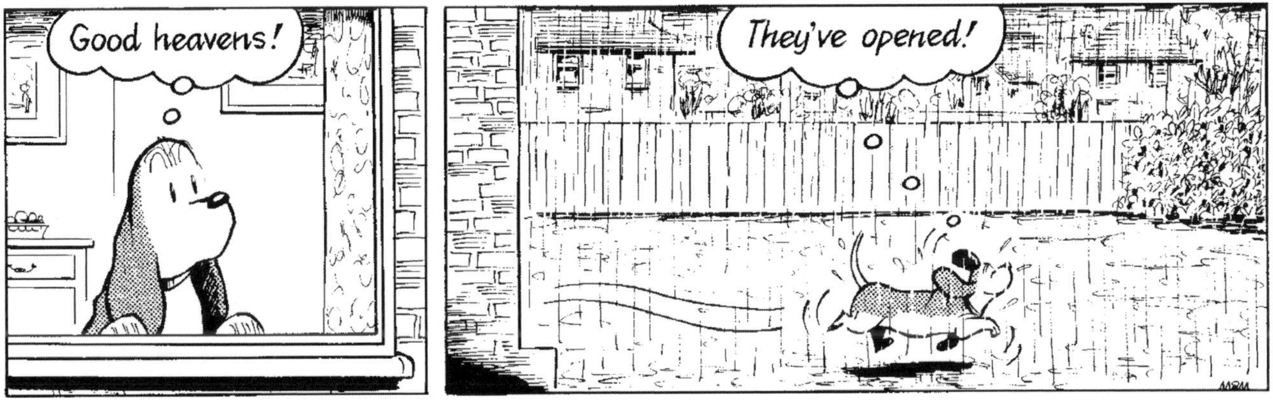
Good heavens!
They've opened!

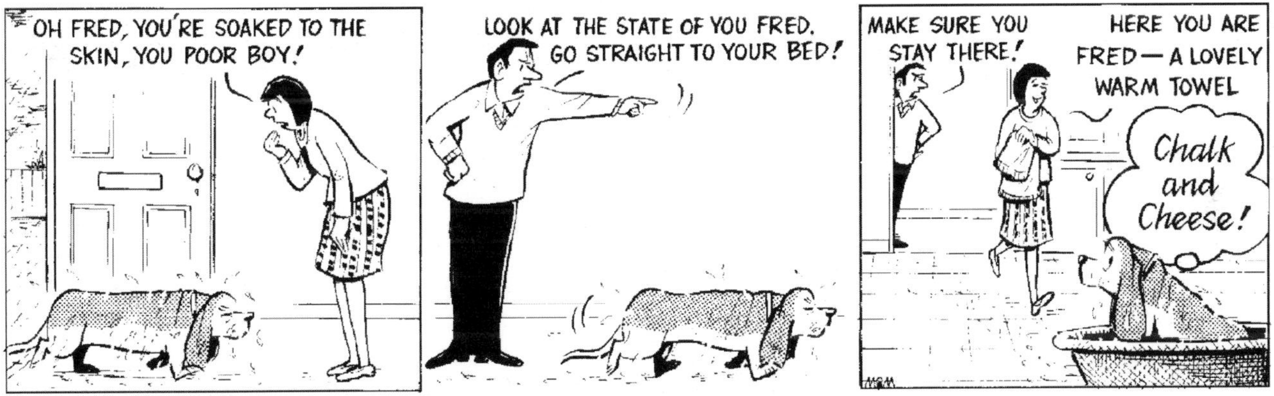
OH FRED, YOU'RE SOAKED TO THE SKIN, YOU POOR BOY!
LOOK AT THE STATE OF YOU FRED. GO STRAIGHT TO YOUR BED!
MAKE SURE YOU STAY THERE!
HERE YOU ARE FRED — A LOVELY WARM TOWEL
Chalk and Cheese!

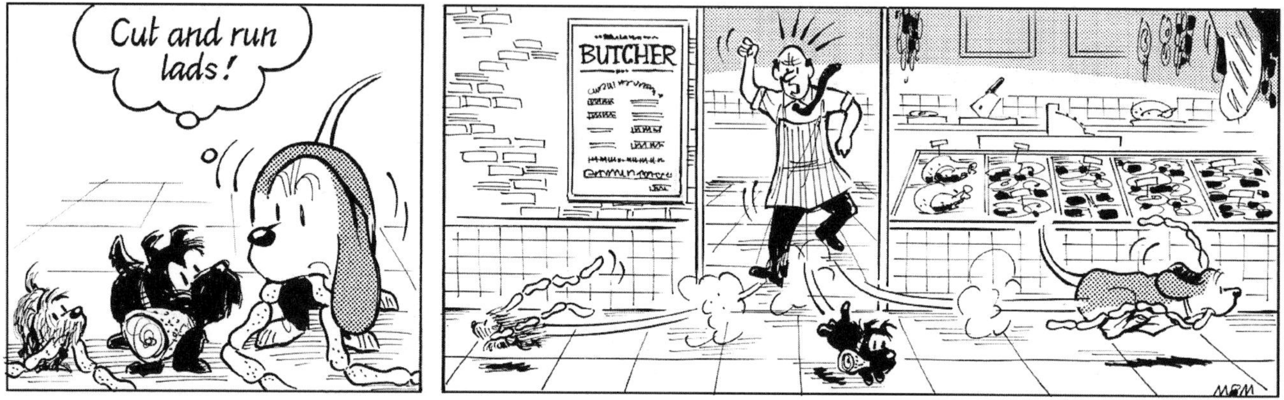
Cut and run lads!
BUTCHER
MBM

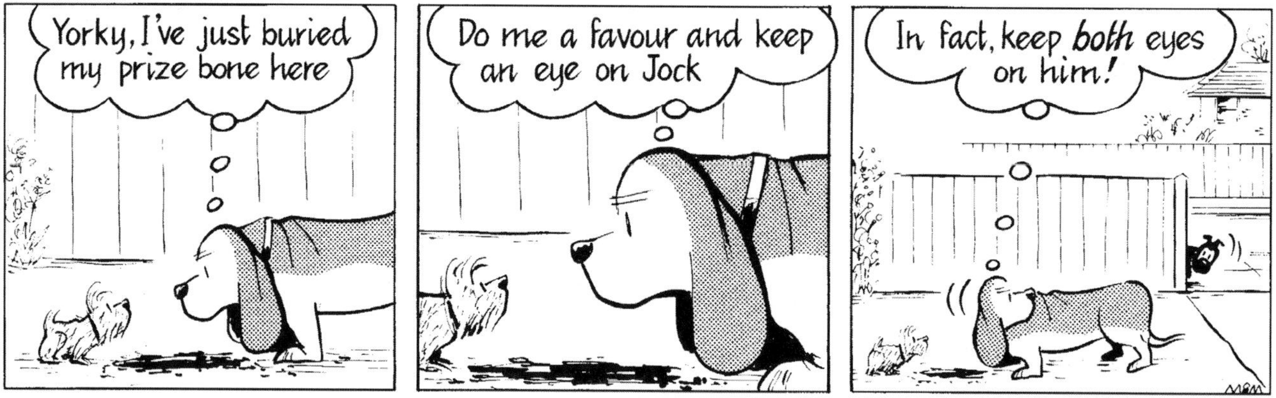
Yorky, I've just buried my prize bone here
Do me a favour and keep an eye on Jock
In fact, keep *both* eyes on him!
MBM

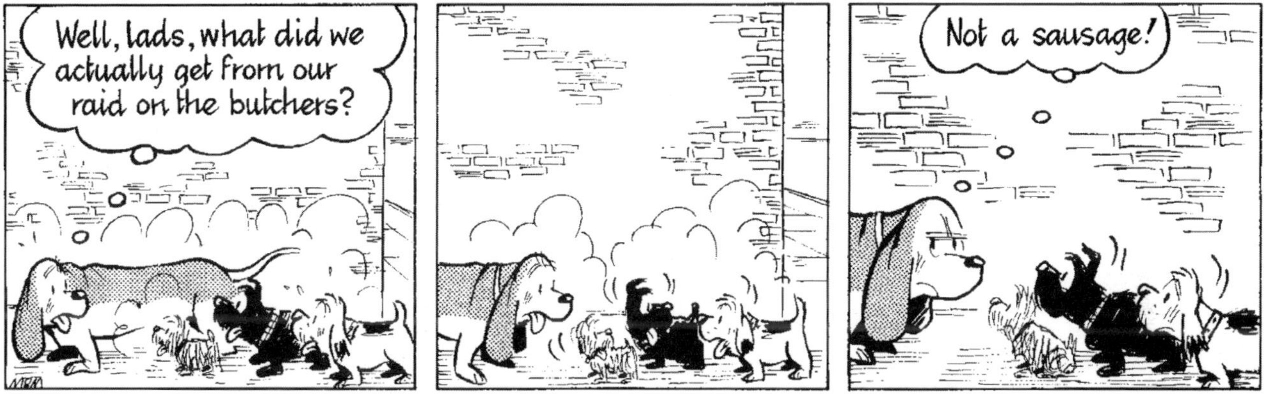
Well, lads, what did we actually get from our raid on the butchers?
Not a sausage!

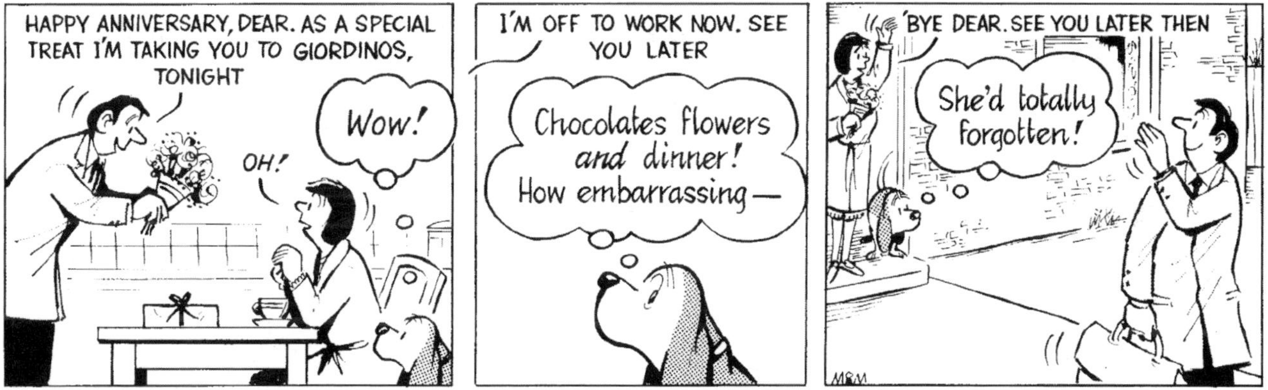
HAPPY ANNIVERSARY, DEAR. AS A SPECIAL TREAT I'M TAKING YOU TO GIORDINOS, TONIGHT
OH!
Wow!
I'M OFF TO WORK NOW. SEE YOU LATER
Chocolates flowers *and* dinner! How embarrassing—
'BYE DEAR. SEE YOU LATER THEN
She'd totally forgotten!

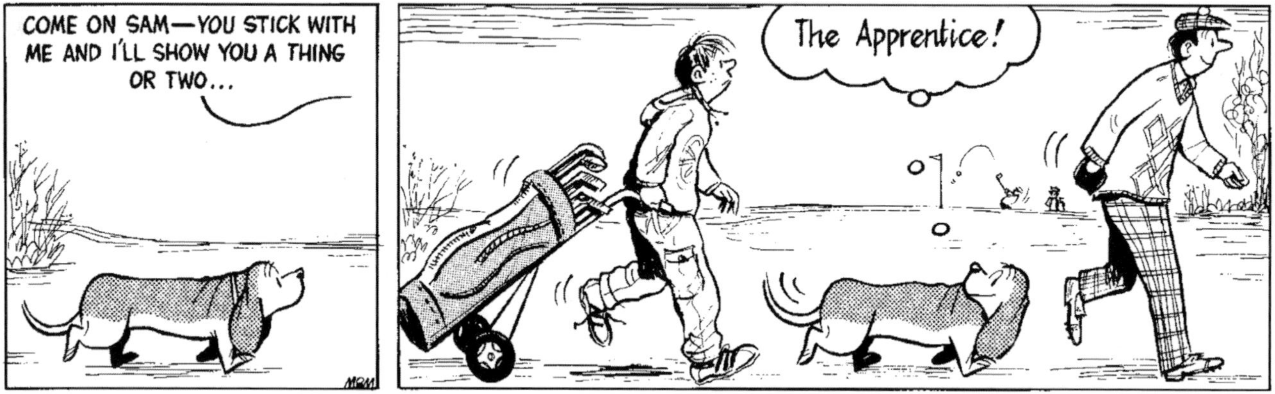
COME ON SAM—YOU STICK WITH ME AND I'LL SHOW YOU A THING OR TWO...
The Apprentice!

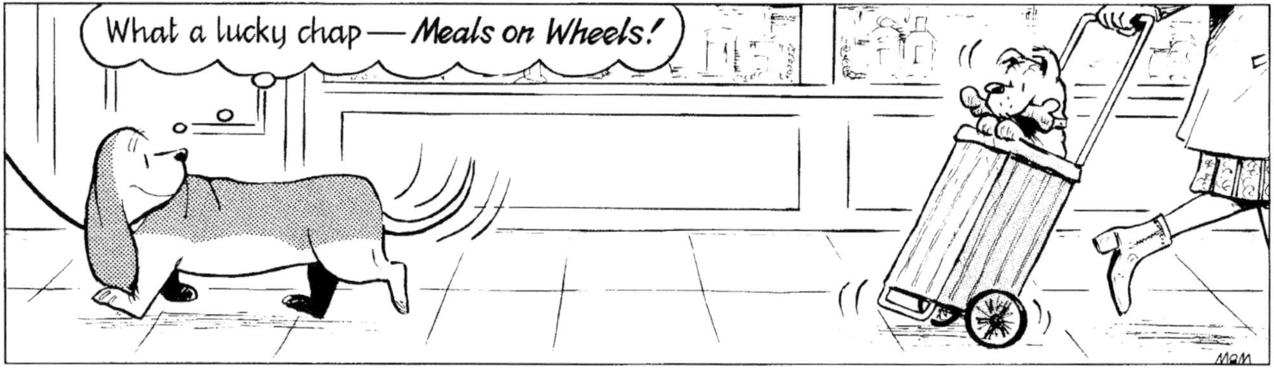
What a lucky chap—*Meals on Wheels!*

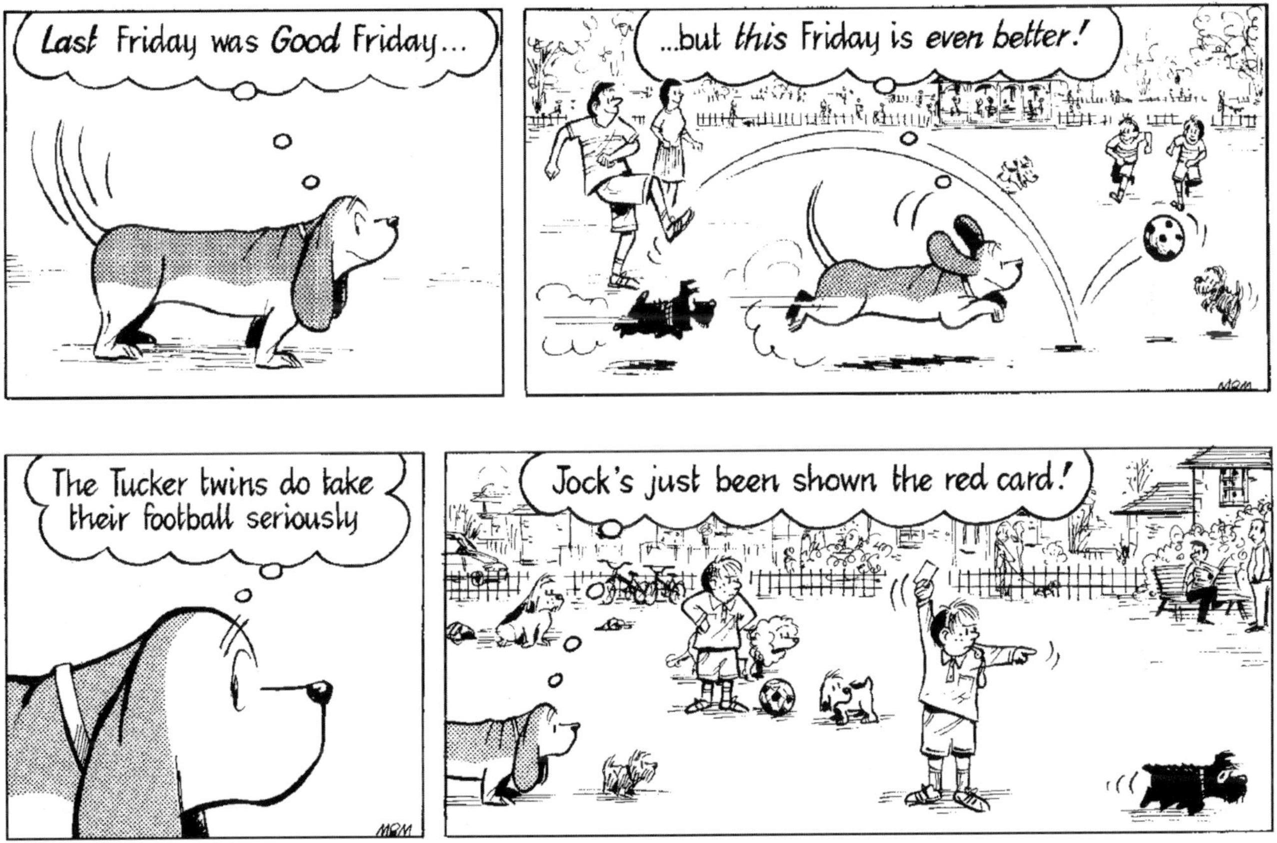

Last Friday was *Good* Friday...
...but *this* Friday is *even better!*
The Tucker twins do take their football seriously
Jock's just been shown the red card!

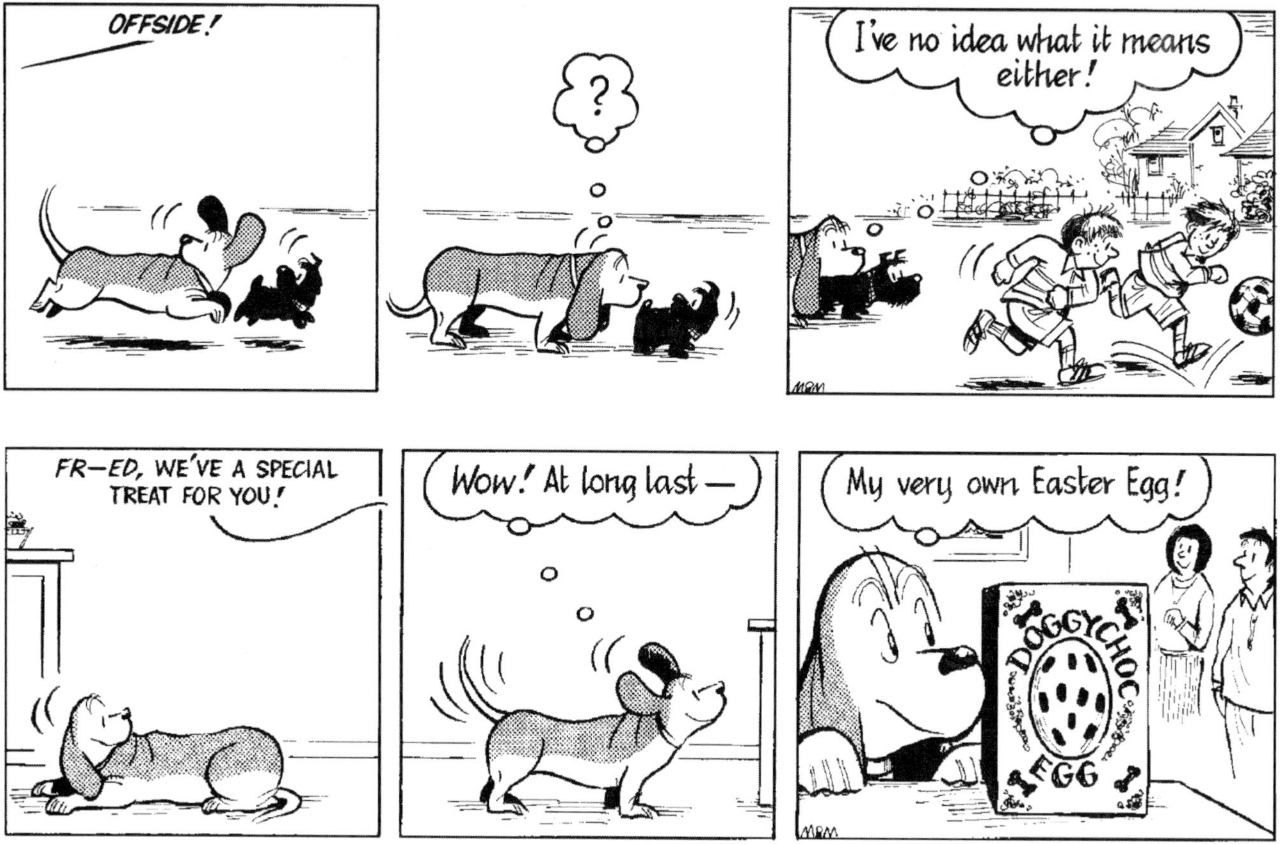

OFFSIDE!
?
I've no idea what it means either!
MRM
FR—ED, WE'VE A SPECIAL TREAT FOR YOU!
Wow! At long last—
My very own Easter Egg!
DOGGYCHOC EGG
MRM

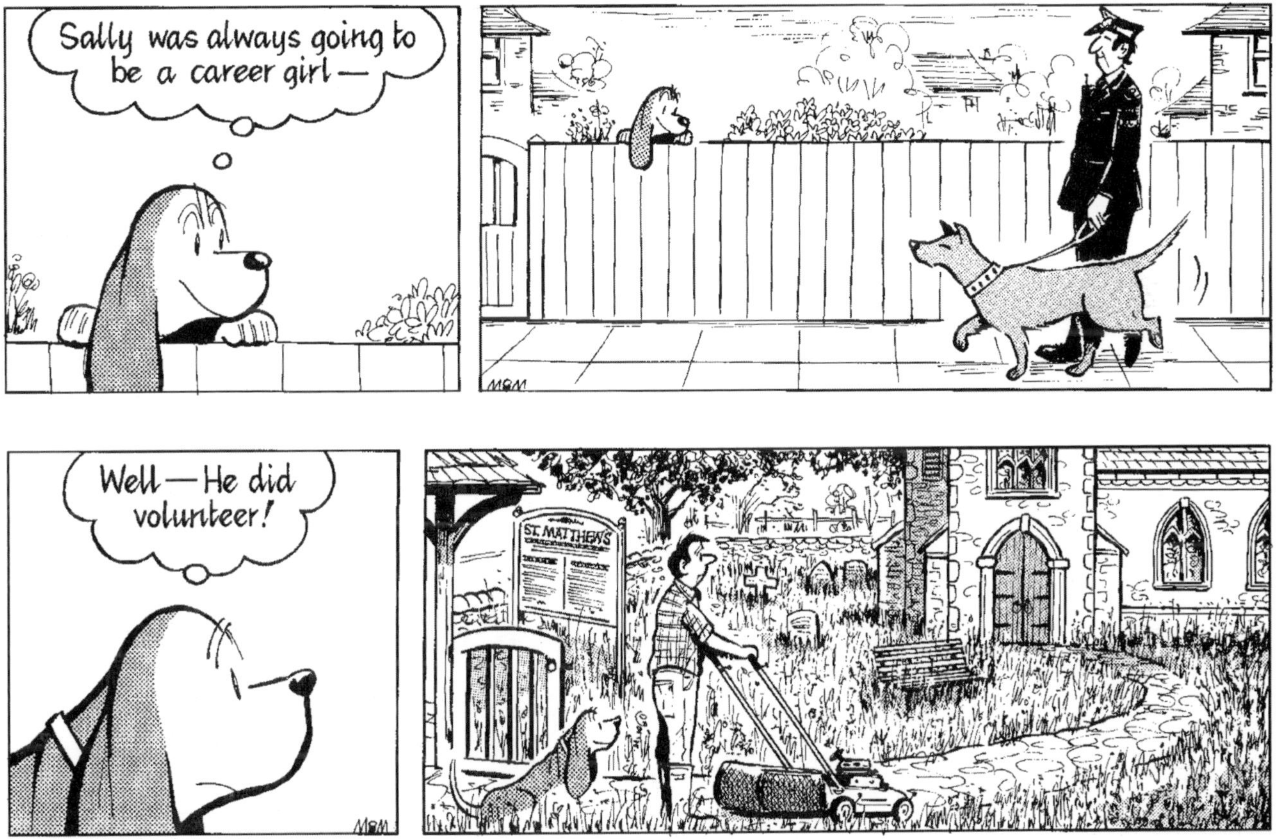
Sally was always going to be a career girl—
Well—He did volunteer!
ST. MATTHEWS

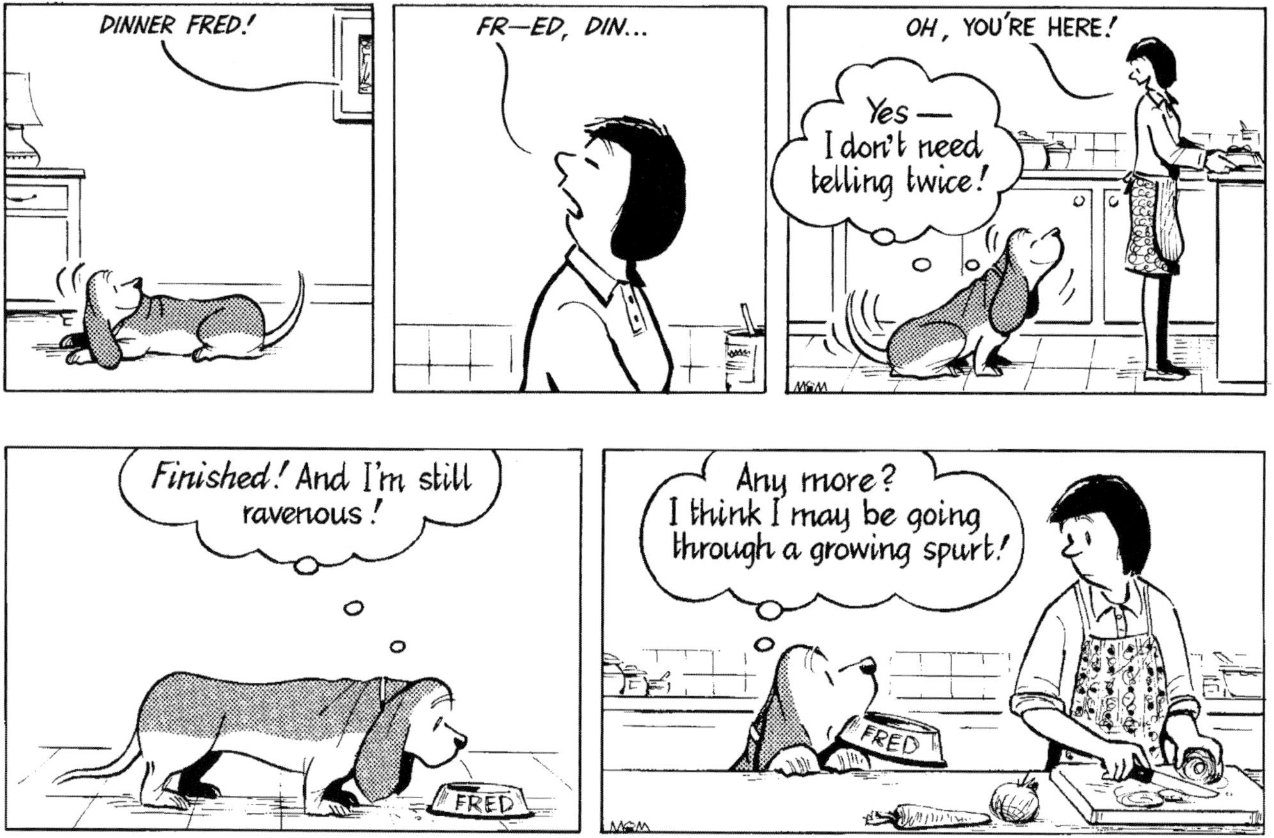
DINNER FRED!
FR—ED, DIN...
OH, YOU'RE HERE!
Yes — I don't need telling twice!
MGM
Finished! And I'm still ravenous!
FRED
Any more? I think I may be going through a growing spurt!
FRED
MGM

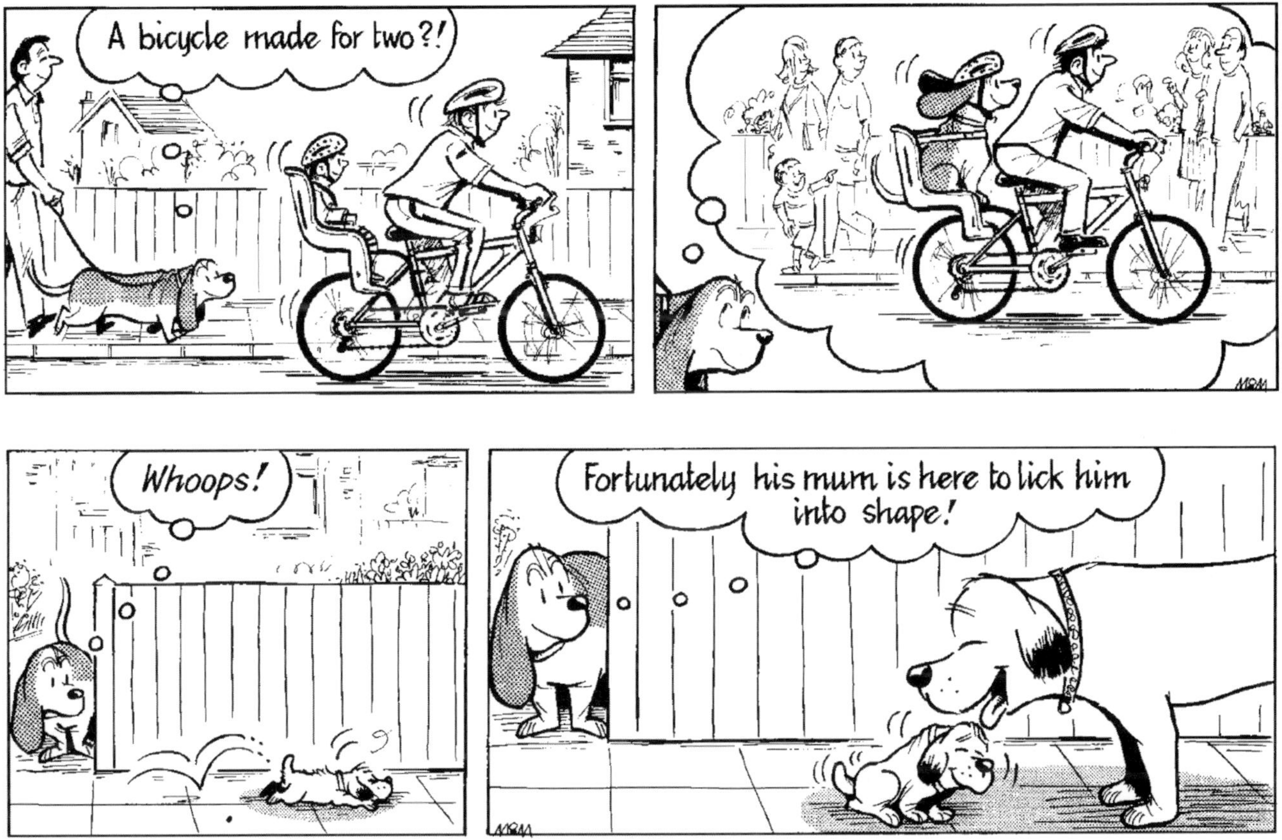
A bicycle made for two?!
Whoops!
Fortunately his mum is here to lick him into shape!

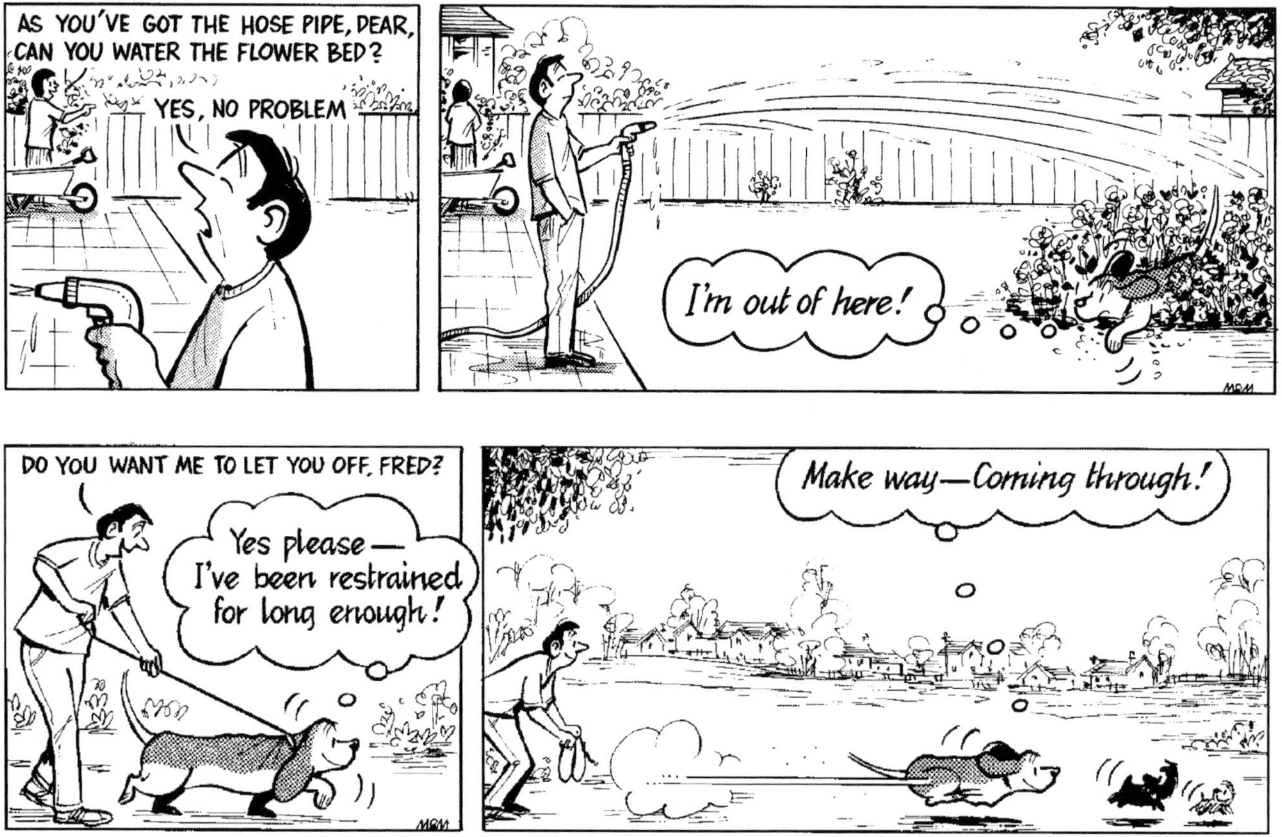
AS YOU'VE GOT THE HOSE PIPE, DEAR, CAN YOU WATER THE FLOWER BED?
YES, NO PROBLEM
I'm out of here!
MGM
DO YOU WANT ME TO LET YOU OFF, FRED?
Yes please — I've been restrained for long enough!
MGM
Make way—Coming through!

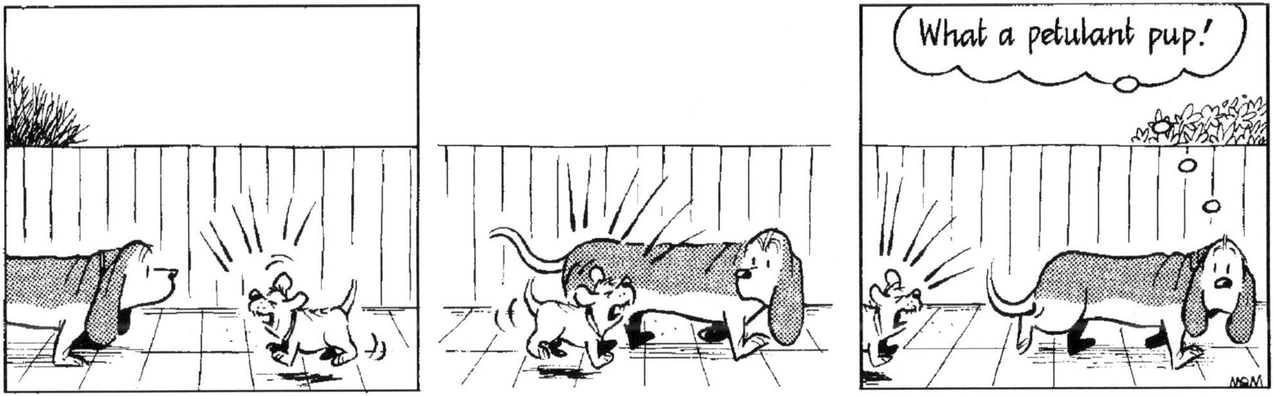
What a petulant pup!

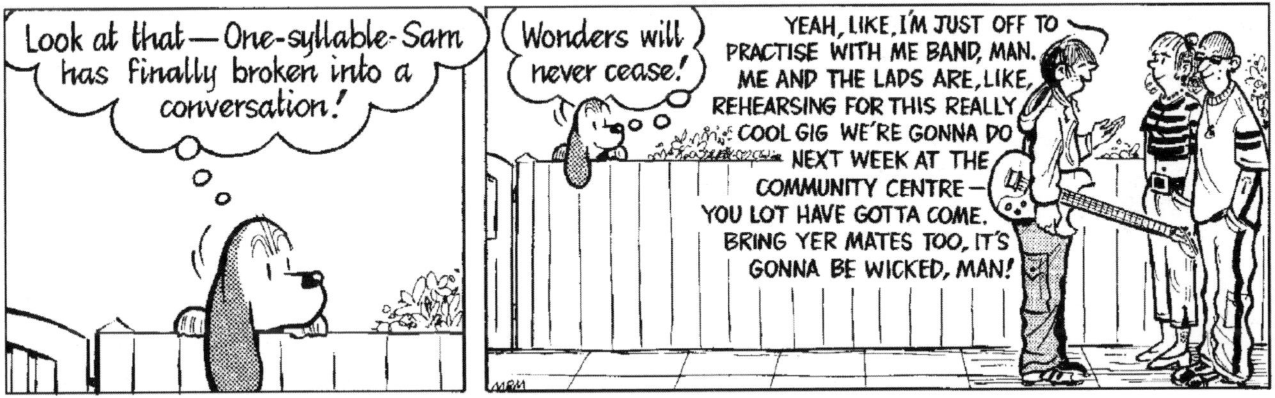
Look at that—One-syllable-Sam has finally broken into a conversation!
Wonders will never cease!
YEAH, LIKE, I'M JUST OFF TO PRACTISE WITH ME BAND, MAN. ME AND THE LADS ARE, LIKE, REHEARSING FOR THIS REALLY COOL GIG WE'RE GONNA DO NEXT WEEK AT THE COMMUNITY CENTRE—YOU LOT HAVE GOTTA COME. BRING YER MATES TOO, IT'S GONNA BE WICKED, MAN!

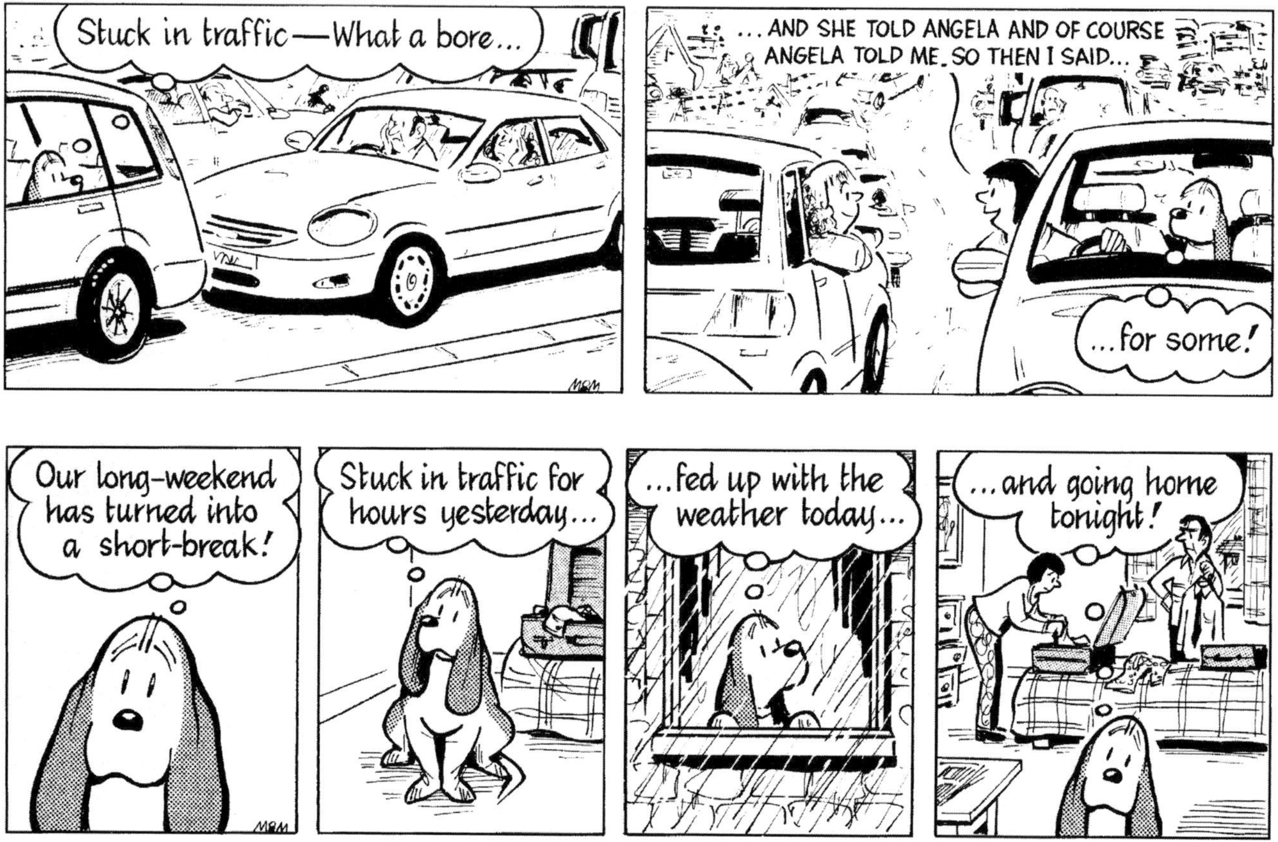
Stuck in traffic—What a bore...
... AND SHE TOLD ANGELA AND OF COURSE ANGELA TOLD ME. SO THEN I SAID...
...for some!
Our long-weekend has turned into a short-break!
Stuck in traffic for hours yesterday...
...fed up with the weather today...
...and going home tonight!

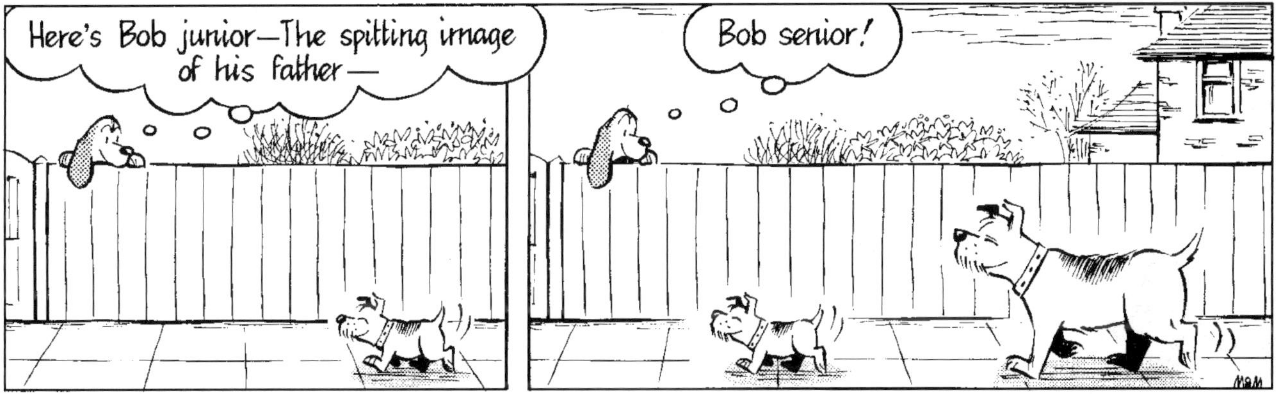
Here's Bob junior—The spitting image of his father—
Bob senior!

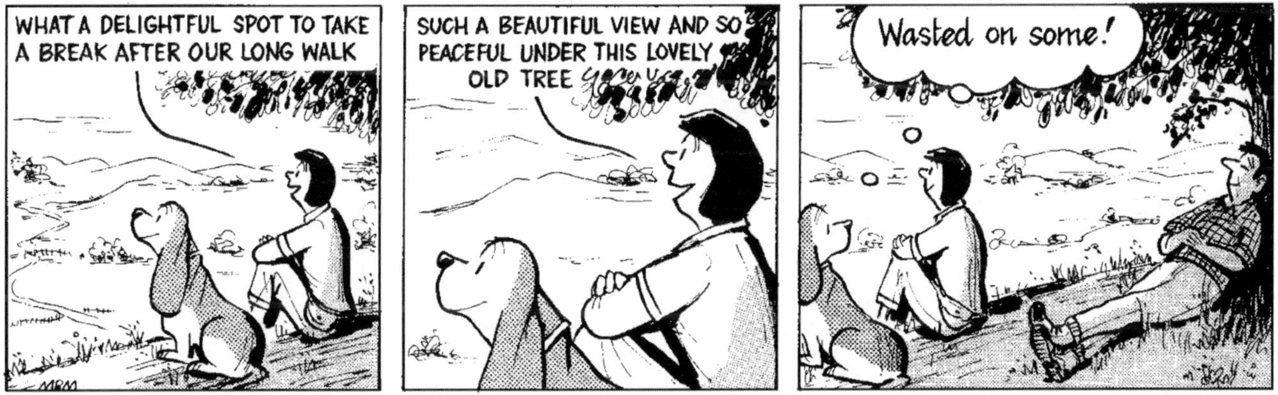
WHAT A DELIGHTFUL SPOT TO TAKE A BREAK AFTER OUR LONG WALK
SUCH A BEAUTIFUL VIEW AND SO PEACEFUL UNDER THIS LOVELY OLD TREE
Wasted on some!

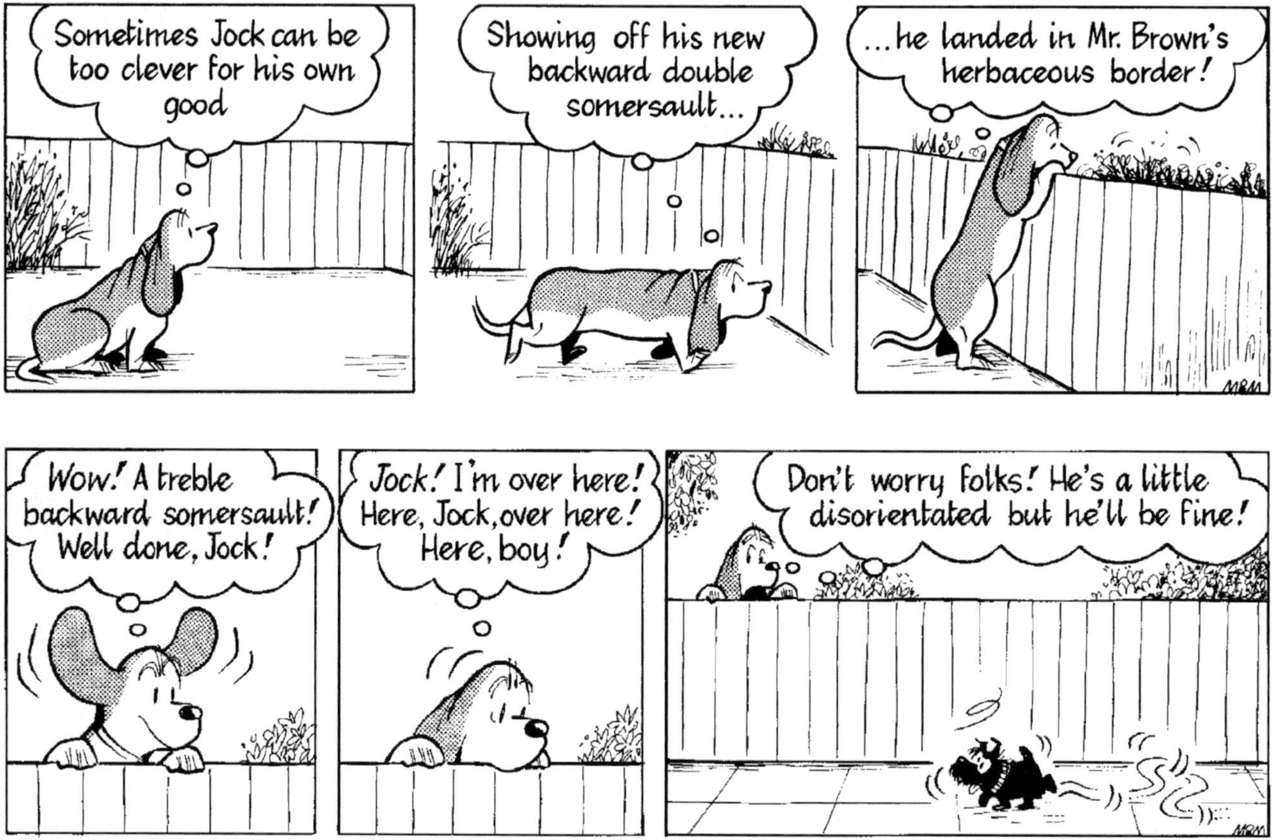
Sometimes Jock can be too clever for his own good
Showing off his new backward double somersault...
...he landed in Mr. Brown's herbaceous border!
MBM
Wow! A treble backward somersault! Well done, Jock!
Jock! I'm over here! Here, Jock, over here! Here, boy!
Don't worry folks! He's a little disorientated but he'll be fine!
MBM

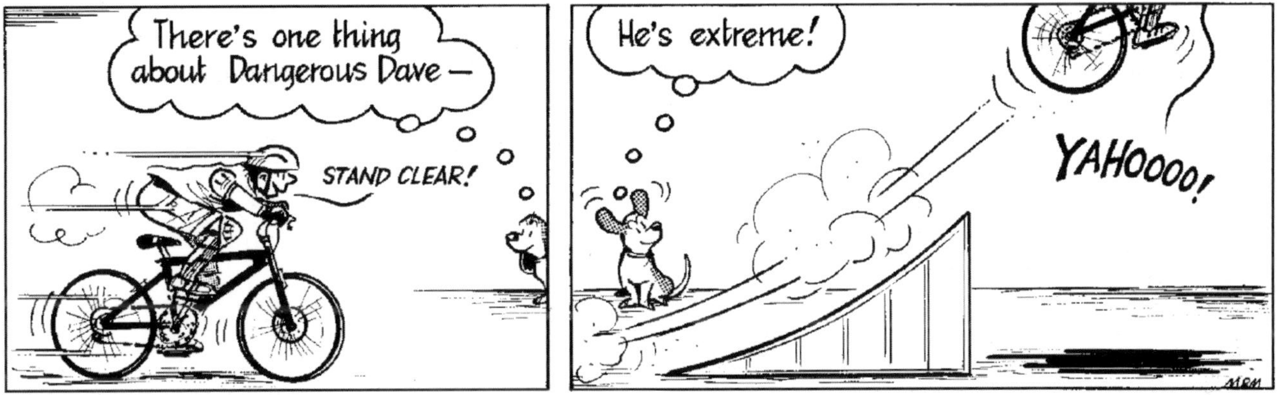
There's one thing about Dangerous Dave –
STAND CLEAR!
He's extreme!
YAHOOOO!
MRM

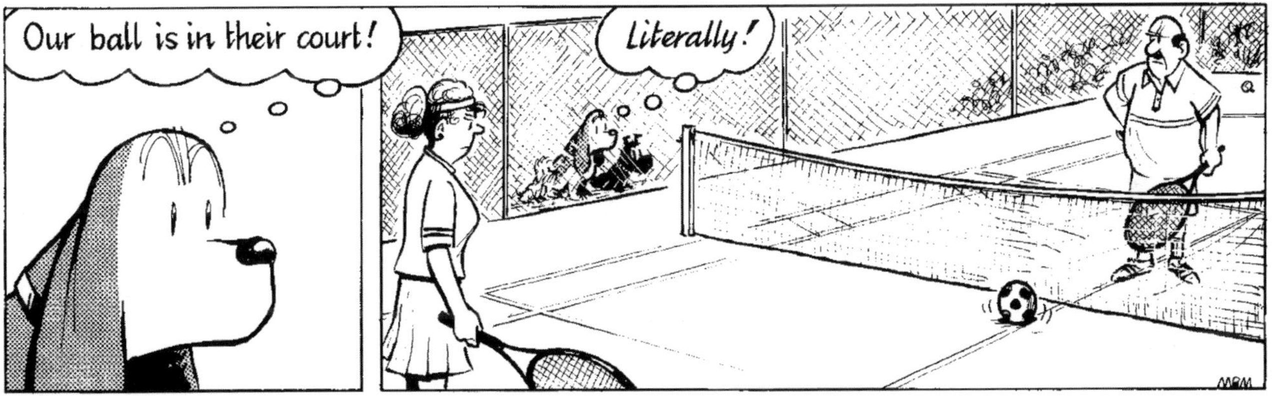
Our ball is in their court!
Literally!
MRM

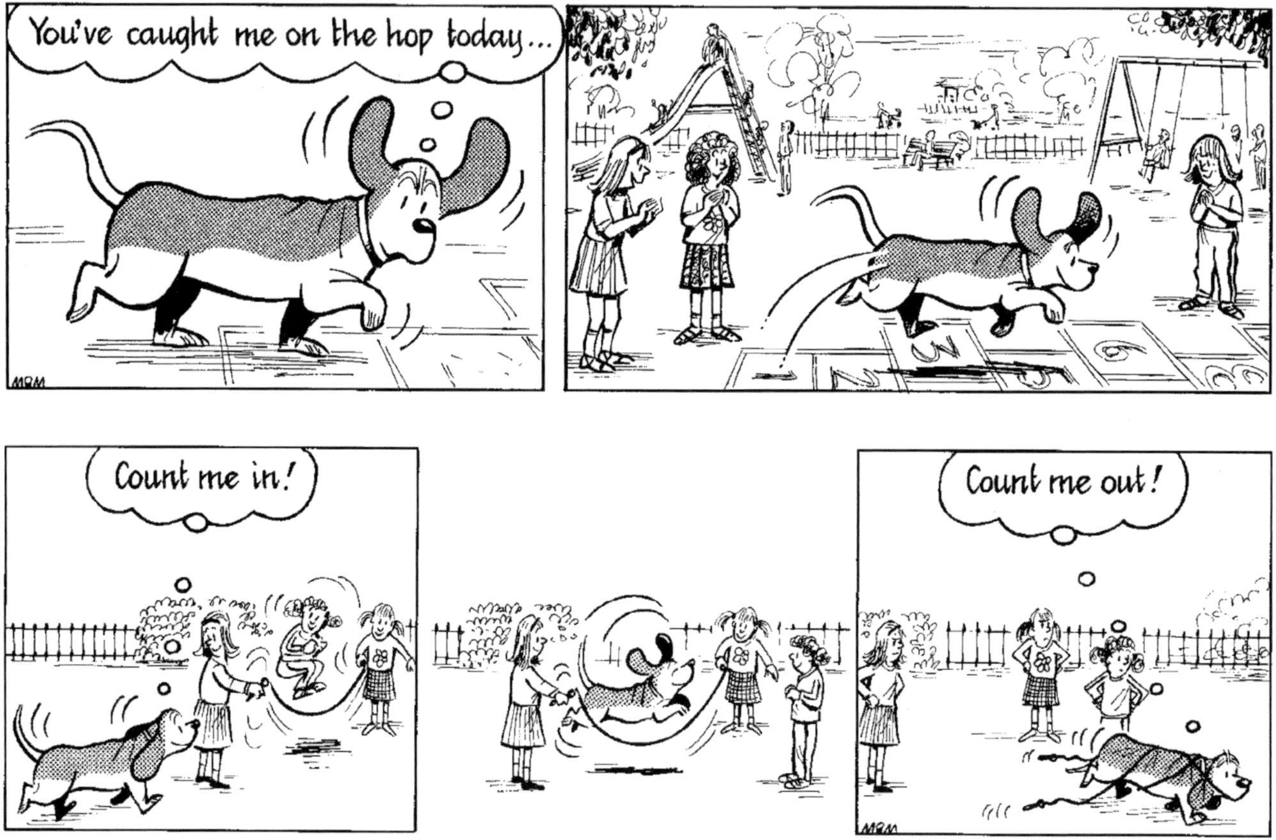

You've caught me on the hop today...
MGM
Count me in!
Count me out!
MGM

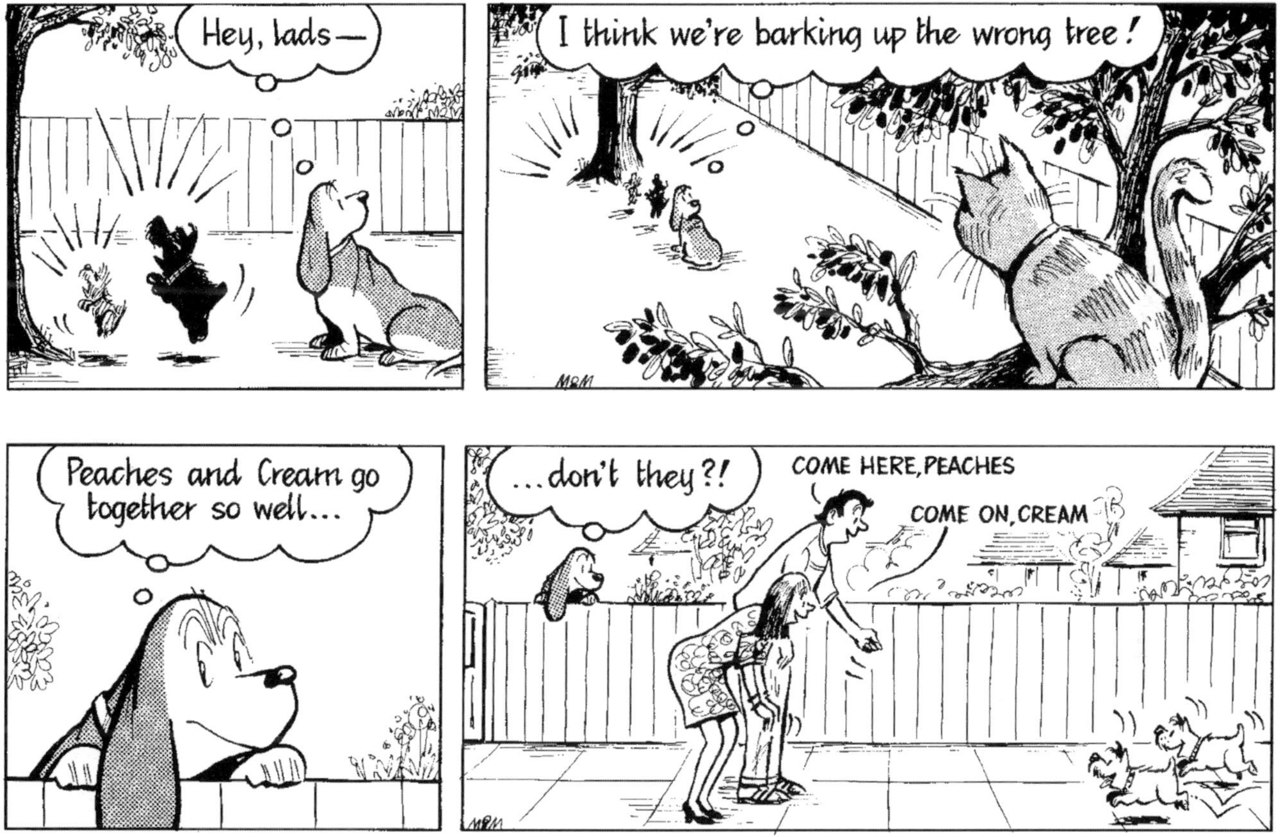
Hey, lads—
I think we're barking up the wrong tree!
MSM
Peaches and Cream go together so well...
...don't they?!
COME HERE, PEACHES
COME ON, CREAM
MSM

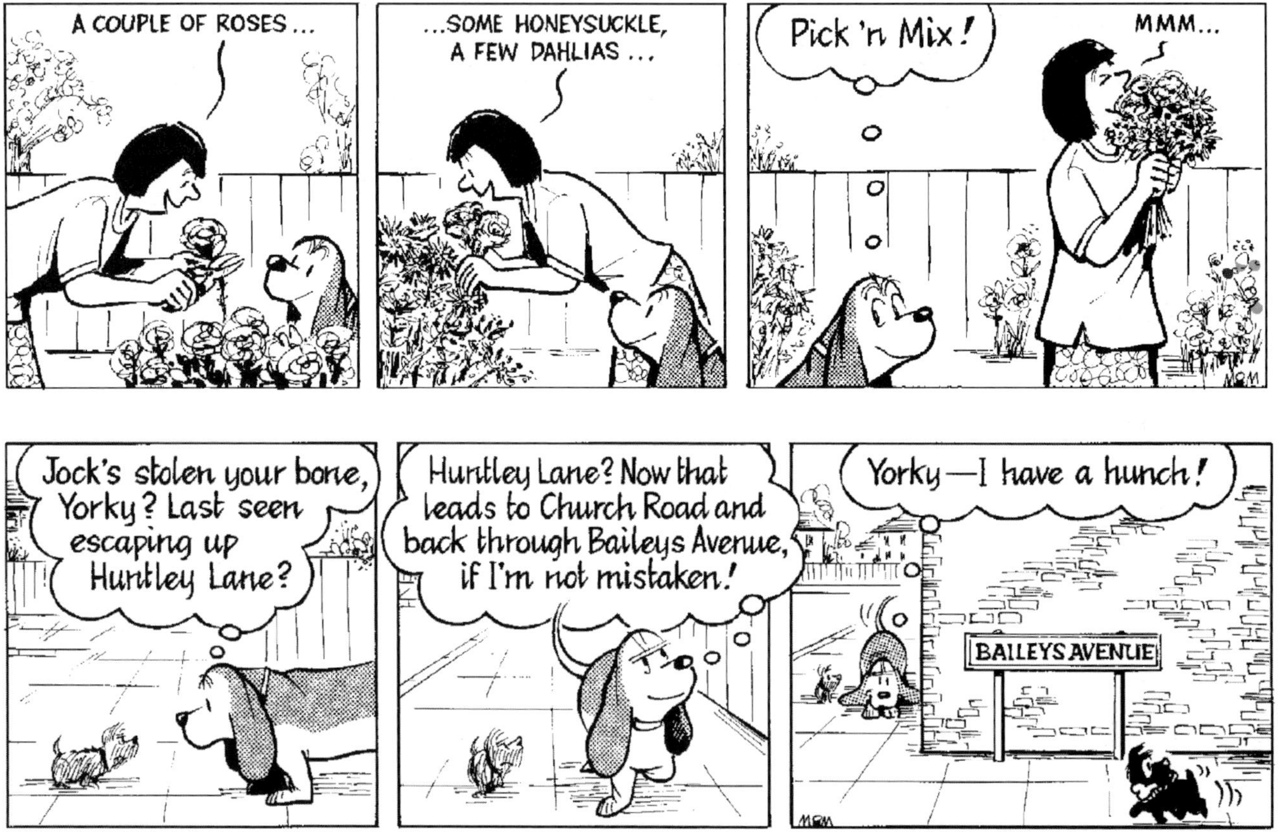
A COUPLE OF ROSES ...
...SOME HONEYSUCKLE, A FEW DAHLIAS ...
Pick 'n Mix!
MMM...
Jock's stolen your bone, Yorky? Last seen escaping up Huntley Lane?
Huntley Lane? Now that leads to Church Road and back through Baileys Avenue, if I'm not mistaken!
Yorky—I have a hunch!
BAILEYS AVENUE

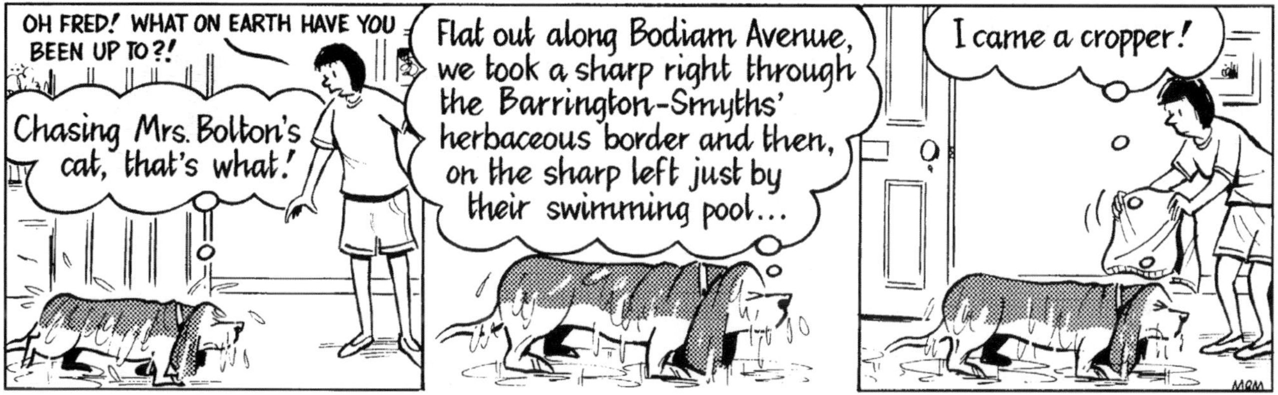
OH FRED! WHAT ON EARTH HAVE YOU BEEN UP TO?!
Chasing Mrs. Bolton's cat, that's what!
Flat out along Bodiam Avenue, we took a sharp right through the Barrington-Smyths' herbaceous border and then, on the sharp left just by their swimming pool...
I came a cropper!

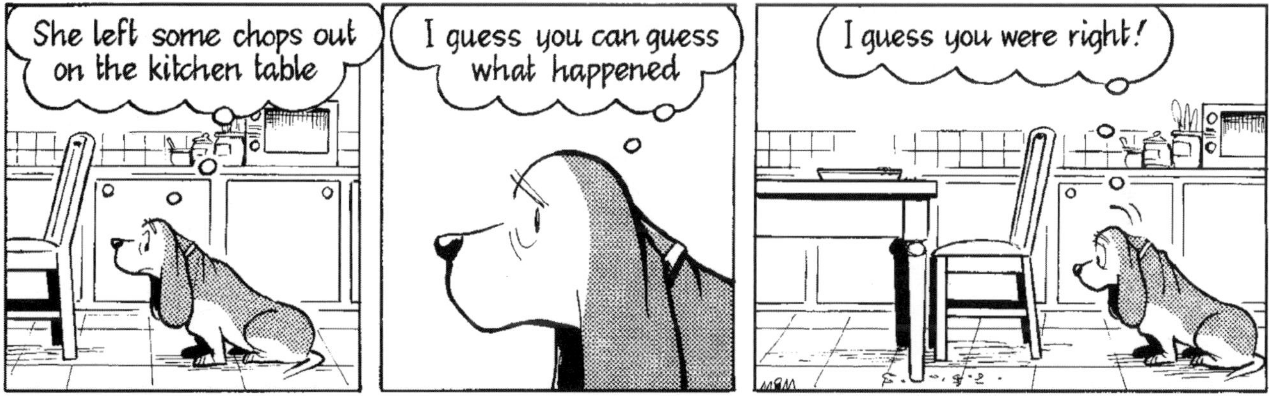
She left some chops out on the kitchen table
I guess you can guess what happened
I guess you were right!

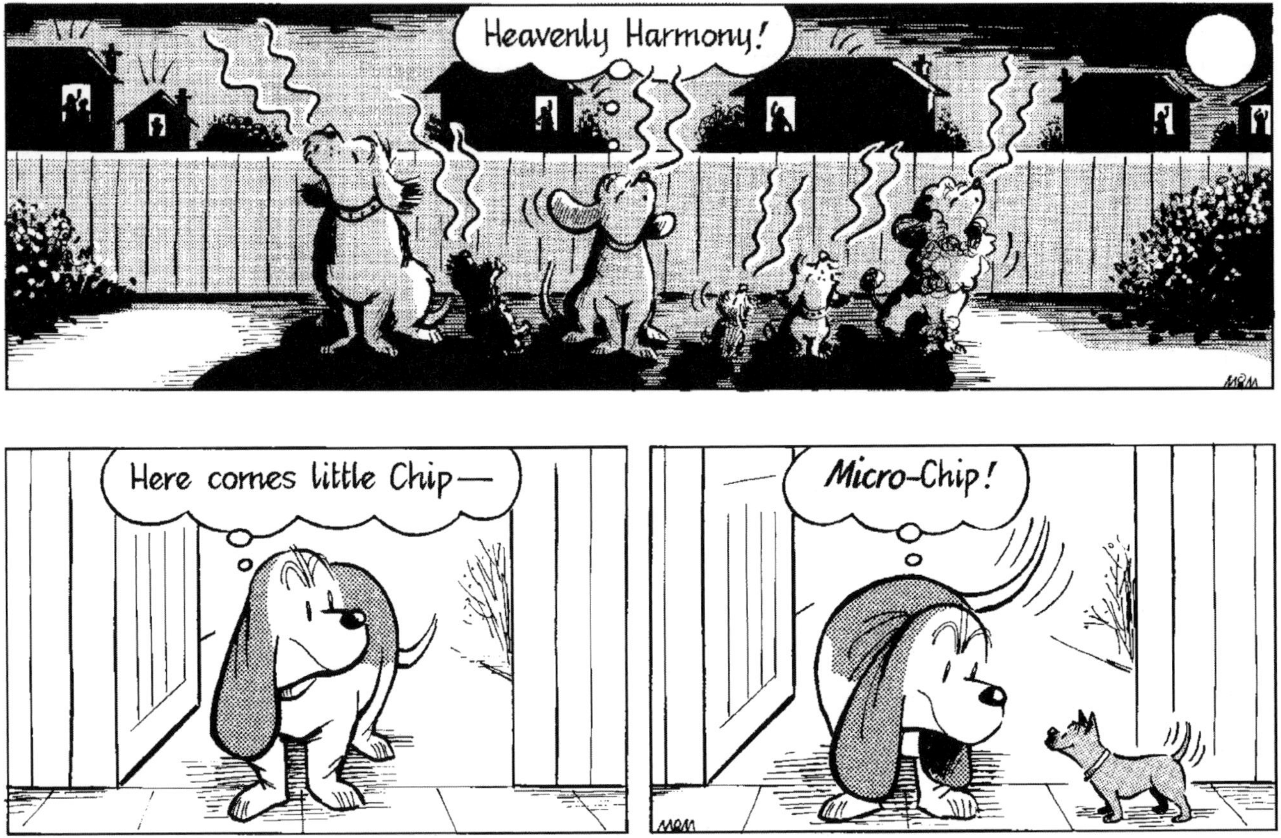
Heavenly Harmony!
Here comes little Chip—
Micro-Chip!

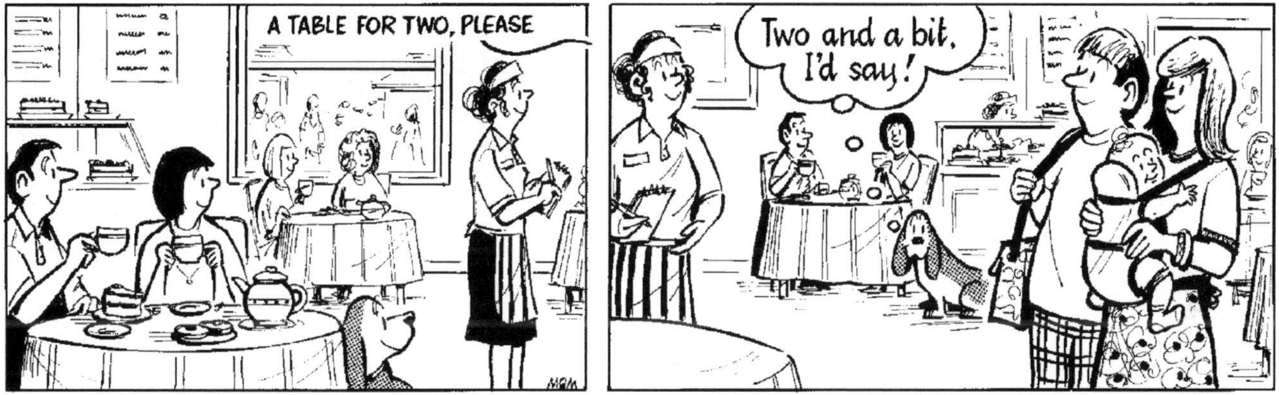
A TABLE FOR TWO, PLEASE
Two and a bit, I'd say!
MGM

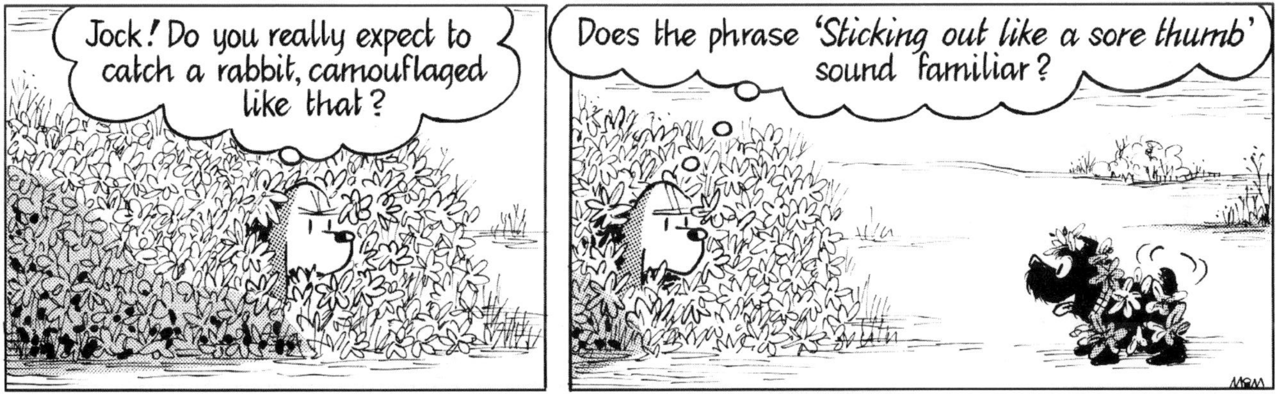
Jock! Do you really expect to catch a rabbit, camouflaged like that?
Does the phrase *'Sticking out like a sore thumb'* sound familiar?
MGM

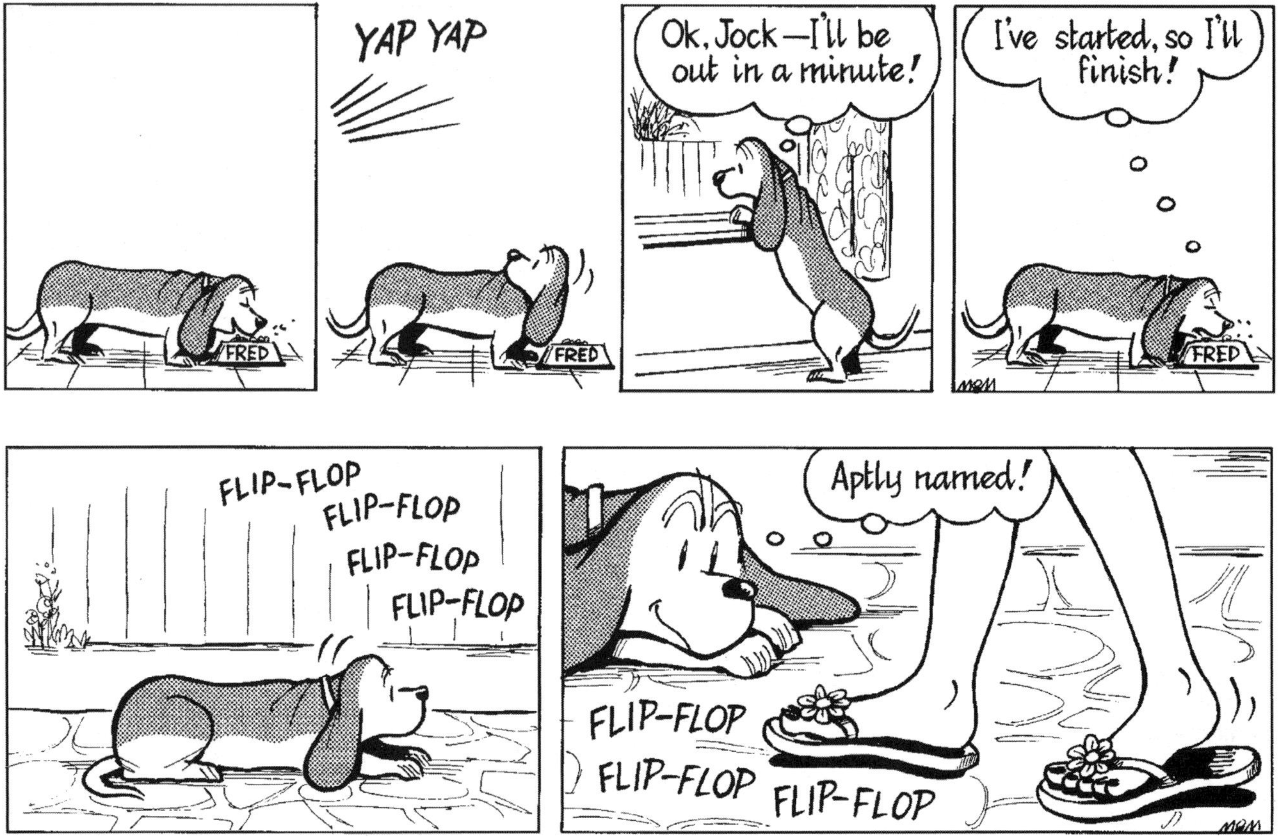
YAP YAP
Ok, Jock—I'll be out in a minute!
I've started, so I'll finish!
FRED
FLIP-FLOP FLIP-FLOP FLIP-FLOP FLIP-FLOP
Aptly named!
FLIP-FLOP FLIP-FLOP FLIP-FLOP

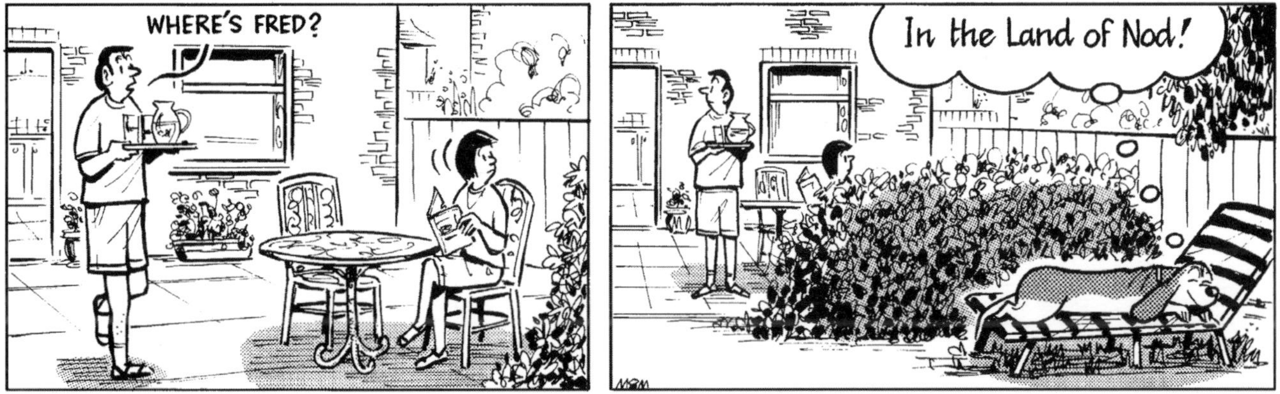
WHERE'S FRED?
In the Land of Nod!

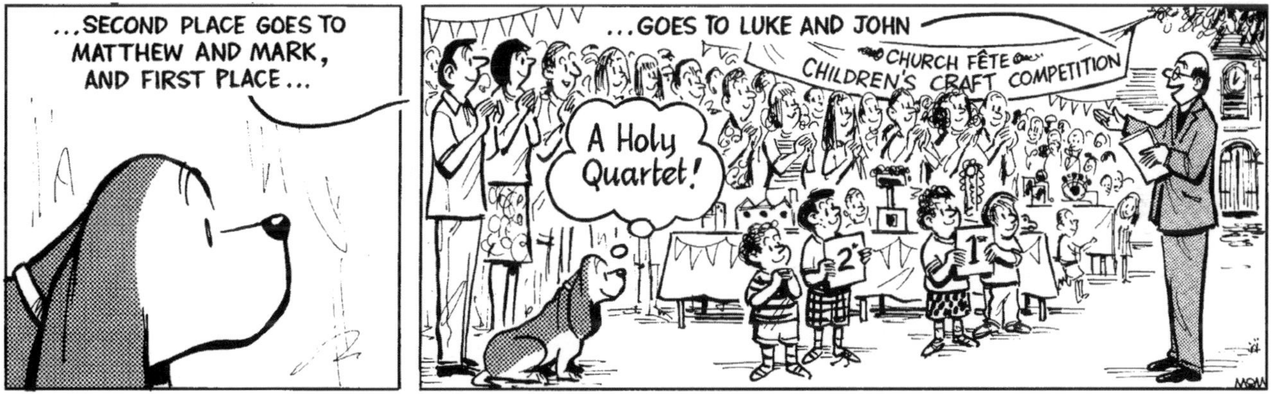
...SECOND PLACE GOES TO MATTHEW AND MARK, AND FIRST PLACE...
...GOES TO LUKE AND JOHN
CHURCH FÊTE
CHILDREN'S CRAFT COMPETITION
A Holy Quartet!

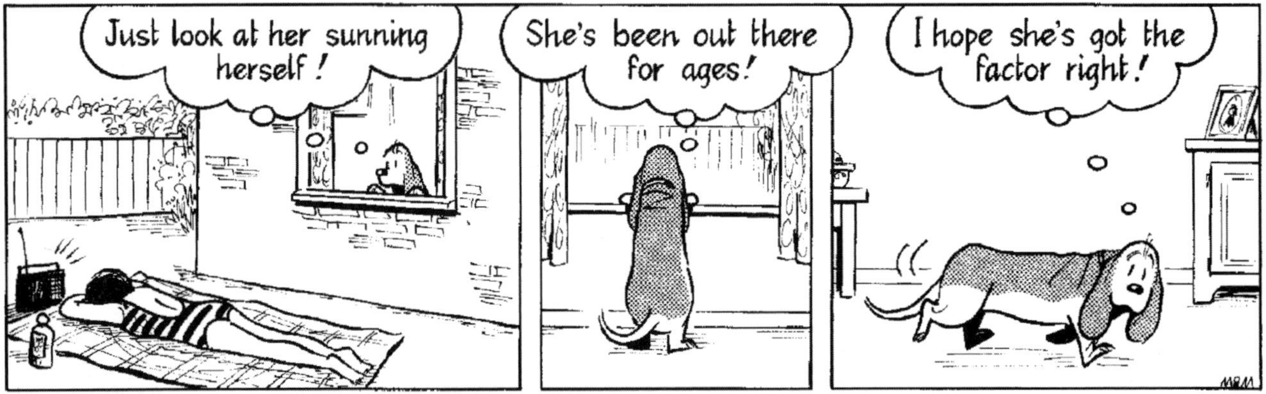
Just look at her sunning herself!
She's been out there for ages!
I hope she's got the factor right!
MRM

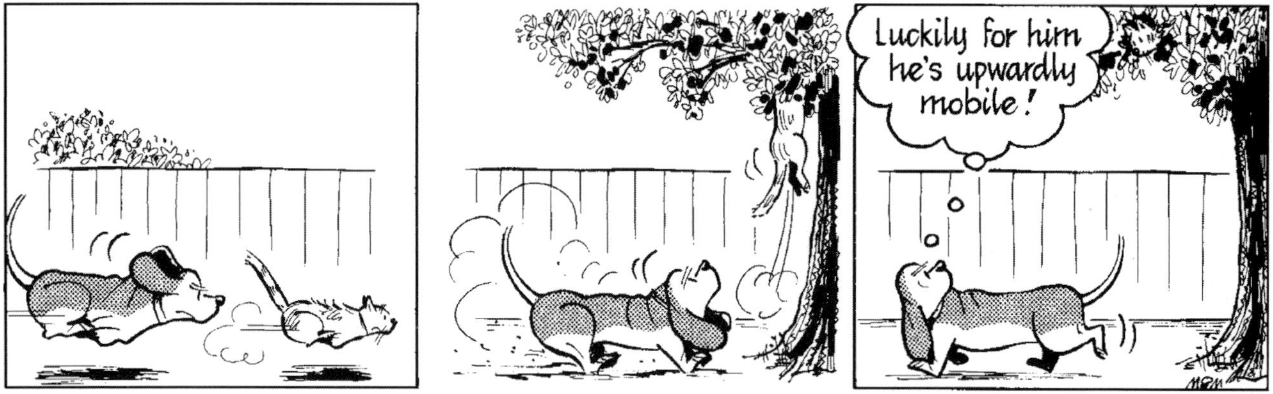
Luckily for him he's upwardly mobile!
MRM

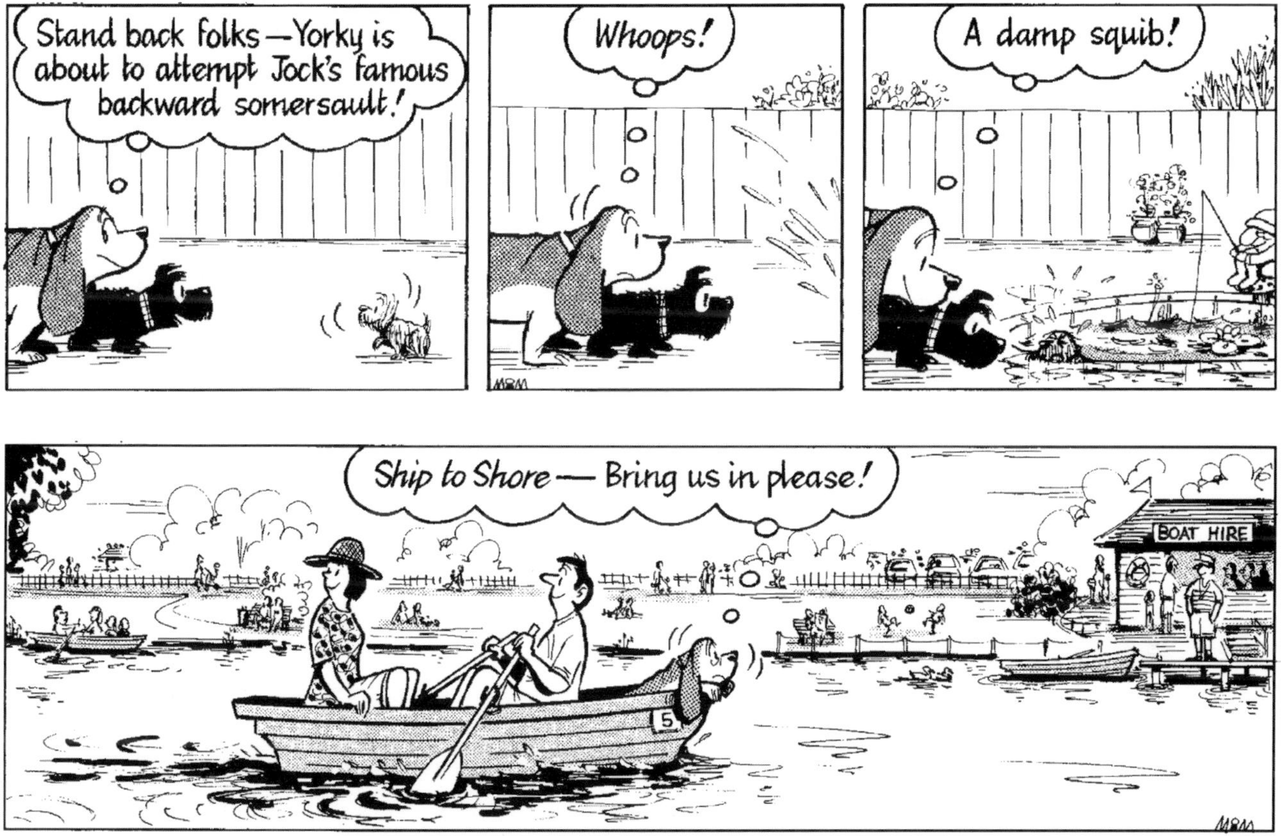
Stand back folks—Yorky is about to attempt Jock's famous backward somersault!
Whoops!
A damp squib!
Ship to Shore— Bring us in please!
BOAT HIRE
5

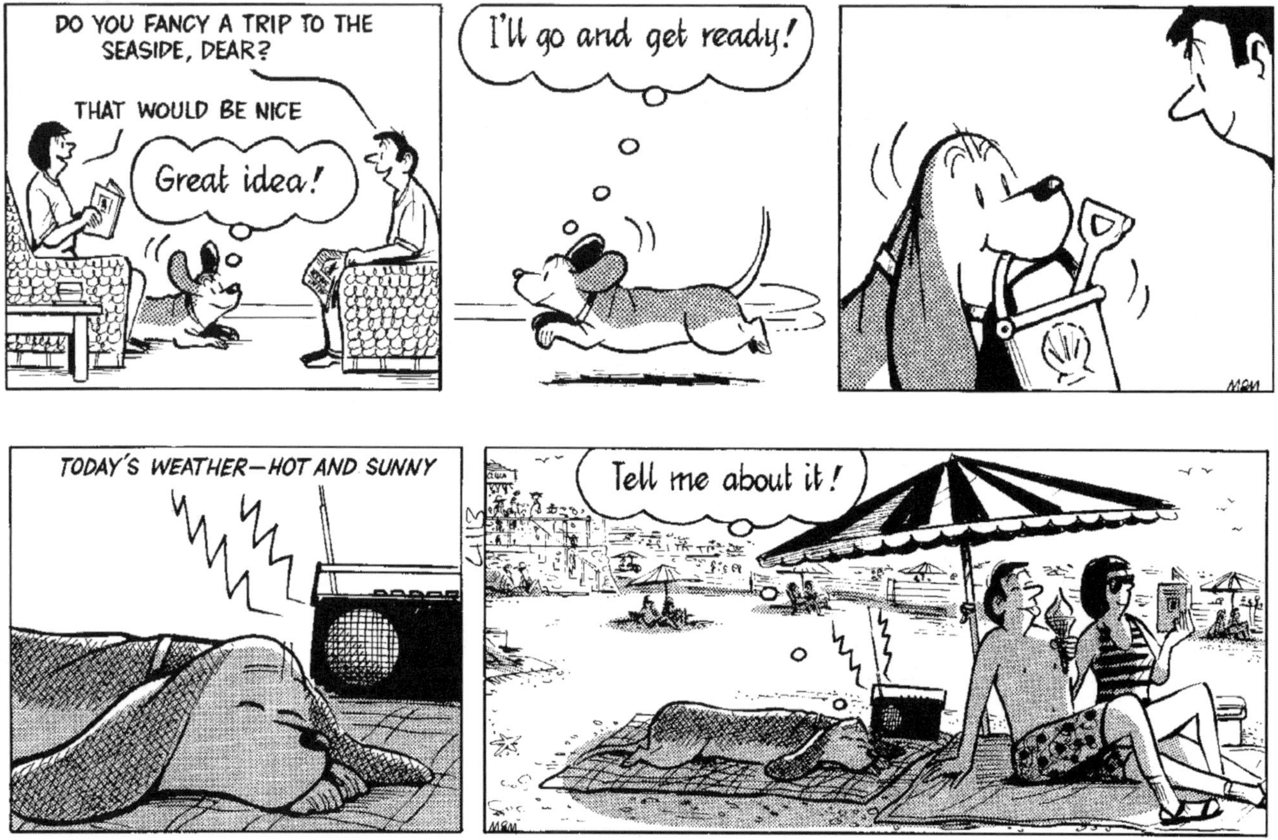
DO YOU FANCY A TRIP TO THE SEASIDE, DEAR?
THAT WOULD BE NICE
Great idea!
I'll go and get ready!
TODAY'S WEATHER—HOT AND SUNNY
Tell me about it!

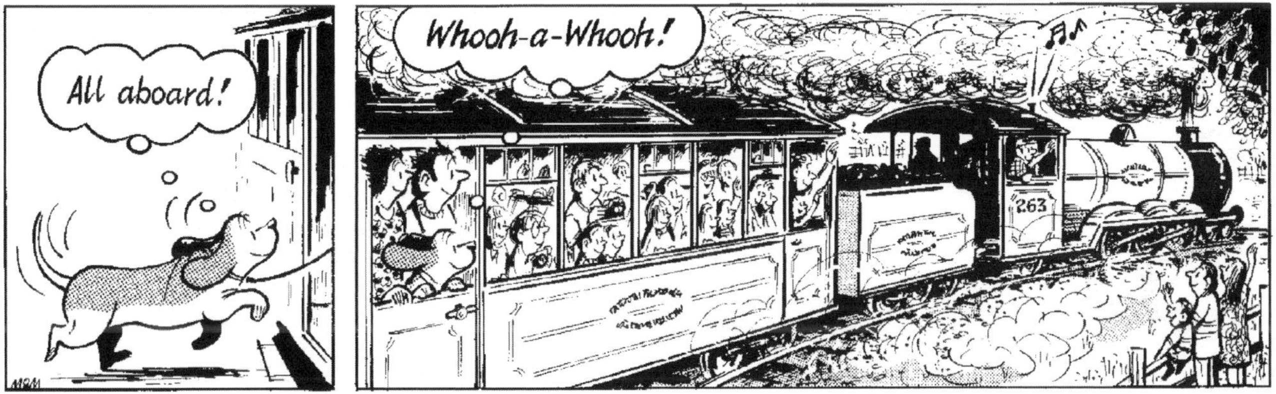
All aboard!
Whooh-a-Whooh!

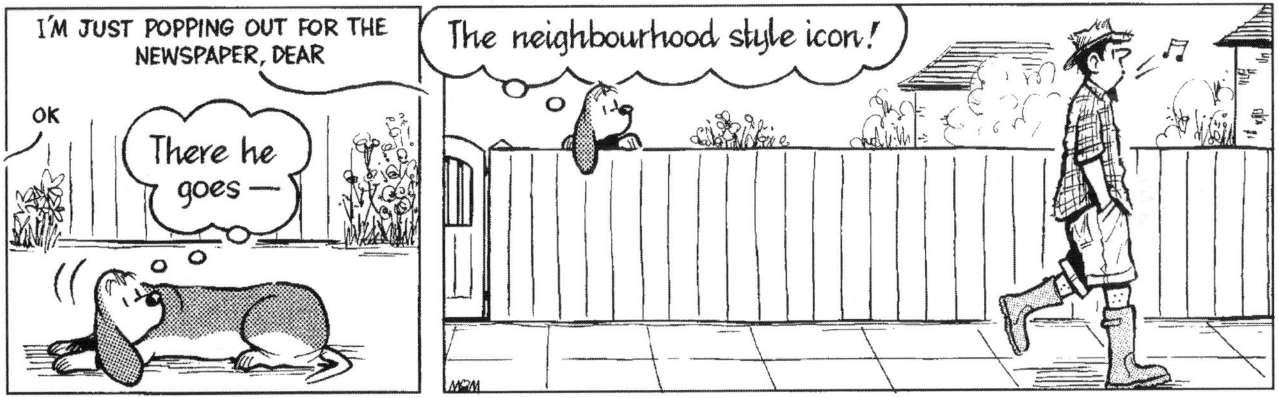
I'M JUST POPPING OUT FOR THE NEWSPAPER, DEAR
OK
There he goes –
The neighbourhood style icon!

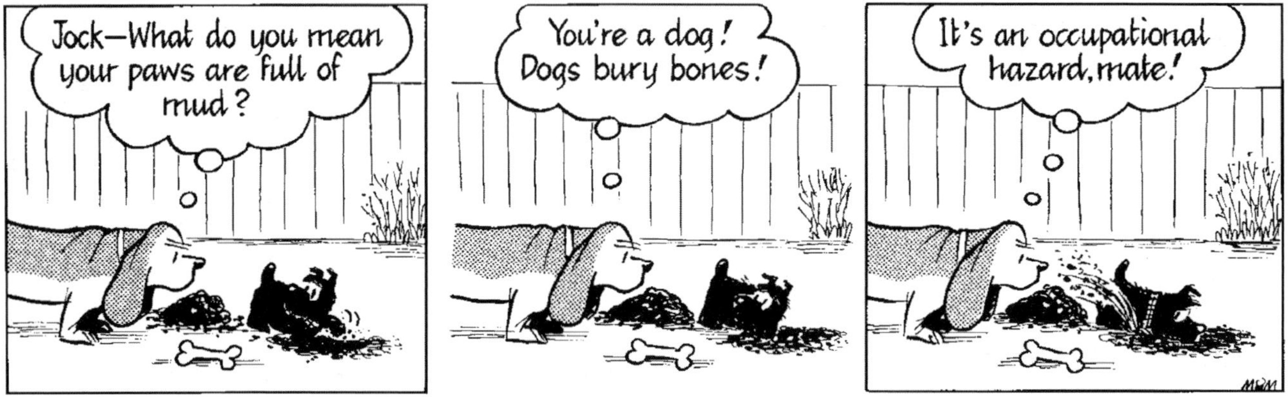
Jock—What do you mean your paws are full of mud?
You're a dog! Dogs bury bones!
It's an occupational hazard, mate!

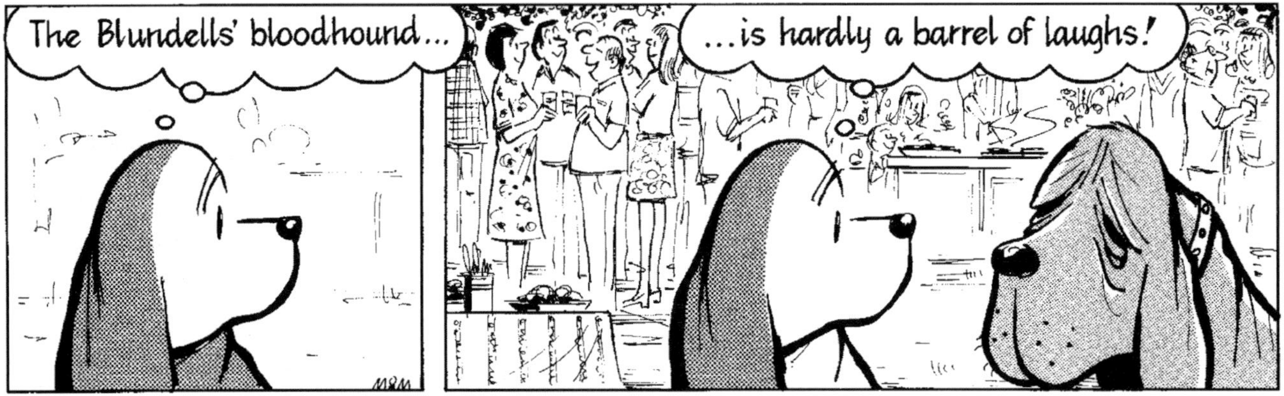
The Blundells' bloodhound...
...is hardly a barrel of laughs!

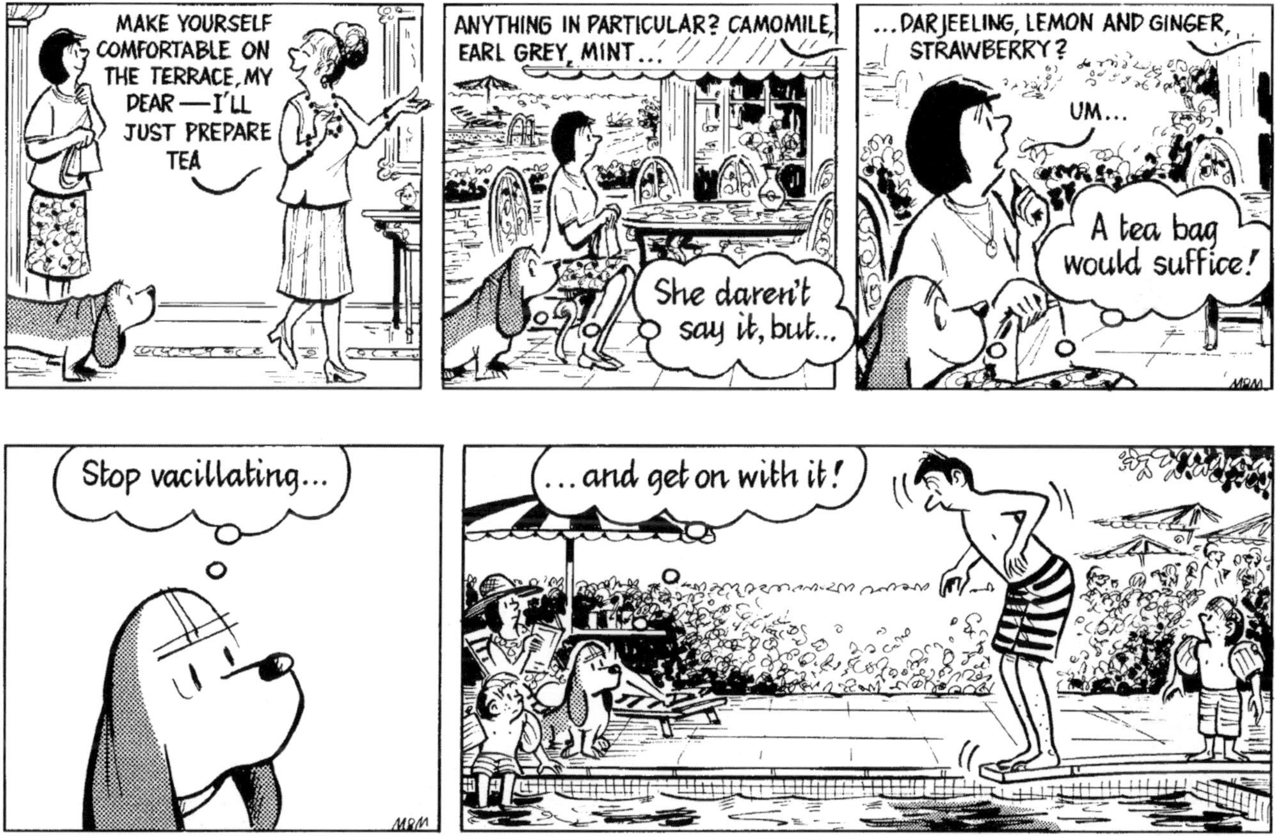
MAKE YOURSELF COMFORTABLE ON THE TERRACE, MY DEAR — I'LL JUST PREPARE TEA
ANYTHING IN PARTICULAR? CAMOMILE, EARL GREY, MINT...
She daren't say it, but...
...DARJEELING, LEMON AND GINGER, STRAWBERRY?
UM...
A tea bag would suffice!
MBM
Stop vacillating...
MBM
...and get on with it!

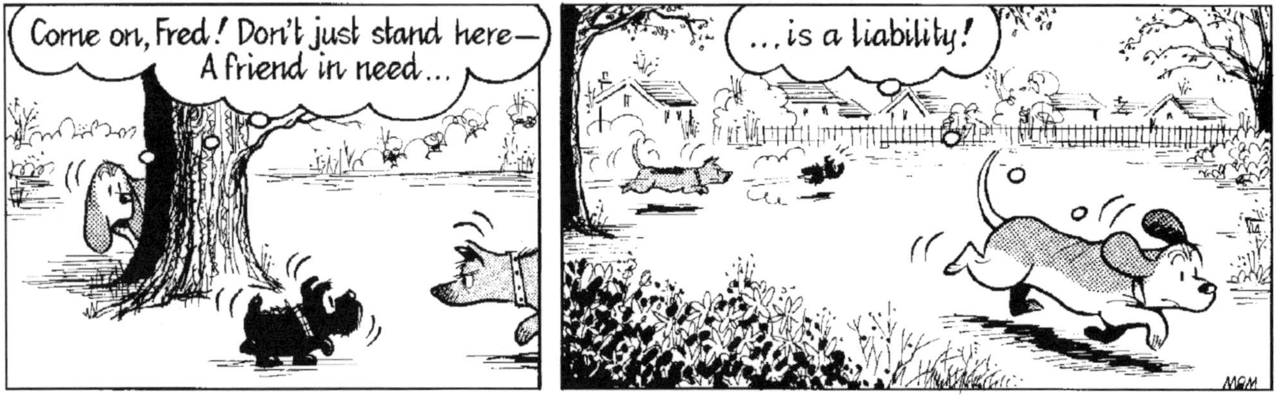
Come on, Fred! Don't just stand here—
A friend in need...
...is a liability!

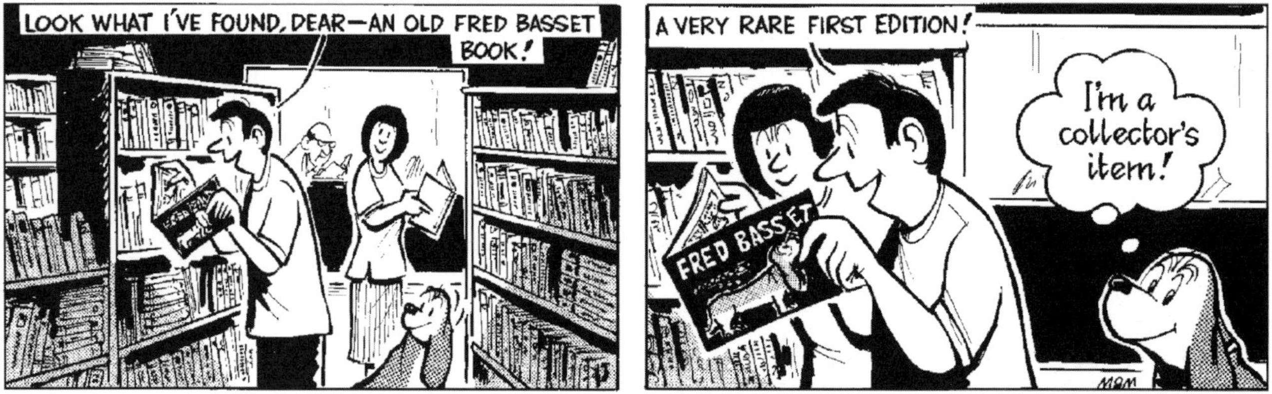
LOOK WHAT I'VE FOUND, DEAR—AN OLD FRED BASSET BOOK!
A VERY RARE FIRST EDITION!
FRED BASSET
I'm a collector's item!

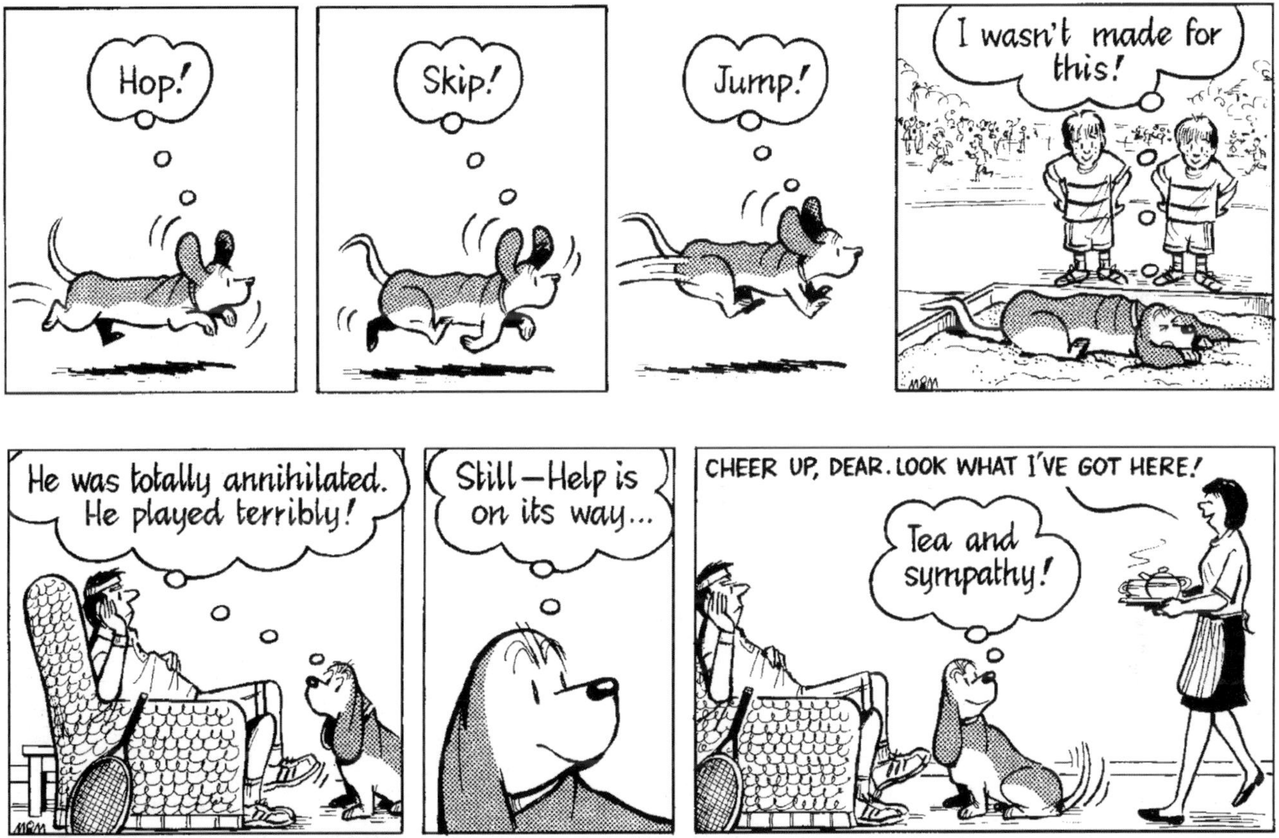

Hop!
Skip!
Jump!
I wasn't made for this!
He was totally annihilated. He played terribly!
Still—Help is on its way...
CHEER UP, DEAR. LOOK WHAT I'VE GOT HERE!
Tea and sympathy!

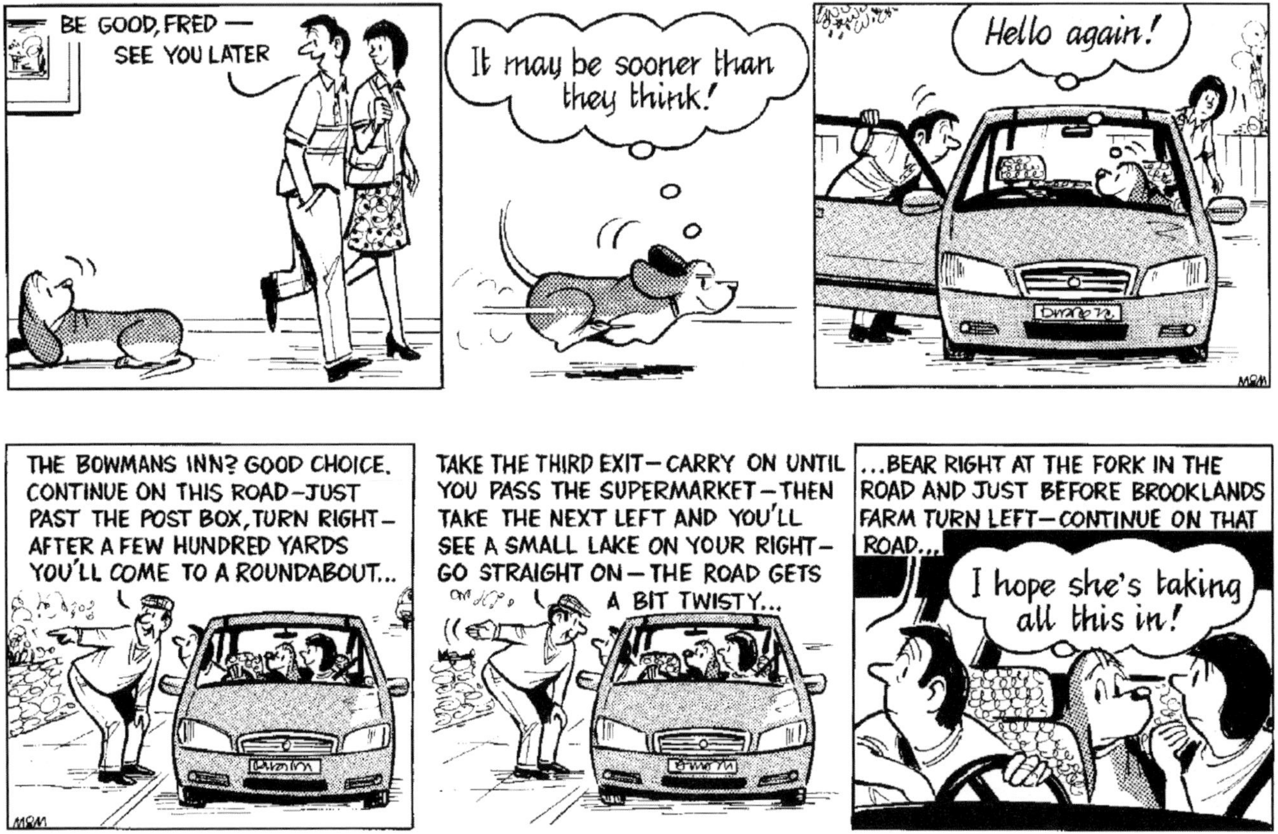
BE GOOD, FRED — SEE YOU LATER
It may be sooner than they think!
Hello again!
MCM
THE BOWMANS INN? GOOD CHOICE. CONTINUE ON THIS ROAD—JUST PAST THE POST BOX, TURN RIGHT—AFTER A FEW HUNDRED YARDS YOU'LL COME TO A ROUNDABOUT...
MCM
TAKE THE THIRD EXIT—CARRY ON UNTIL YOU PASS THE SUPERMARKET—THEN TAKE THE NEXT LEFT AND YOU'LL SEE A SMALL LAKE ON YOUR RIGHT—GO STRAIGHT ON—THE ROAD GETS A BIT TWISTY...
...BEAR RIGHT AT THE FORK IN THE ROAD AND JUST BEFORE BROOKLANDS FARM TURN LEFT—CONTINUE ON THAT ROAD...
I hope she's taking all this in!

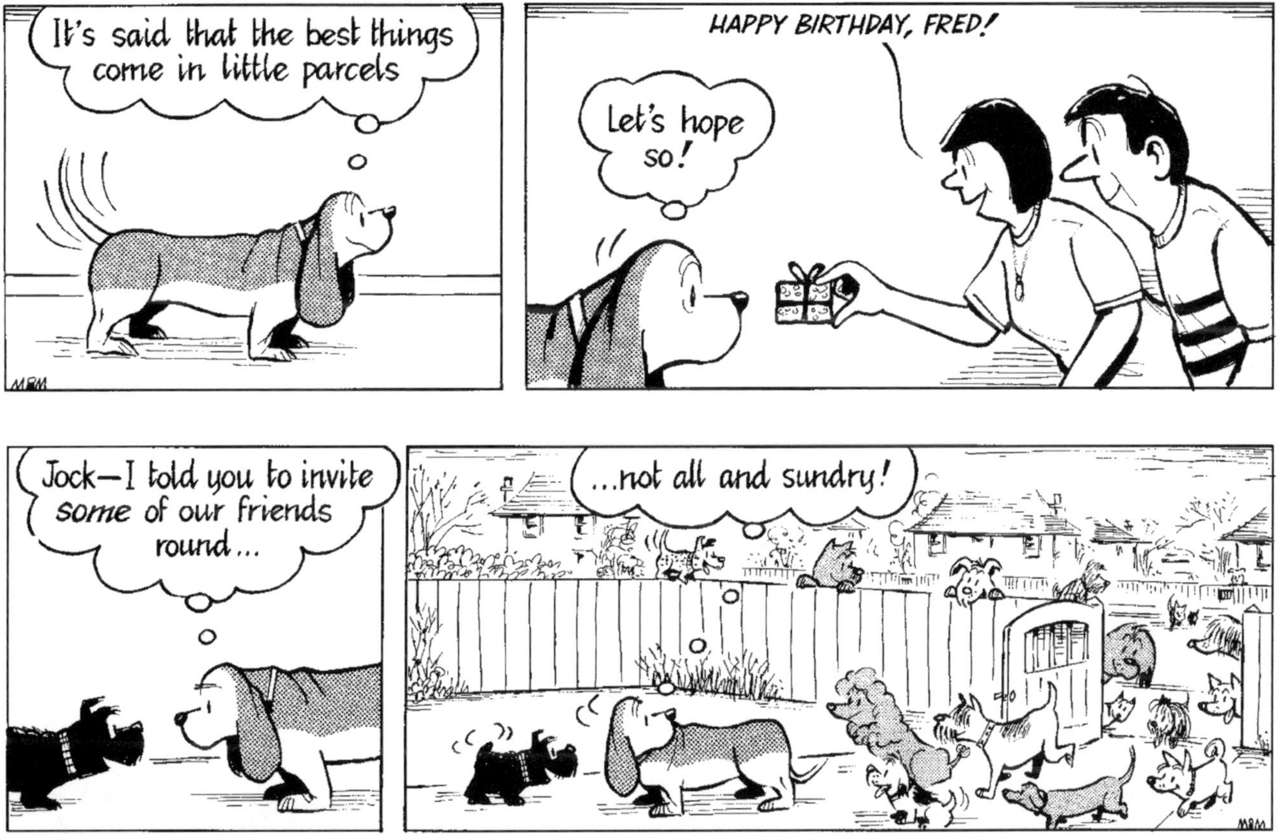
It's said that the best things come in little parcels
HAPPY BIRTHDAY, FRED!
Let's hope so!
Jock—I told you to invite *some* of our friends round...
...not all and sundry!

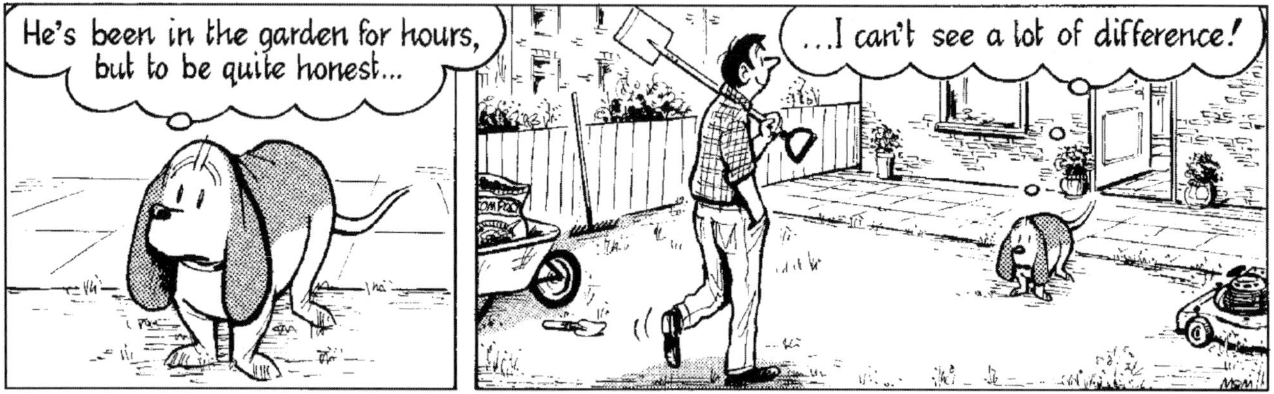
He's been in the garden for hours, but to be quite honest...
...I can't see a lot of difference!

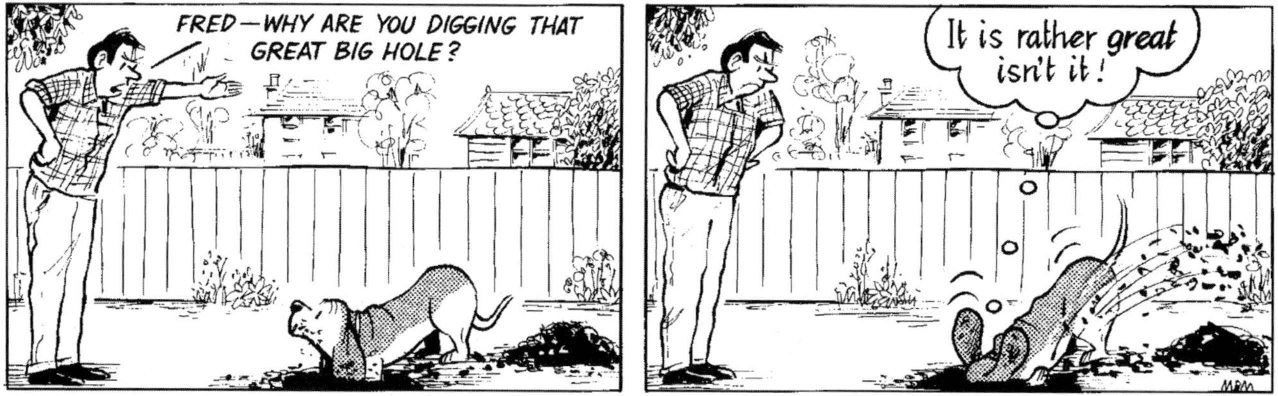
FRED—WHY ARE YOU DIGGING THAT GREAT BIG HOLE?
It is rather great isn't it!

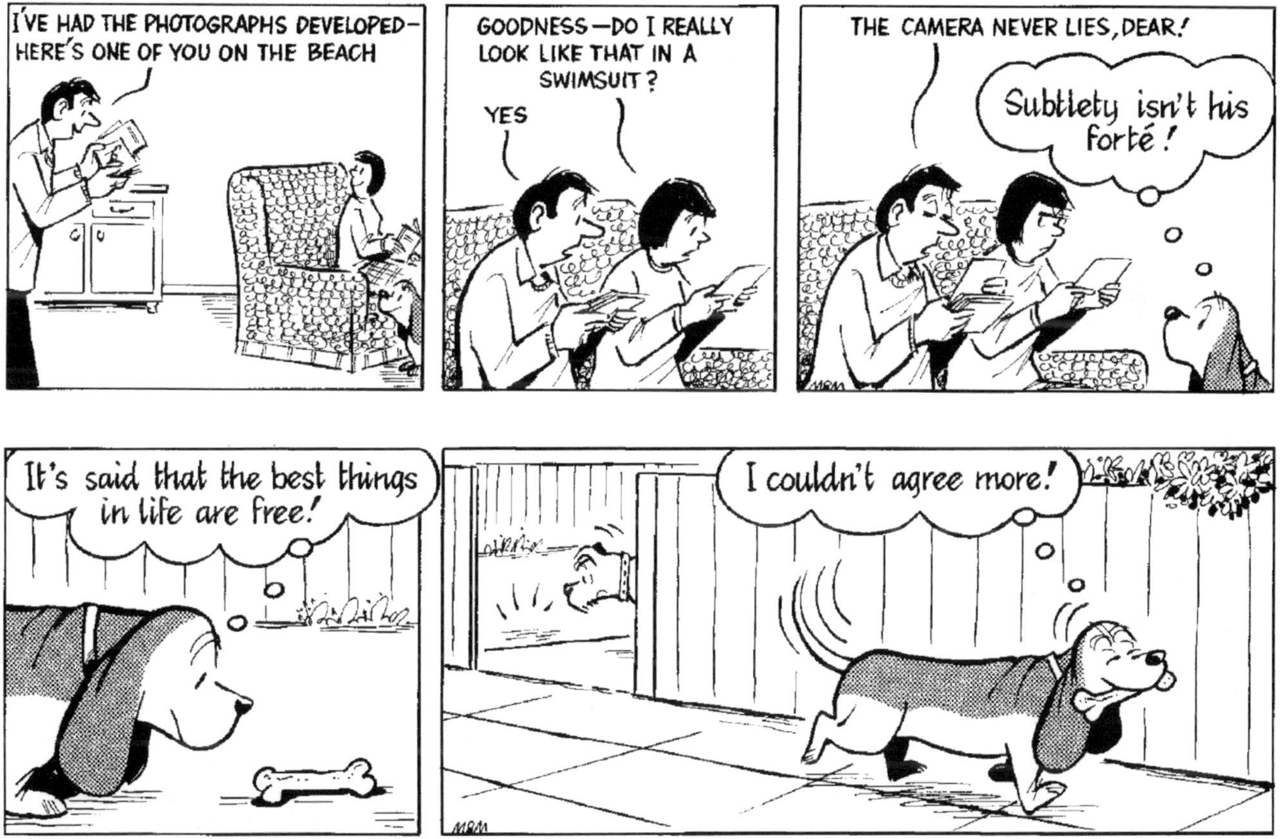
I'VE HAD THE PHOTOGRAPHS DEVELOPED– HERE'S ONE OF YOU ON THE BEACH
GOODNESS—DO I REALLY LOOK LIKE THAT IN A SWIMSUIT?
YES
THE CAMERA NEVER LIES, DEAR!
Subtlety isn't his forté!
It's said that the best things in life are free!
I couldn't agree more!
MBM
MBM

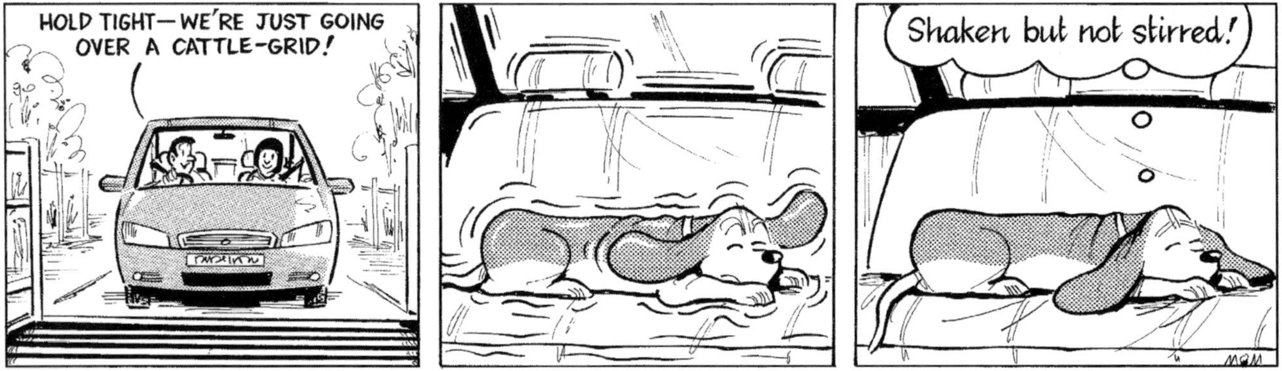
HOLD TIGHT—WE'RE JUST GOING OVER A CATTLE-GRID!
Shaken but not stirred!
MGM

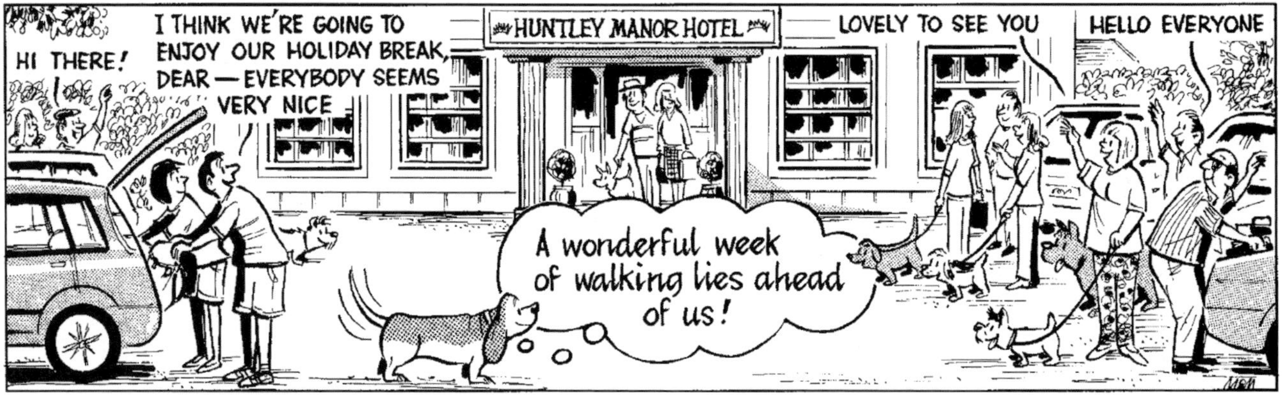
HUNTLEY MANOR HOTEL
HI THERE!
I THINK WE'RE GOING TO ENJOY OUR HOLIDAY BREAK, DEAR—EVERYBODY SEEMS VERY NICE
LOVELY TO SEE YOU
HELLO EVERYONE
A wonderful week of walking lies ahead of us!
MGM

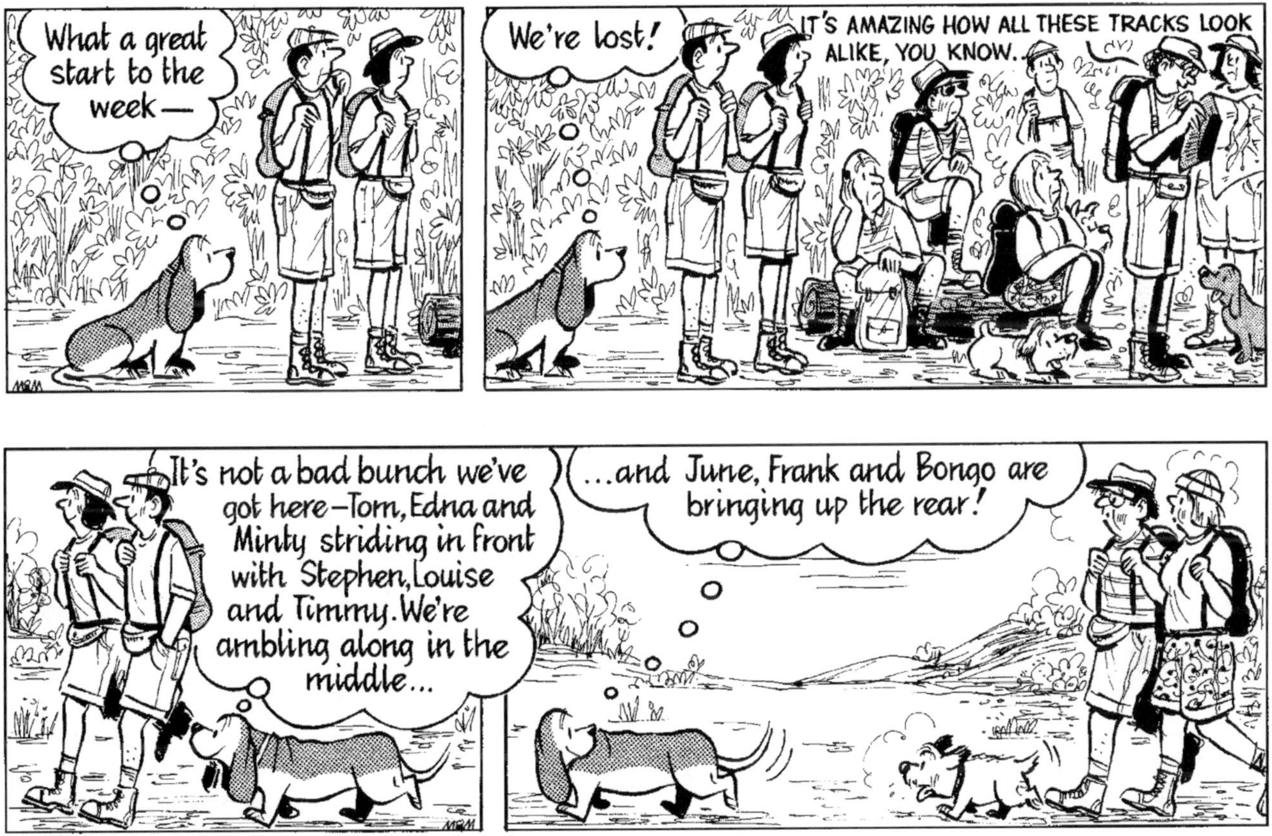
What a great start to the week—
We're lost!
IT'S AMAZING HOW ALL THESE TRACKS LOOK ALIKE, YOU KNOW...
It's not a bad bunch we've got here—Tom, Edna and Minty striding in front with Stephen, Louise and Timmy. We're ambling along in the middle...
...and June, Frank and Bongo are bringing up the rear!

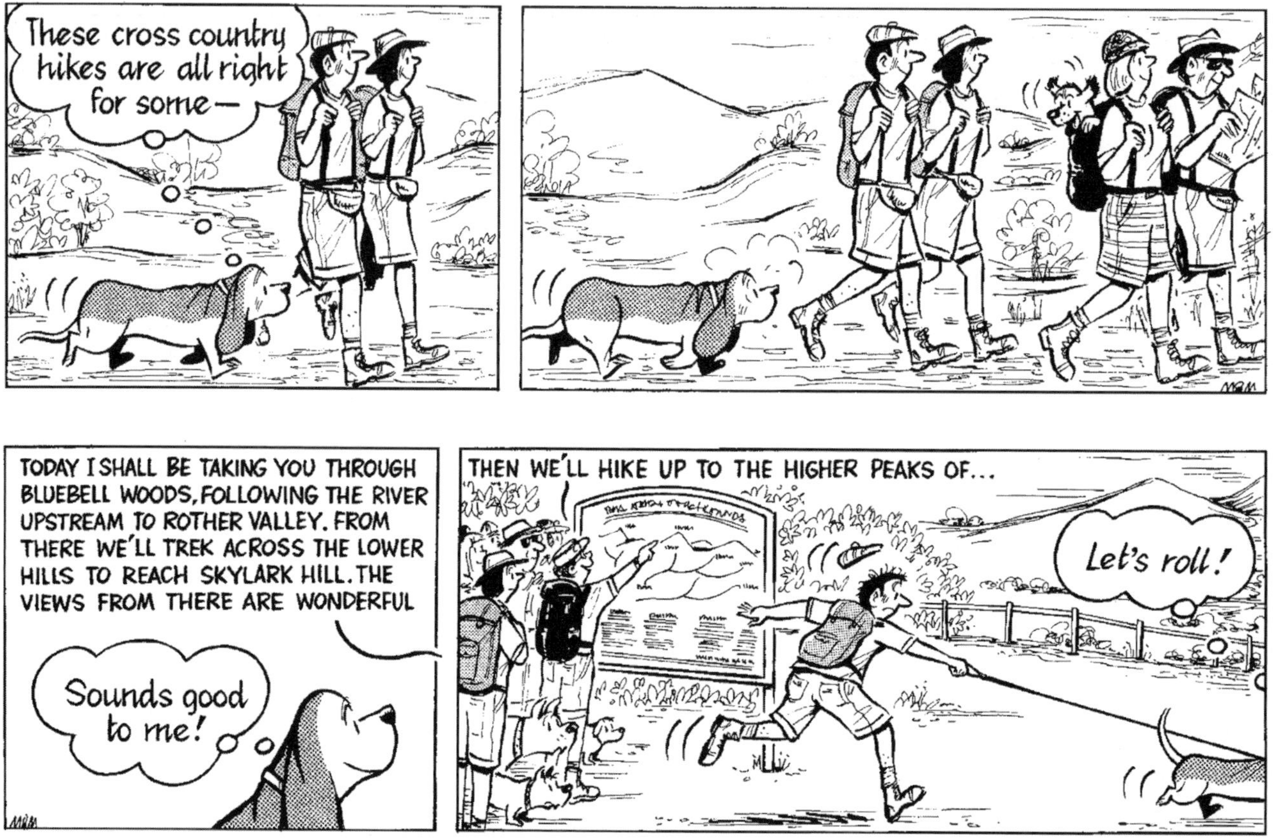
These cross country hikes are all right for some—
TODAY I SHALL BE TAKING YOU THROUGH BLUEBELL WOODS, FOLLOWING THE RIVER UPSTREAM TO ROTHER VALLEY. FROM THERE WE'LL TREK ACROSS THE LOWER HILLS TO REACH SKYLARK HILL. THE VIEWS FROM THERE ARE WONDERFUL
Sounds good to me!
THEN WE'LL HIKE UP TO THE HIGHER PEAKS OF...
Let's roll!

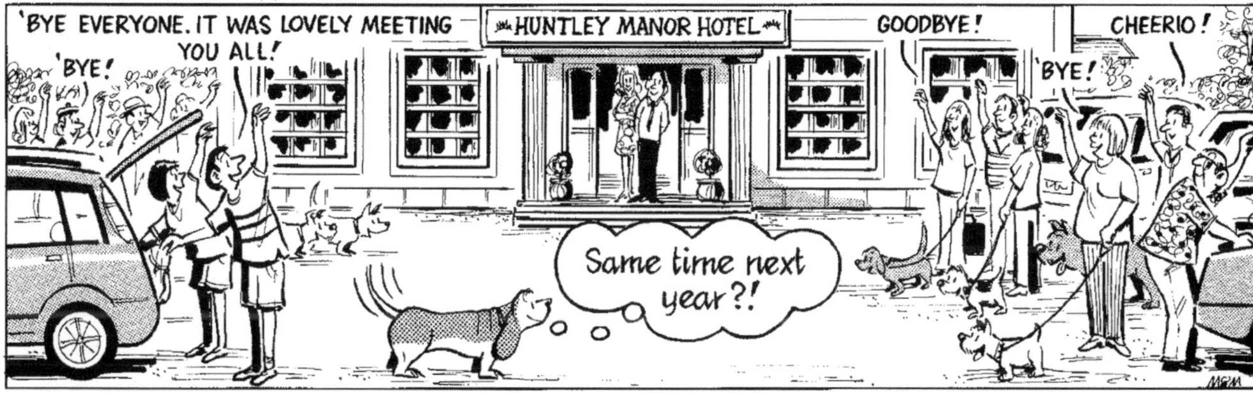
HUNTLEY MANOR HOTEL
'BYE EVERYONE. IT WAS LOVELY MEETING YOU ALL!
'BYE!
GOODBYE!
'BYE!
CHEERIO!
Same time next year?!
MGM

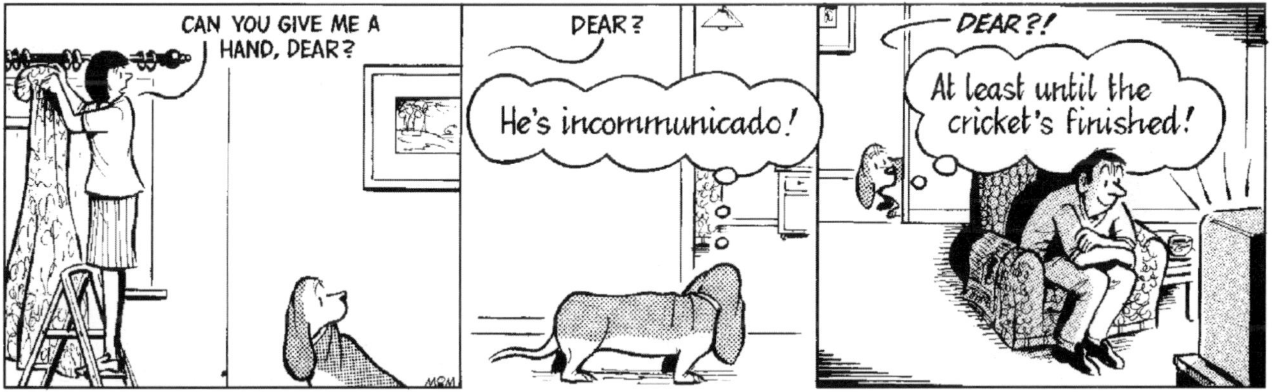
CAN YOU GIVE ME A HAND, DEAR?
MGM
DEAR?
He's incommunicado!
DEAR?!
At least until the cricket's finished!

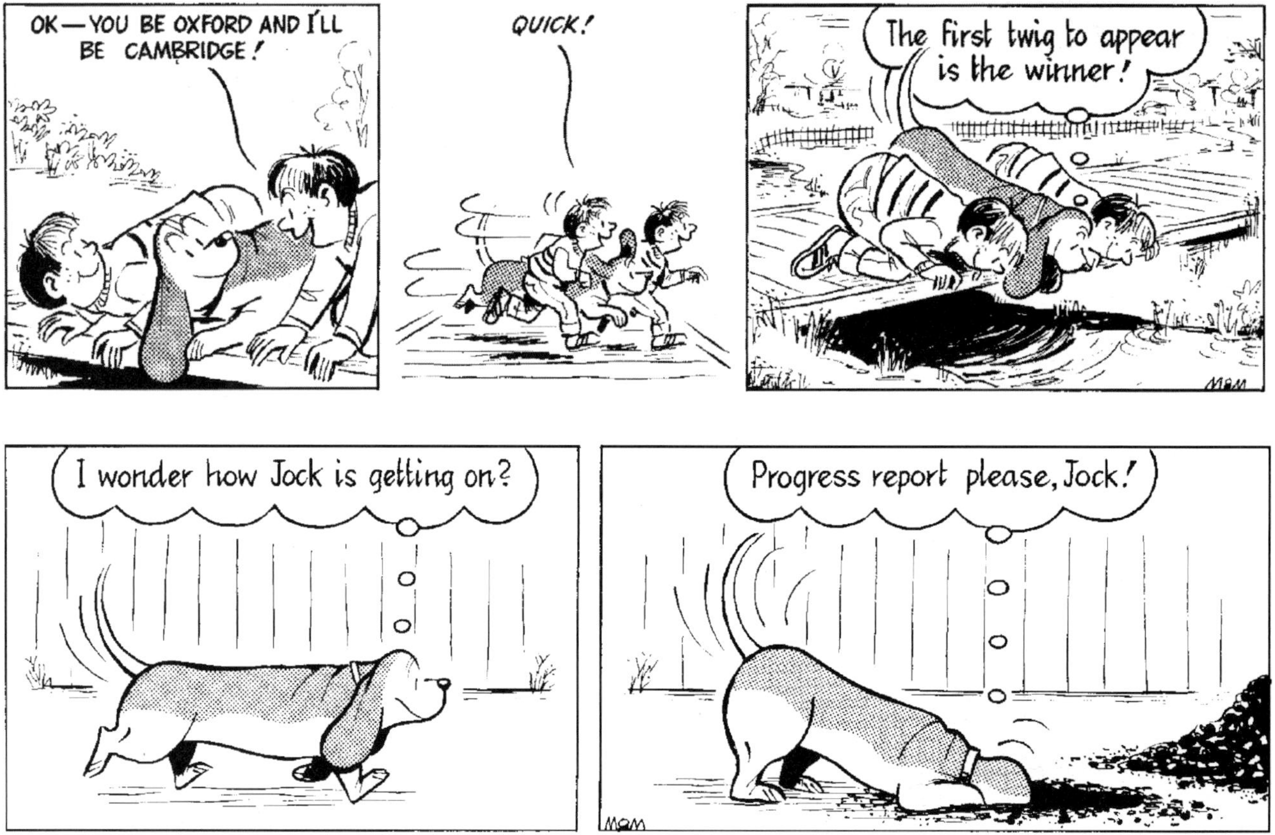
OK—YOU BE OXFORD AND I'LL BE CAMBRIDGE!
QUICK!
The first twig to appear is the winner!
I wonder how Jock is getting on?
Progress report please, Jock!

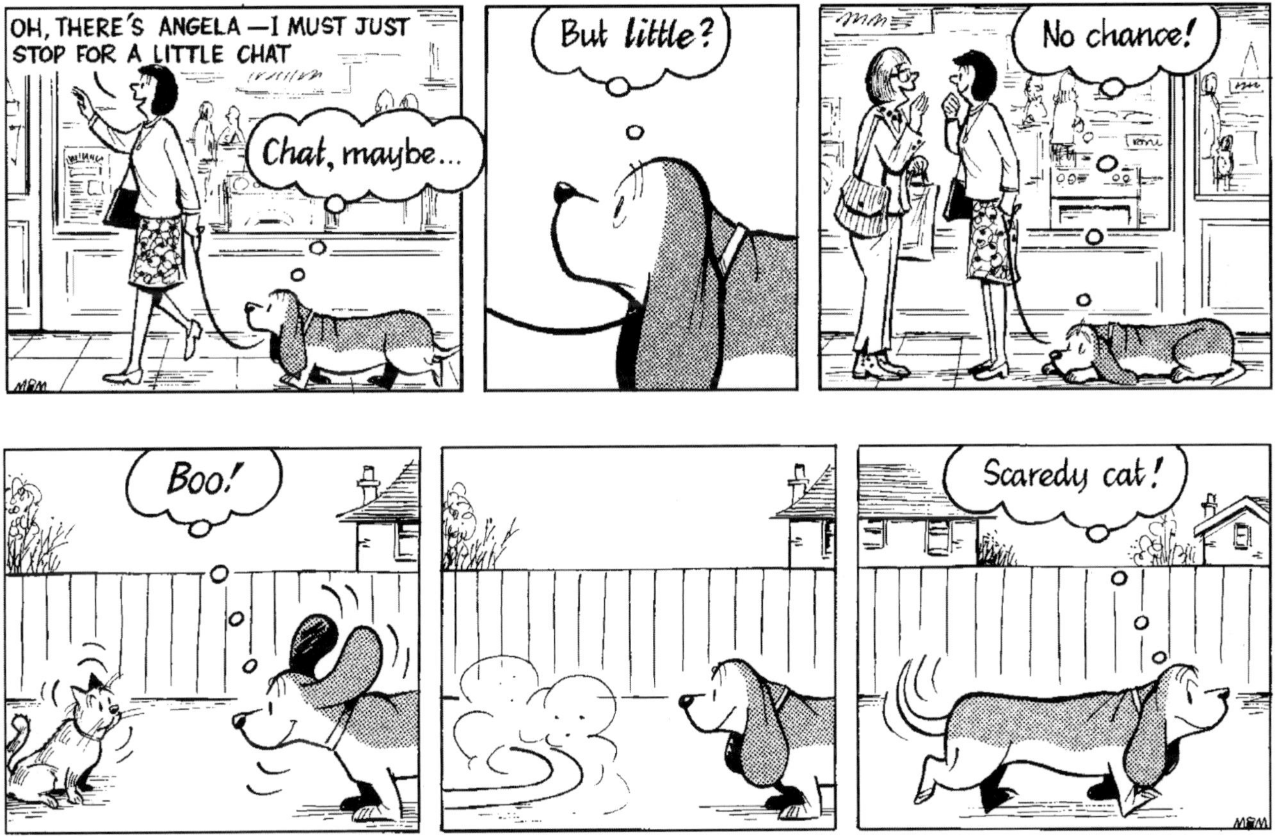
OH, THERE'S ANGELA —I MUST JUST STOP FOR A LITTLE CHAT
Chat, maybe...
But little?
No chance!
Boo!
Scaredy cat!

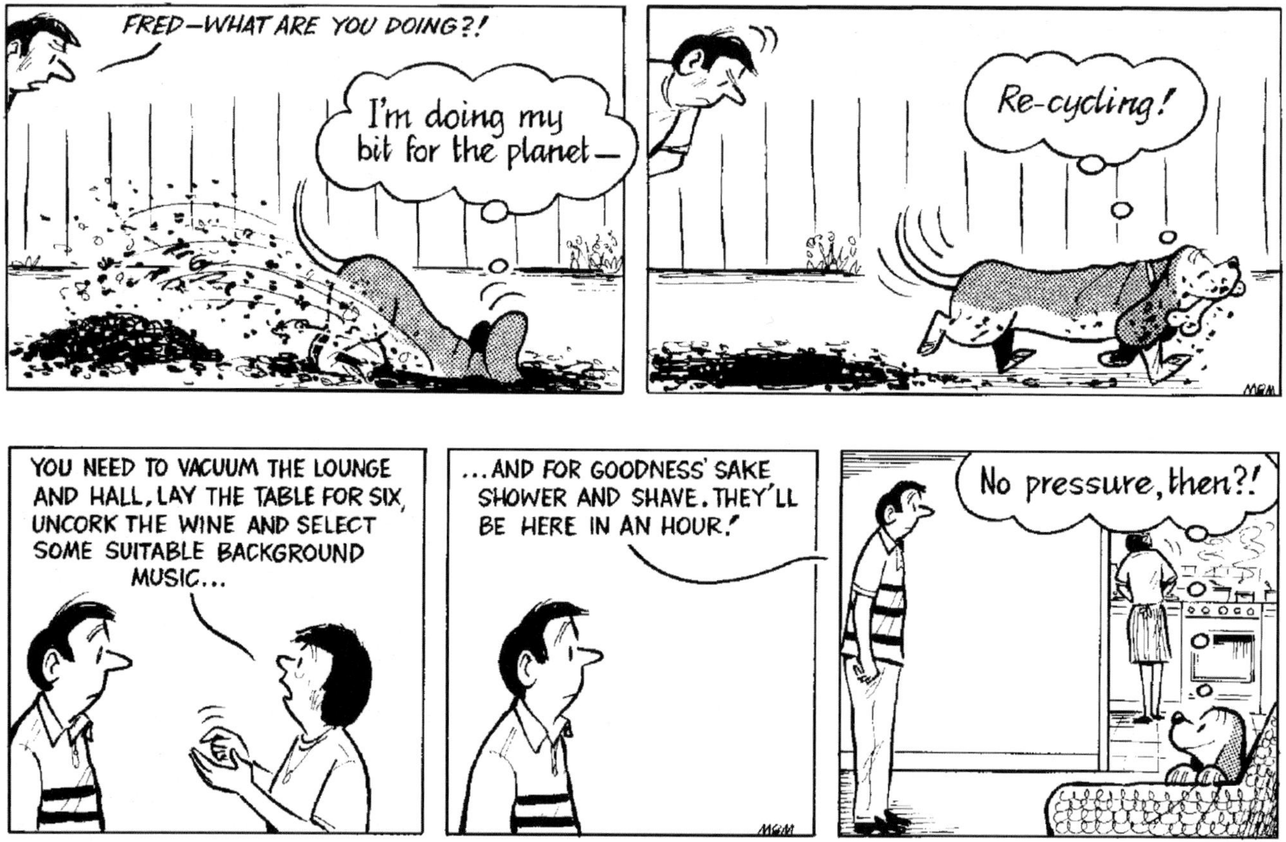
FRED—WHAT ARE YOU DOING?!
I'm doing my bit for the planet—
Re-cycling!
MGM
YOU NEED TO VACUUM THE LOUNGE AND HALL, LAY THE TABLE FOR SIX, UNCORK THE WINE AND SELECT SOME SUITABLE BACKGROUND MUSIC...
...AND FOR GOODNESS' SAKE SHOWER AND SHAVE. THEY'LL BE HERE IN AN HOUR!
MGM
No pressure, then?!

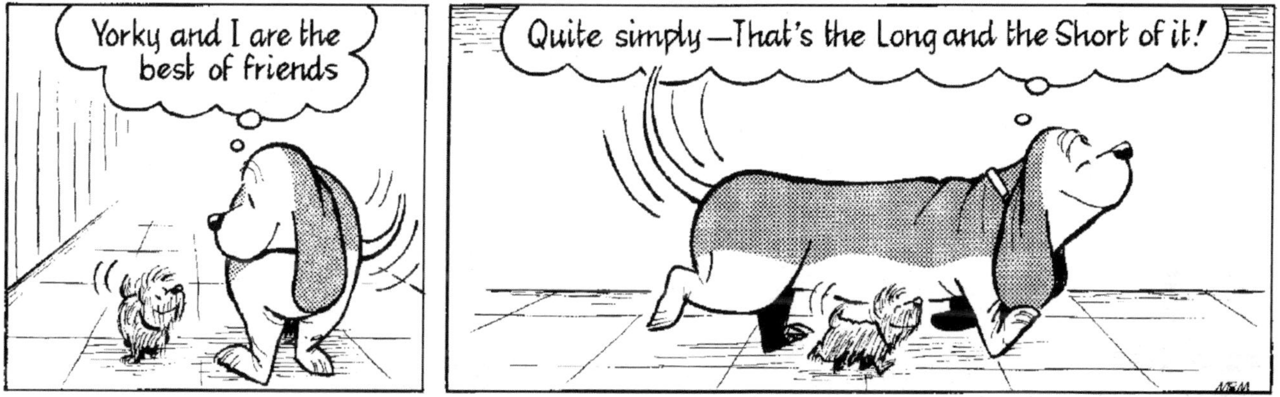
Yorky and I are the best of friends
Quite simply—That's the Long and the Short of it!

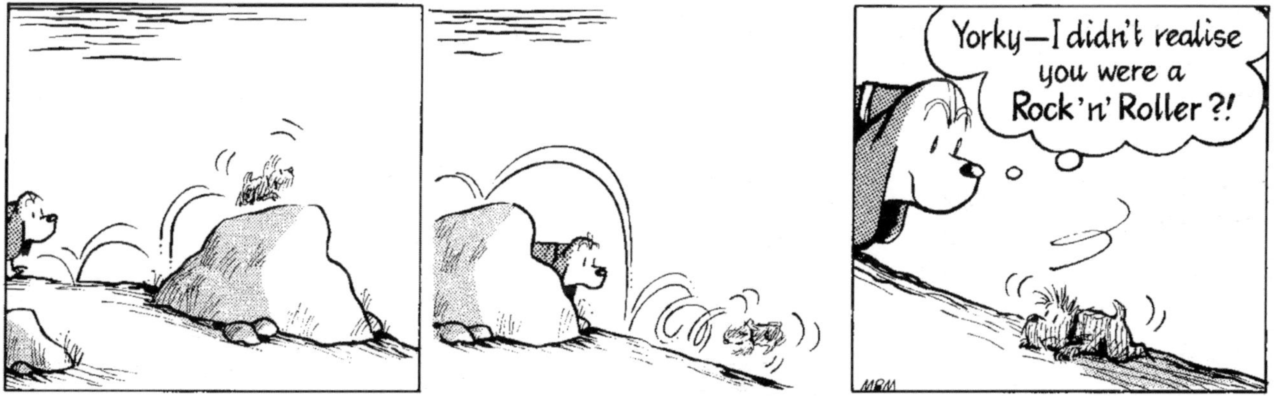
Yorky—I didn't realise you were a Rock'n' Roller?!

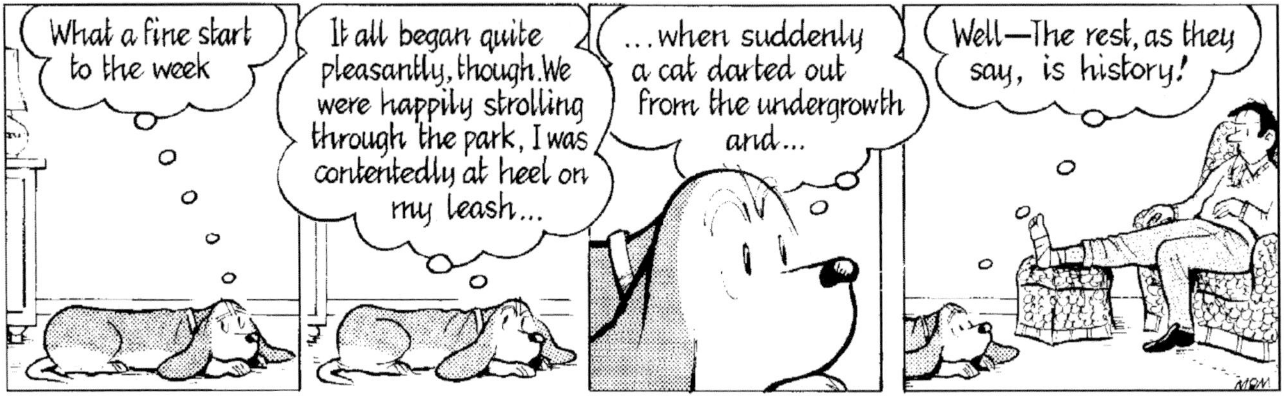
What a fine start to the week
It all began quite pleasantly, though. We were happily strolling through the park, I was contentedly at heel on my leash...
...when suddenly a cat darted out from the undergrowth and...
Well—The rest, as they say, is history!
MGM

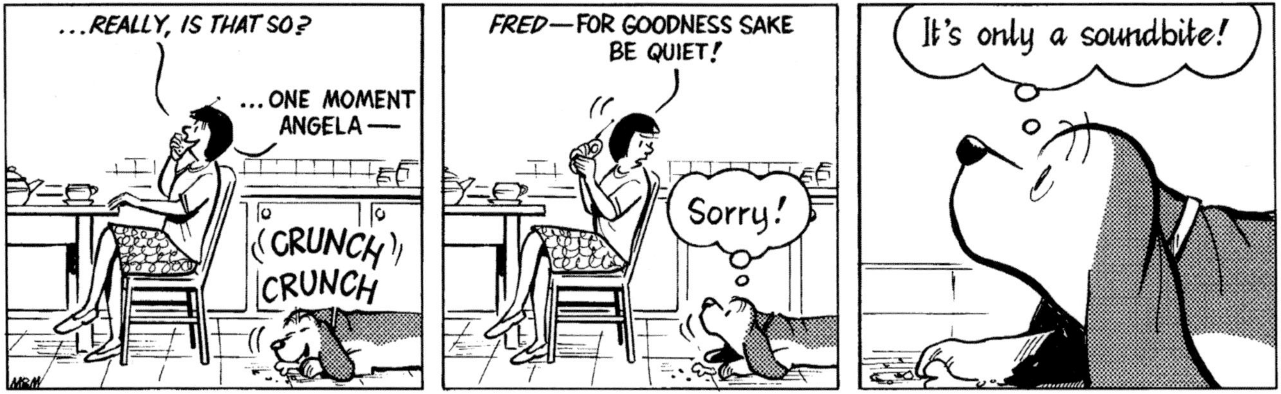
...REALLY, IS THAT SO?
...ONE MOMENT ANGELA—
CRUNCH CRUNCH
MGM
FRED—FOR GOODNESS SAKE BE QUIET!
Sorry!
It's only a soundbite!

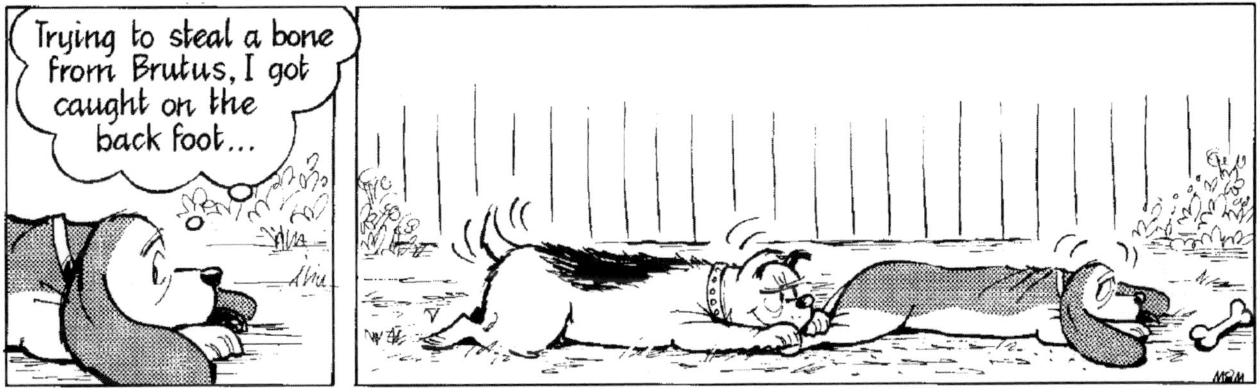
Trying to steal a bone from Brutus, I got caught on the back foot...

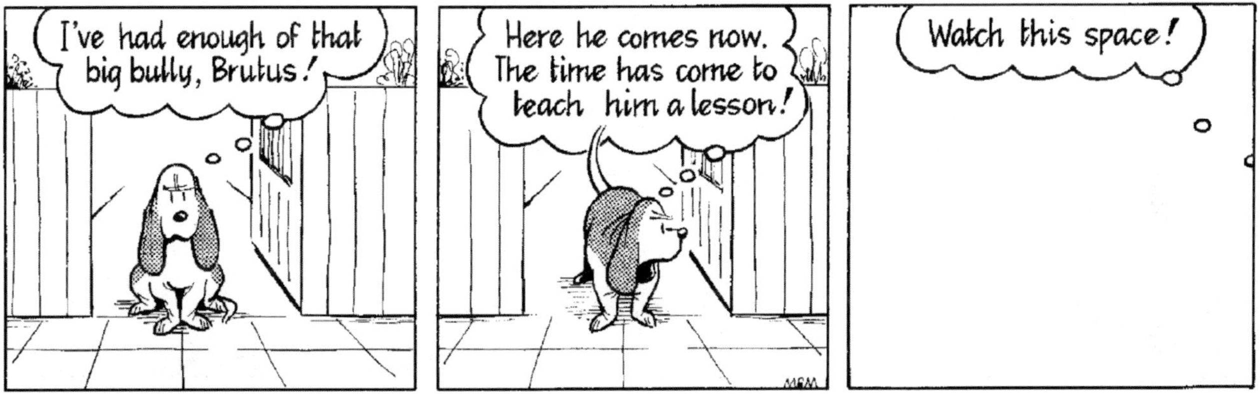
I've had enough of that big bully, Brutus!
Here he comes now. The time has come to teach him a lesson!
Watch this space!

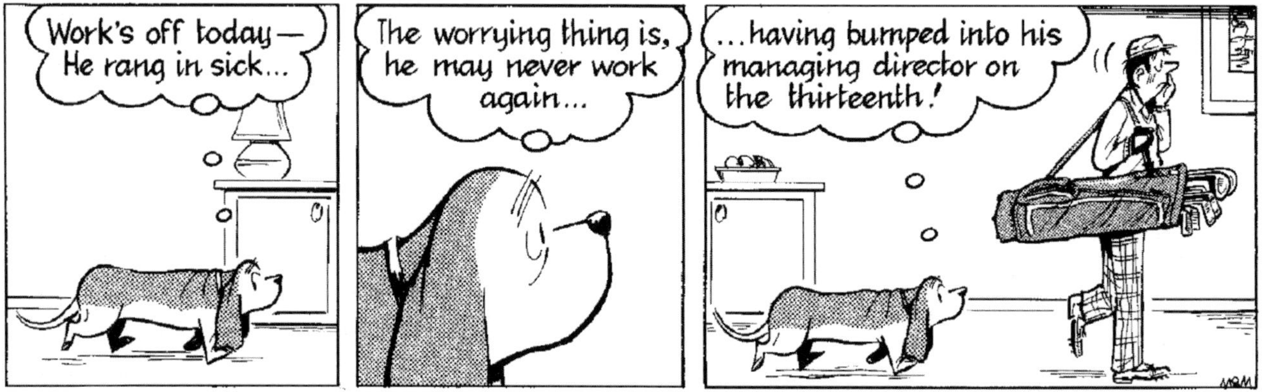
Work's off today— He rang in sick...
The worrying thing is, he may never work again...
...having bumped into his managing director on the thirteenth!

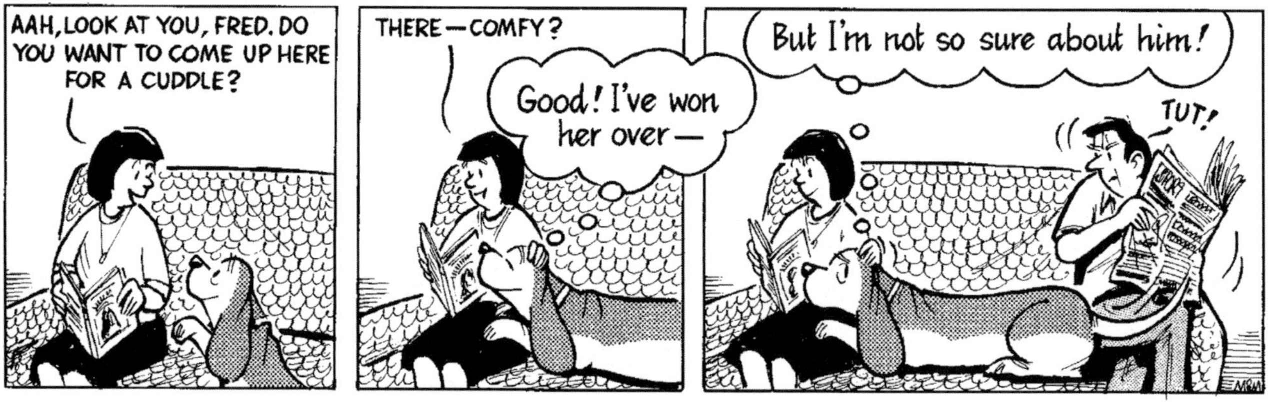
AAH, LOOK AT YOU, FRED. DO YOU WANT TO COME UP HERE FOR A CUDDLE?
THERE—COMFY?
Good! I've won her over—
But I'm not so sure about him!
TUT!

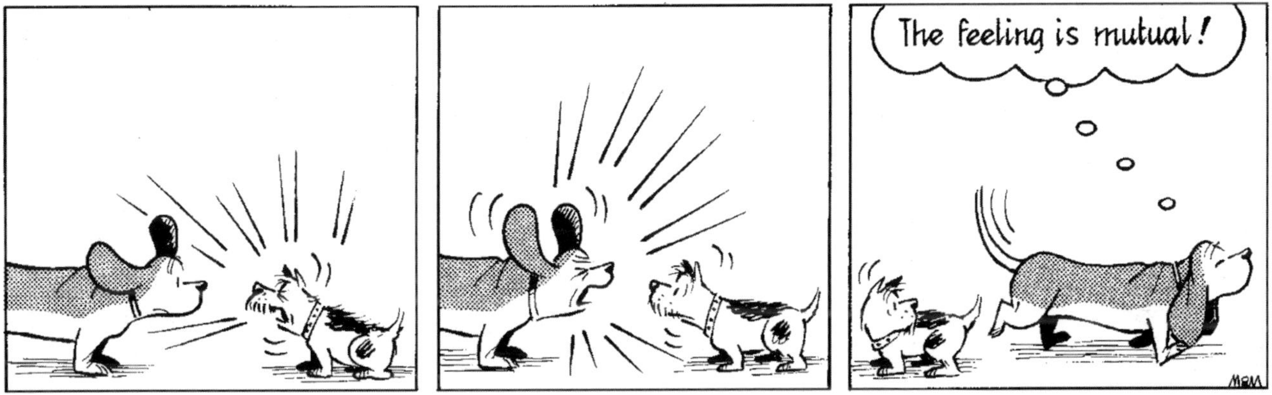
The feeling is mutual!

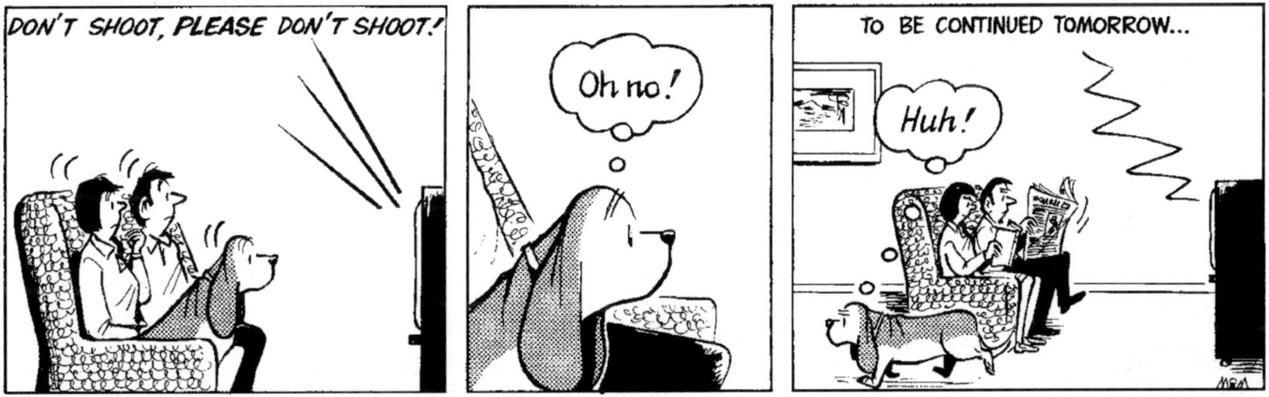
DON'T SHOOT, PLEASE DON'T SHOOT!
Oh no!
TO BE CONTINUED TOMORROW...
Huh!

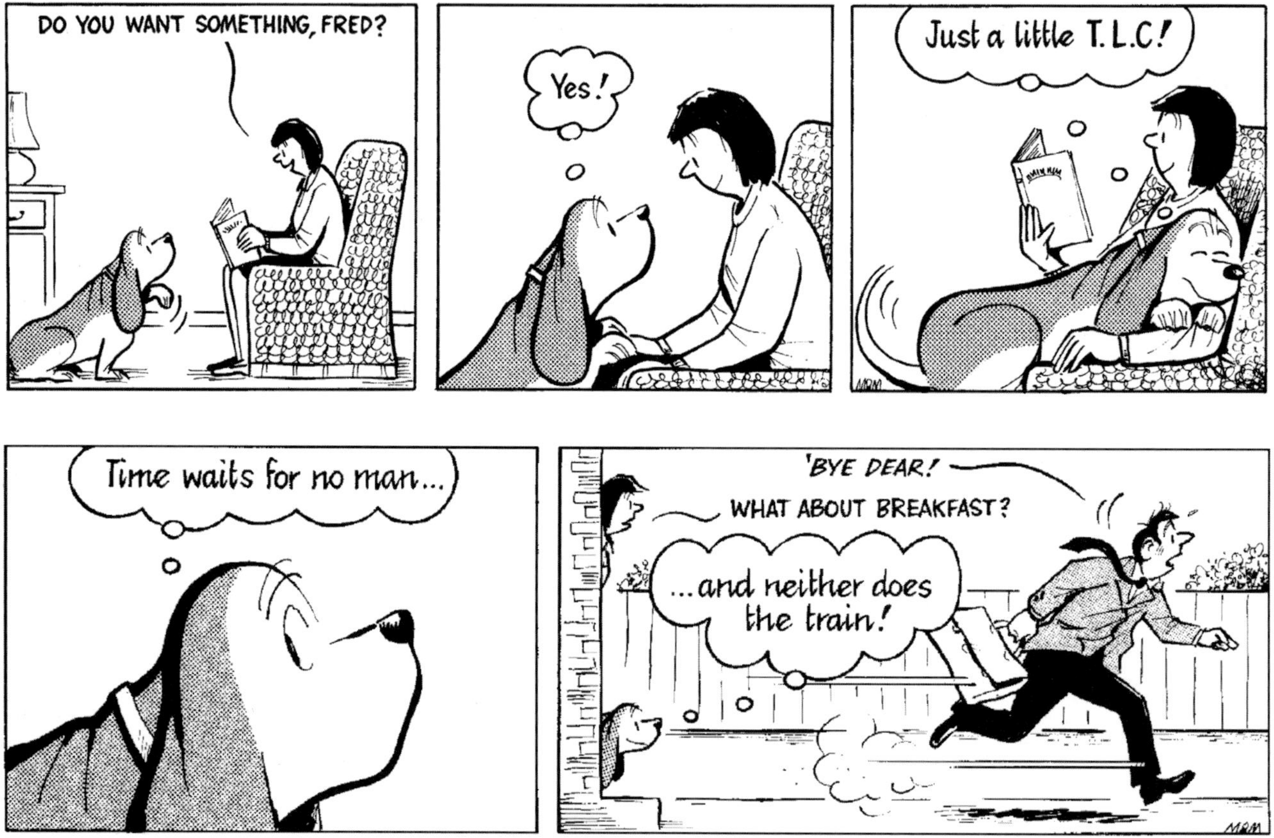

DO YOU WANT SOMETHING, FRED?
Yes!
Just a little T.L.C!
Time waits for no man...
'BYE DEAR!
WHAT ABOUT BREAKFAST?
...and neither does the train!

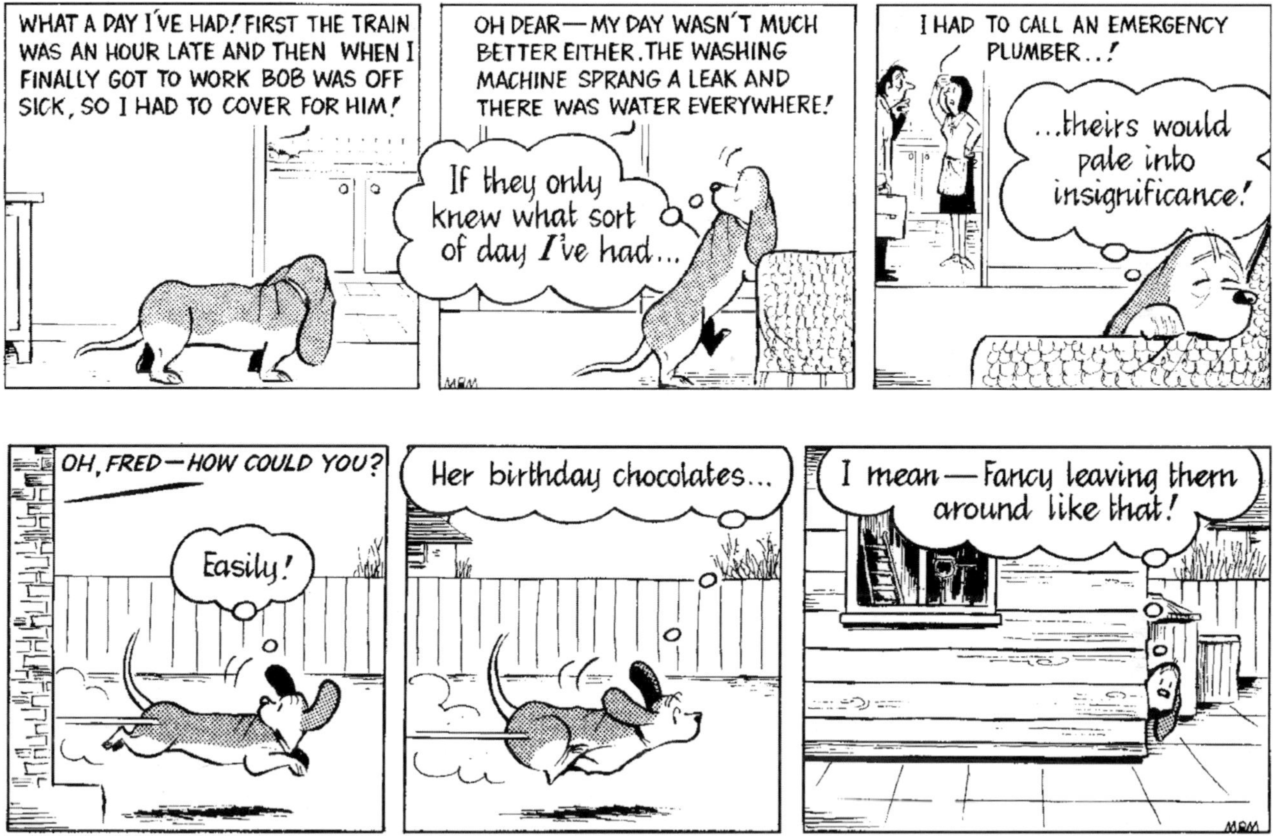
WHAT A DAY I'VE HAD! FIRST THE TRAIN WAS AN HOUR LATE AND THEN WHEN I FINALLY GOT TO WORK BOB WAS OFF SICK, SO I HAD TO COVER FOR HIM!
OH DEAR—MY DAY WASN'T MUCH BETTER EITHER. THE WASHING MACHINE SPRANG A LEAK AND THERE WAS WATER EVERYWHERE!
If they only knew what sort of day *I*'ve had...
MBM
I HAD TO CALL AN EMERGENCY PLUMBER..!
...theirs would pale into insignificance!
OH, FRED—HOW COULD YOU?
Easily!
Her birthday chocolates...
I mean—Fancy leaving them around like that!
MBM

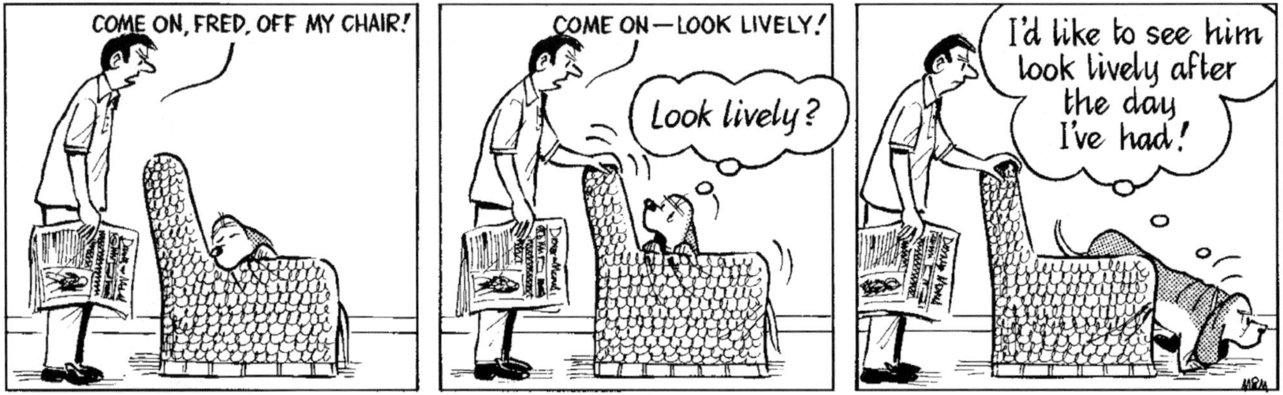
COME ON, FRED, OFF MY CHAIR!
COME ON—LOOK LIVELY!
Look lively?
I'd like to see him look lively after the day I've had!

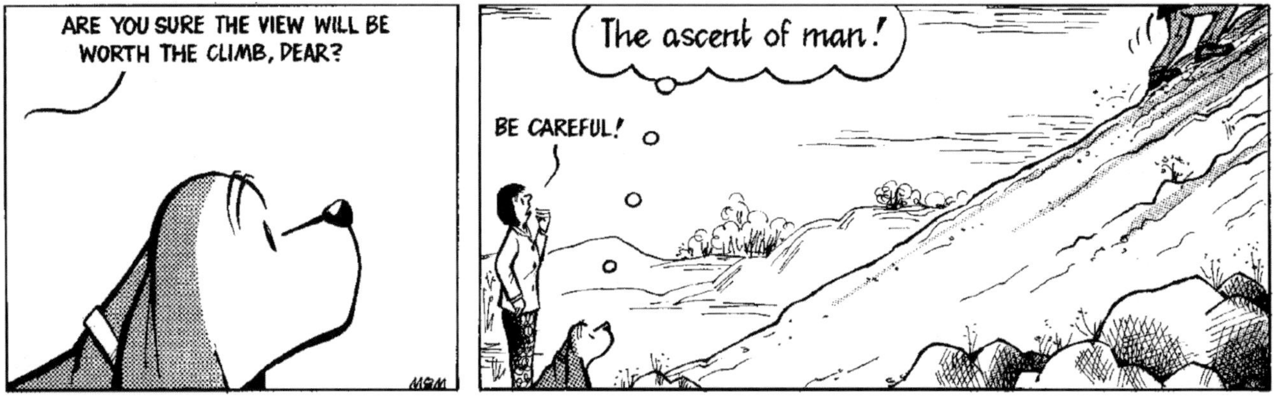
ARE YOU SURE THE VIEW WILL BE WORTH THE CLIMB, DEAR?
The ascent of man!
BE CAREFUL!

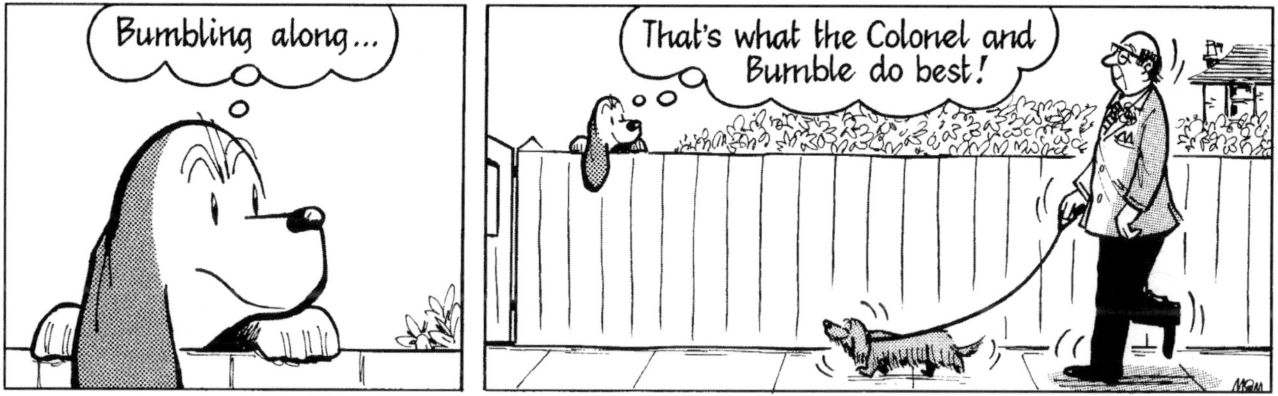
Bumbling along...
That's what the Colonel and Bumble do best!
MGM

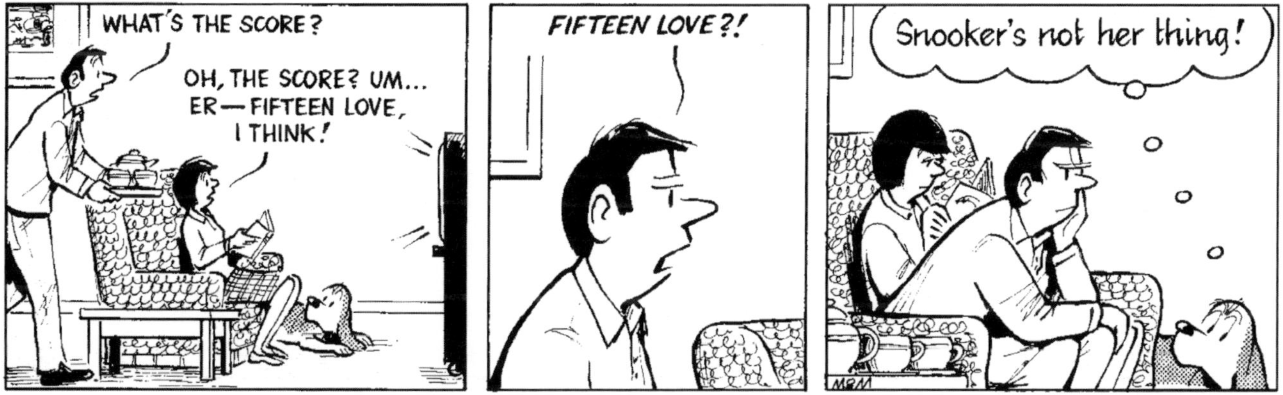
WHAT'S THE SCORE?
OH, THE SCORE? UM... ER—FIFTEEN LOVE, I THINK!
FIFTEEN LOVE?!
Snooker's not her thing!
MGM

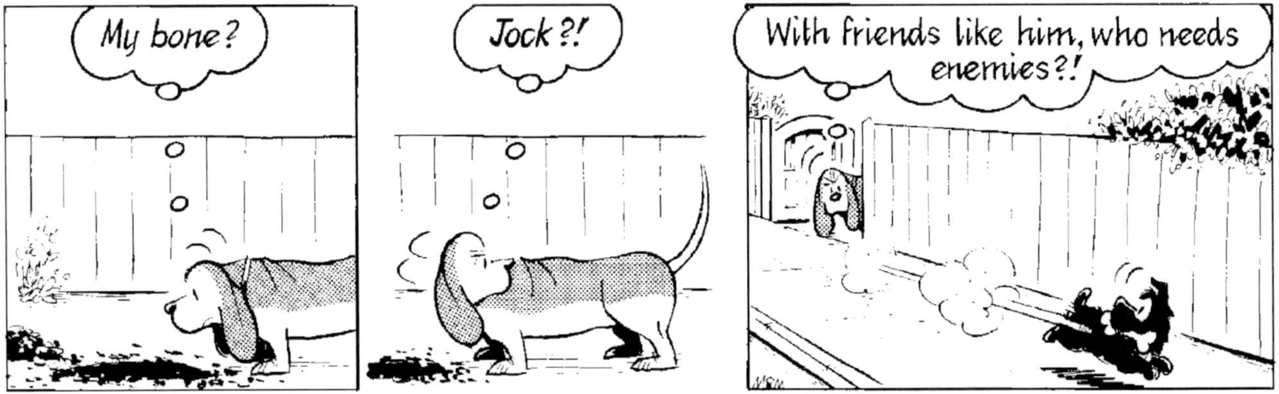
My bone?
Jock?!
With friends like him, who needs enemies?!

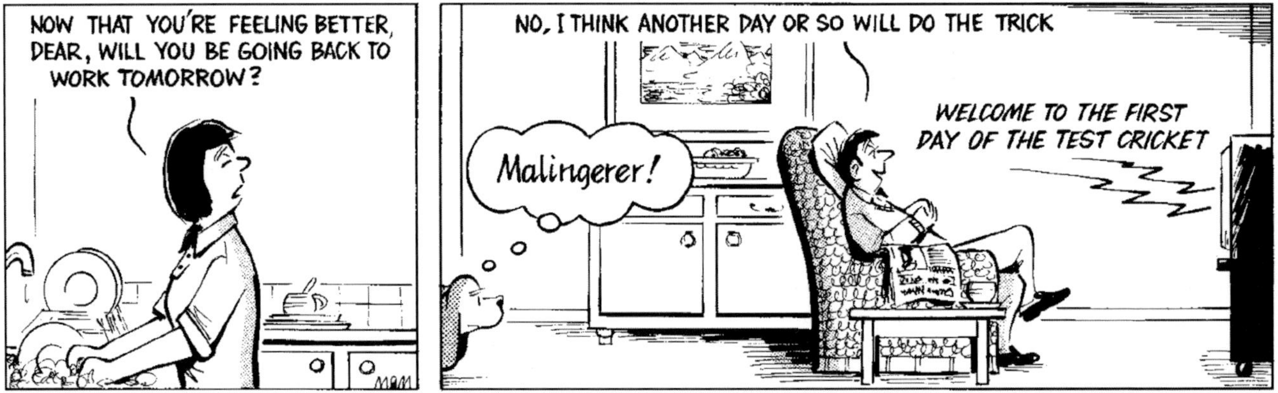
NOW THAT YOU'RE FEELING BETTER, DEAR, WILL YOU BE GOING BACK TO WORK TOMORROW?
NO, I THINK ANOTHER DAY OR SO WILL DO THE TRICK
Malingerer!
WELCOME TO THE FIRST DAY OF THE TEST CRICKET

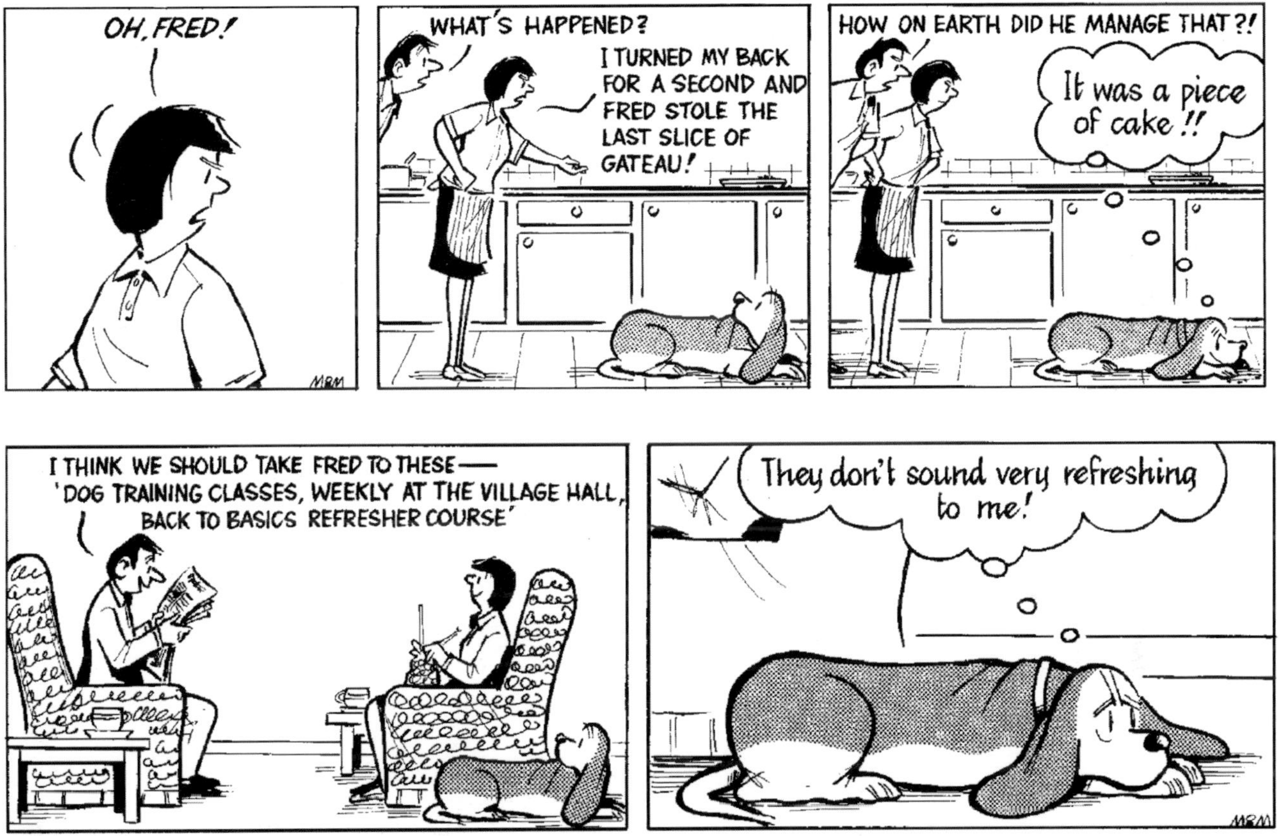
OH, FRED!
WHAT'S HAPPENED?
I TURNED MY BACK FOR A SECOND AND FRED STOLE THE LAST SLICE OF GATEAU!
HOW ON EARTH DID HE MANAGE THAT?!
It was a piece of cake!!
I THINK WE SHOULD TAKE FRED TO THESE— 'DOG TRAINING CLASSES, WEEKLY AT THE VILLAGE HALL, BACK TO BASICS REFRESHER COURSE'
They don't sound very refreshing to me!

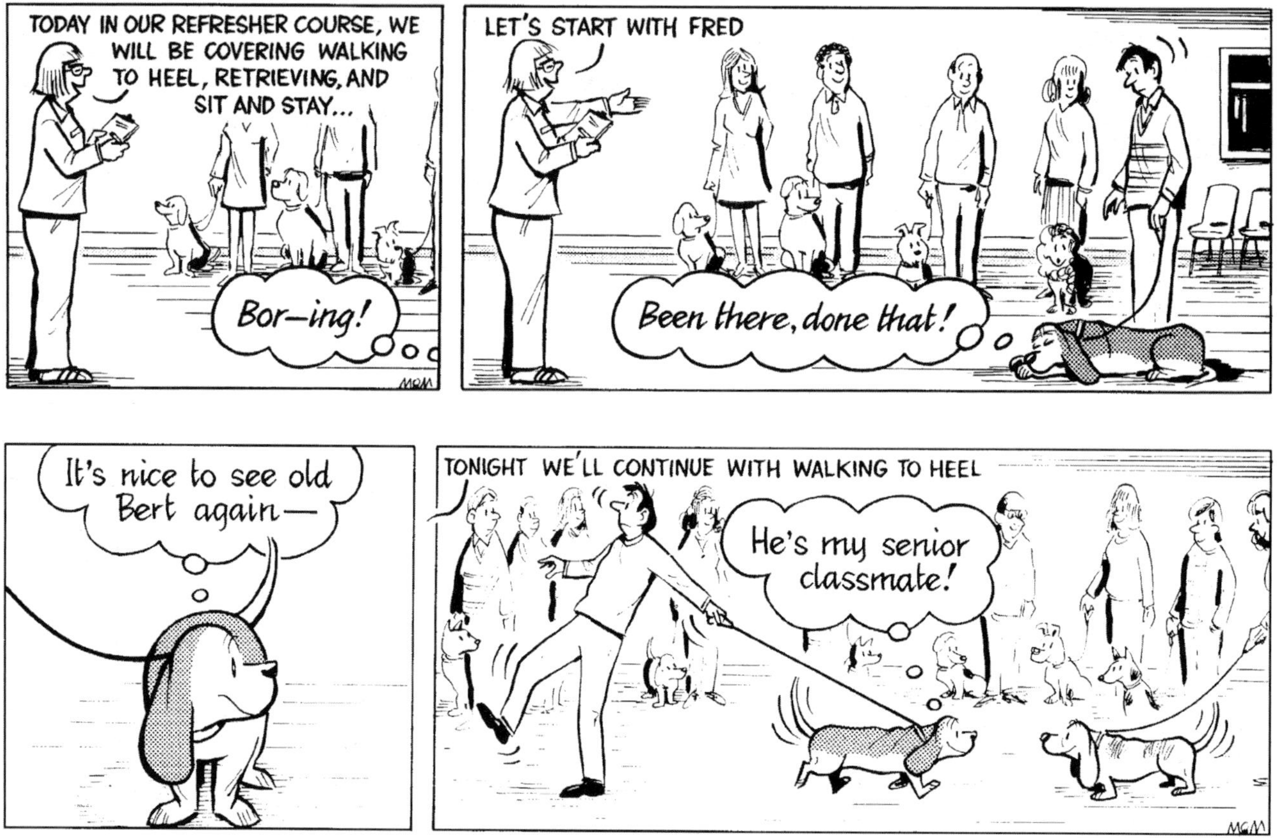
TODAY IN OUR REFRESHER COURSE, WE WILL BE COVERING WALKING TO HEEL, RETRIEVING, AND SIT AND STAY...
Bor–ing!
LET'S START WITH FRED
Been there, done that!
It's nice to see old Bert again—
TONIGHT WE'LL CONTINUE WITH WALKING TO HEEL
He's my senior classmate!
MGM
MGM

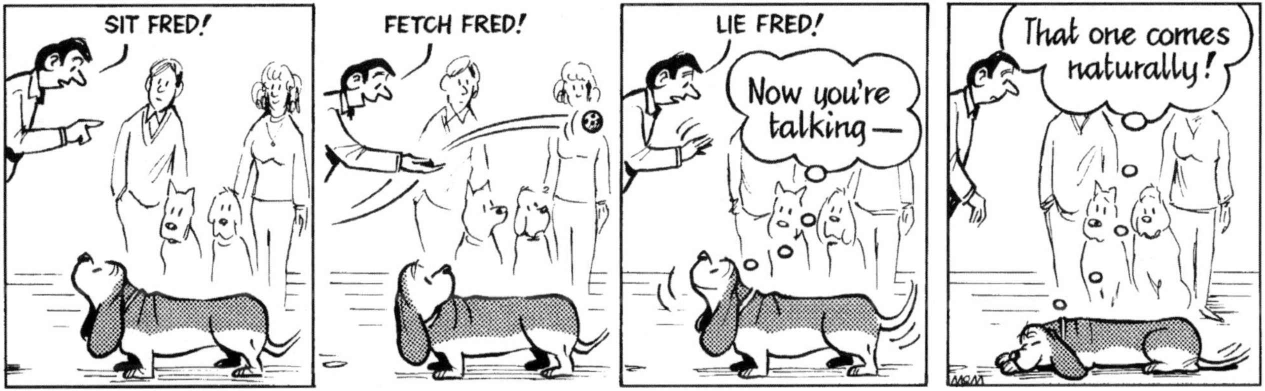
SIT FRED!
FETCH FRED!
LIE FRED!
Now you're talking —
That one comes naturally!

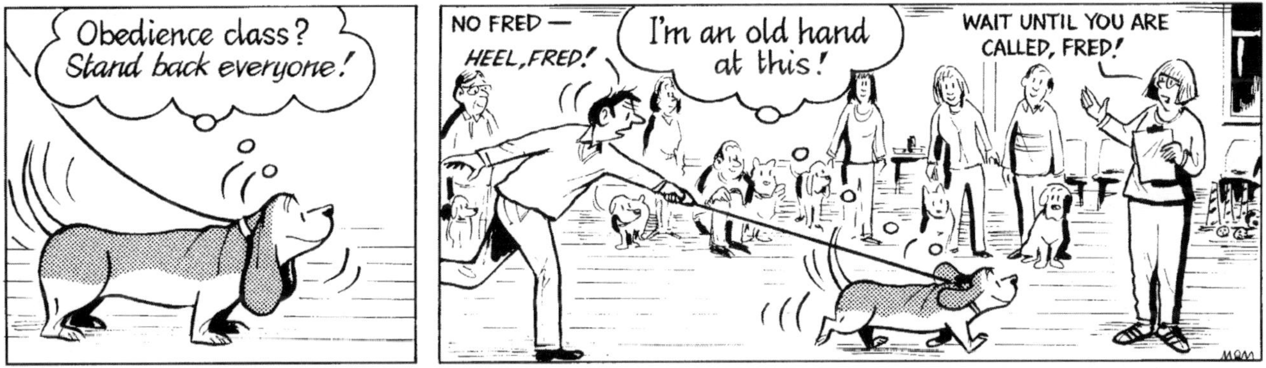
Obedience class? Stand back everyone!
NO FRED —
HEEL, FRED!
I'm an old hand at this!
WAIT UNTIL YOU ARE CALLED, FRED!

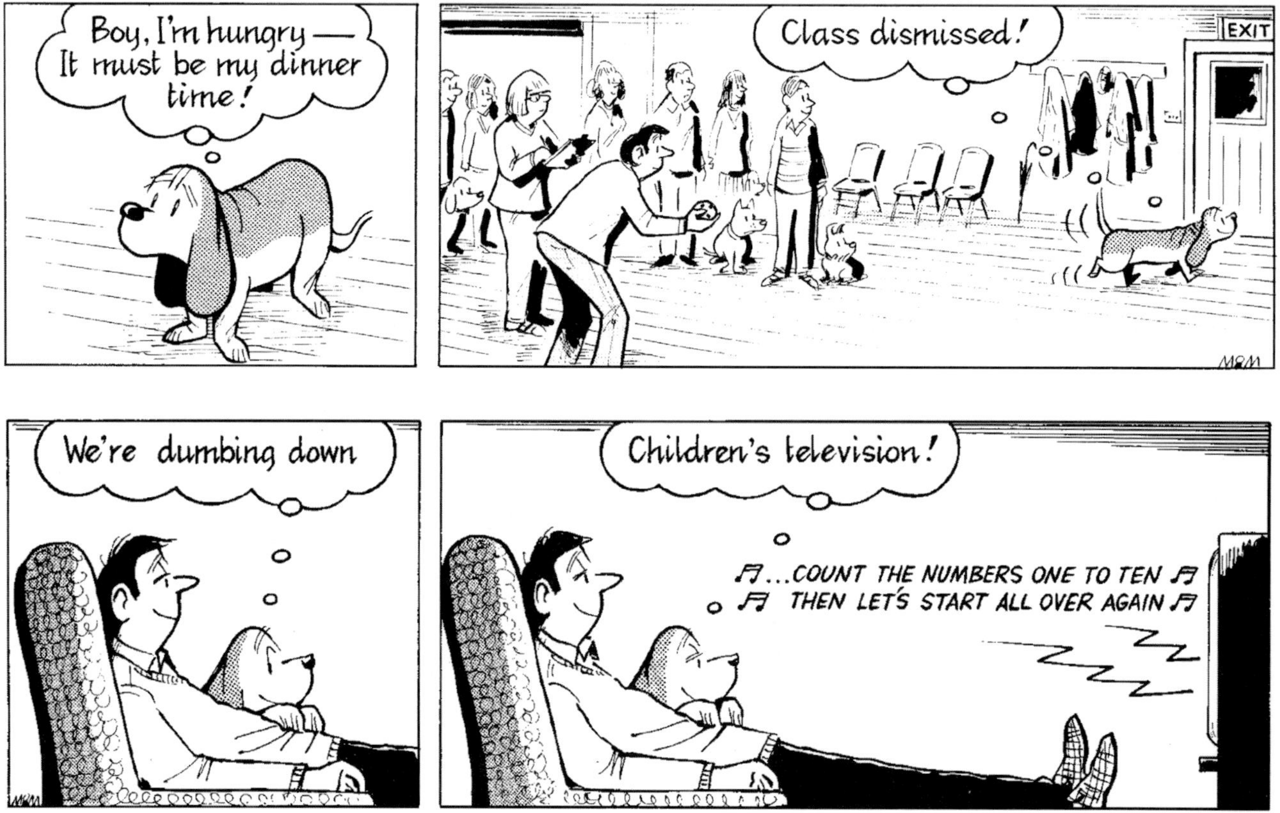
Boy, I'm hungry — It must be my dinner time!
Class dismissed!
EXIT
We're dumbing down
Children's television!
...COUNT THE NUMBERS ONE TO TEN
THEN LET'S START ALL OVER AGAIN

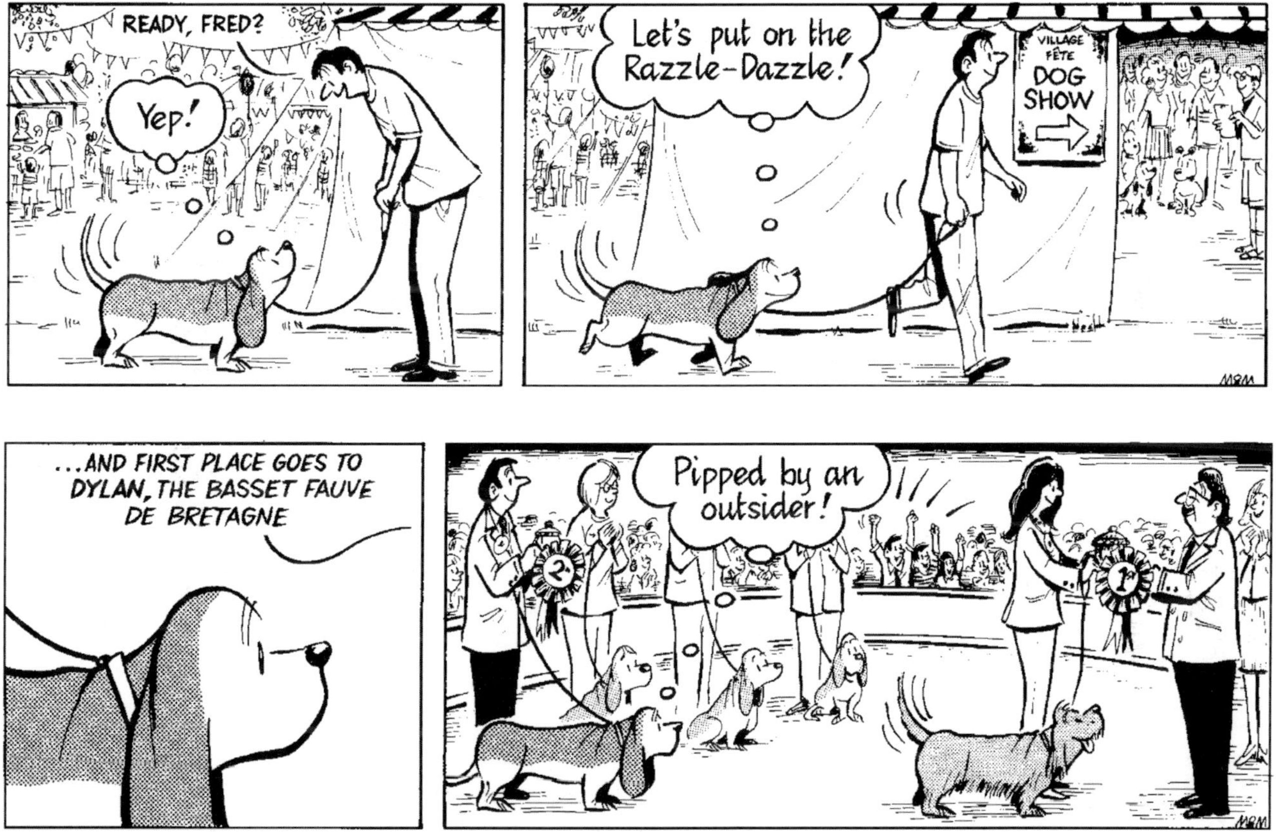
READY, FRED?
Yep!
Let's put on the Razzle-Dazzle!
VILLAGE FÊTE
DOG SHOW
...AND FIRST PLACE GOES TO DYLAN, THE BASSET FAUVE DE BRETAGNE
Pipped by an outsider!

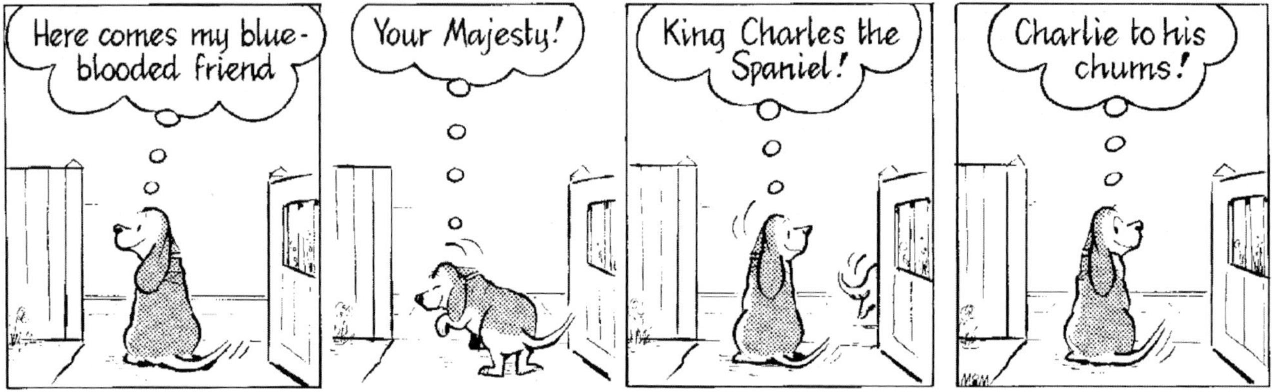
Here comes my blue-blooded friend
Your Majesty!
King Charles the Spaniel!
Charlie to his chums!

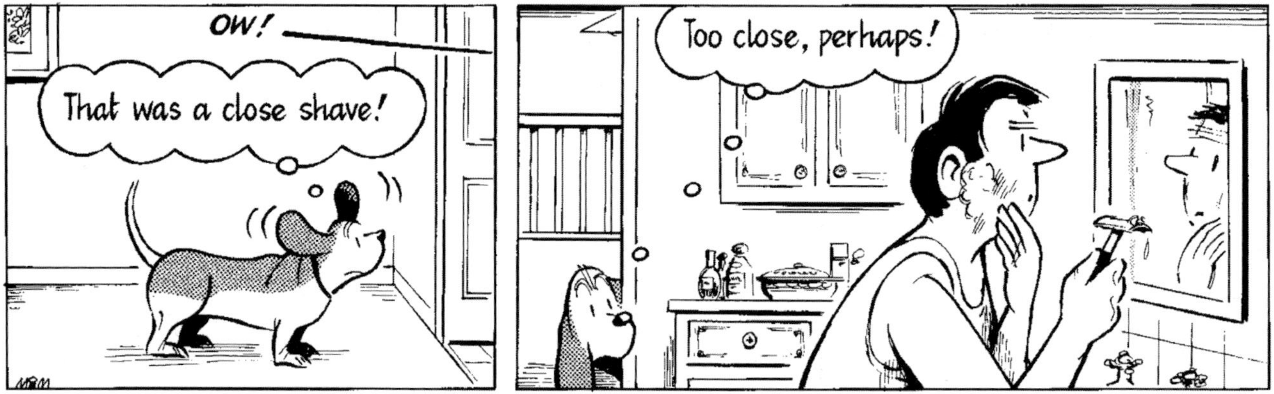
OW!
That was a close shave!
Too close, perhaps!

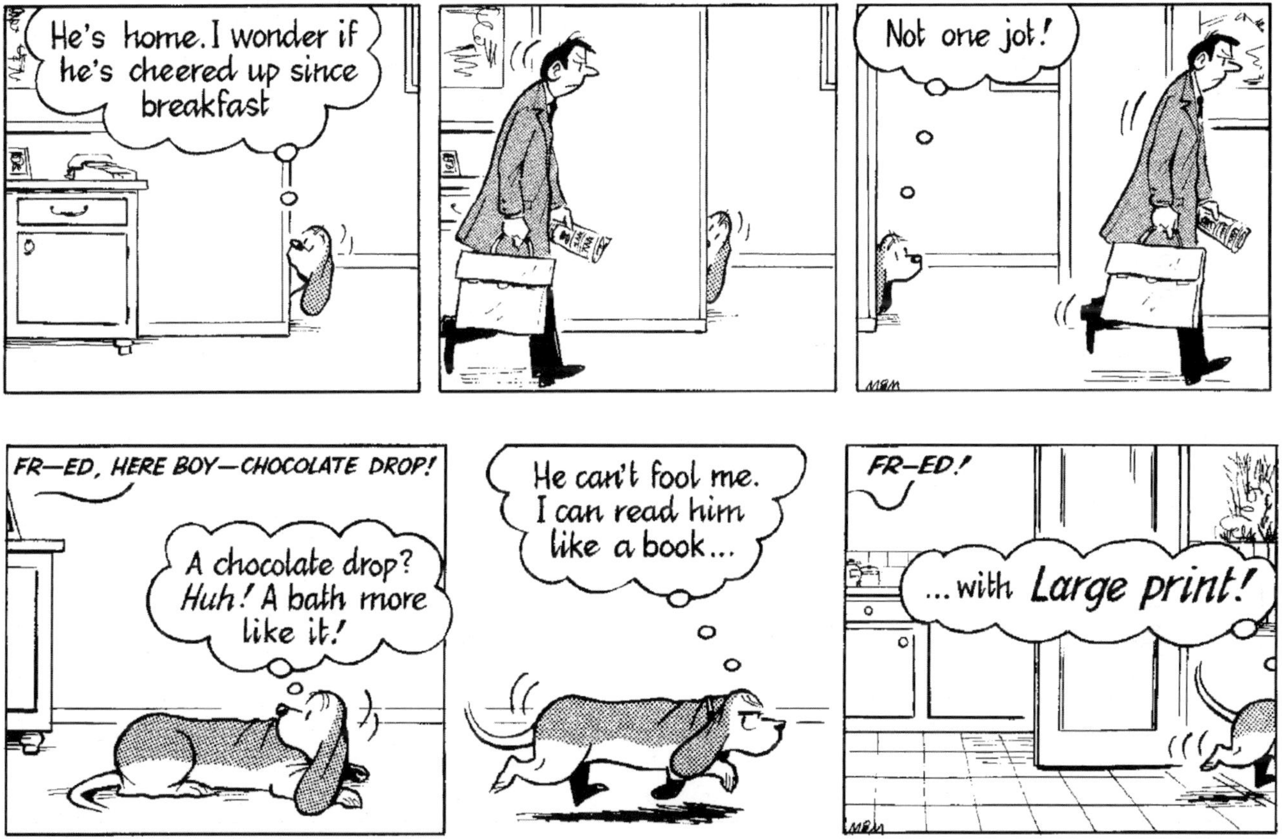
He's home. I wonder if he's cheered up since breakfast
Not one jot!
FR—ED, HERE BOY—CHOCOLATE DROP!
A chocolate drop? Huh! A bath more like it!
He can't fool me. I can read him like a book...
FR—ED!
...with Large print!
MGM
MGM

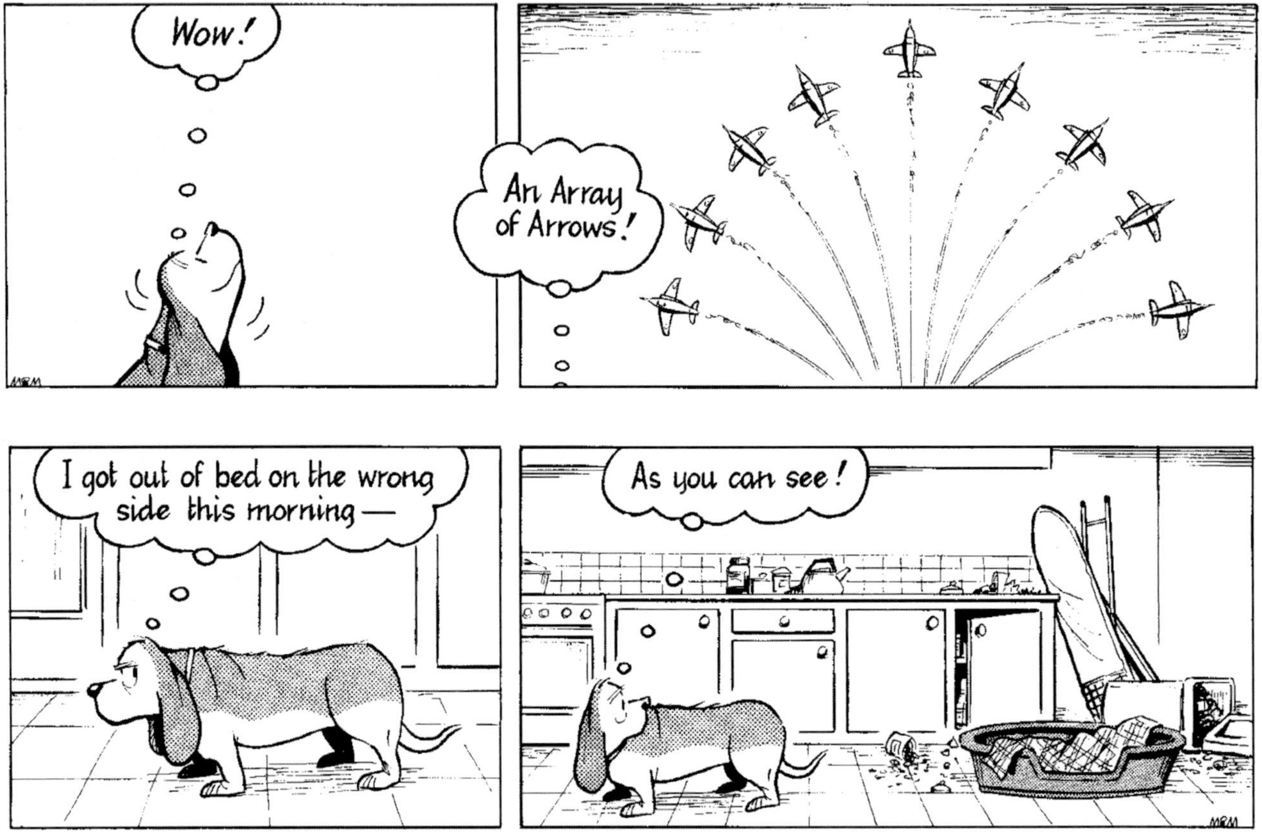
Wow!
An Array of Arrows!
I got out of bed on the wrong side this morning—
As you can see!
MBM
MBM

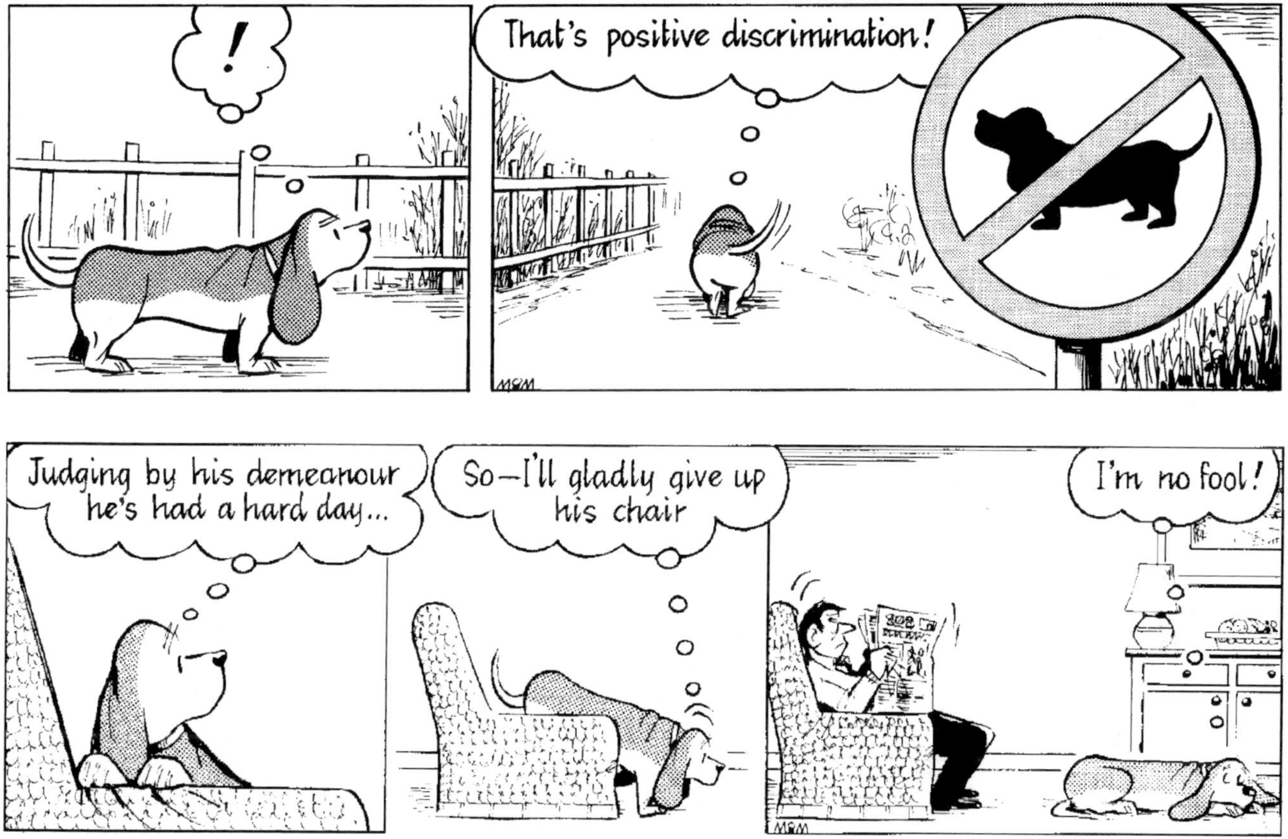
!
That's positive discrimination!
MGM
Judging by his demeanour he's had a hard day...
So—I'll gladly give up his chair
I'm no fool!
MGM

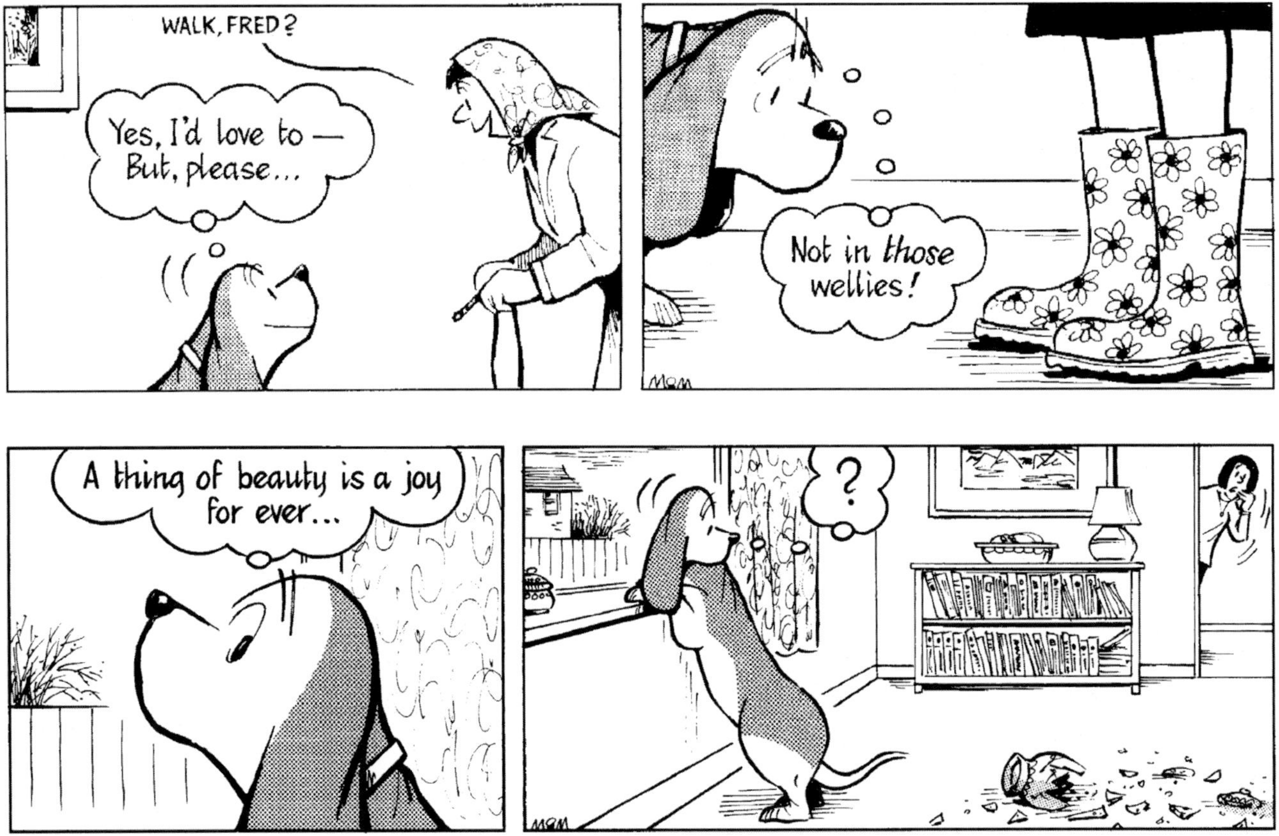
WALK, FRED?
Yes, I'd love to — But, please...
Not in *those* wellies!
A thing of beauty is a joy for ever...
?

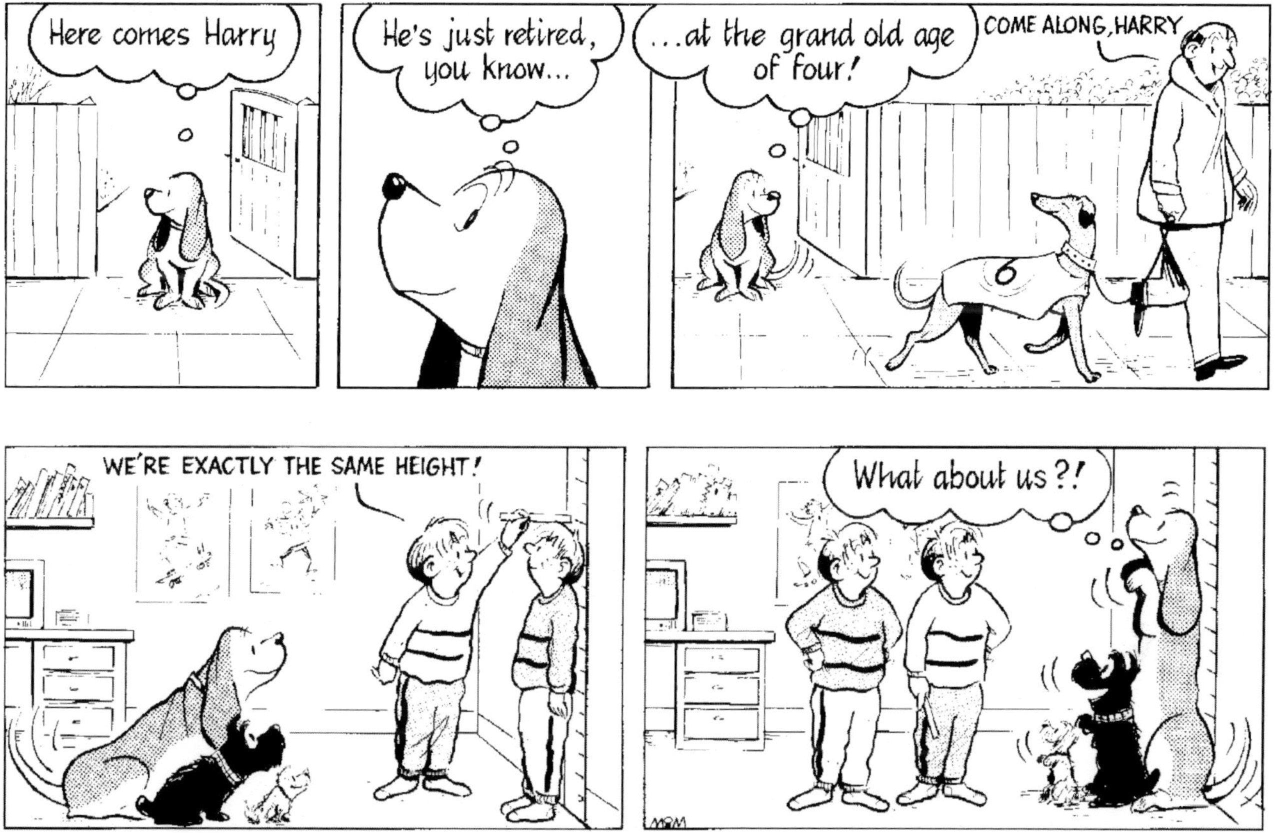
Here comes Harry
He's just retired, you know...
...at the grand old age of four!
COME ALONG, HARRY
WE'RE EXACTLY THE SAME HEIGHT!
What about us?!
MGM

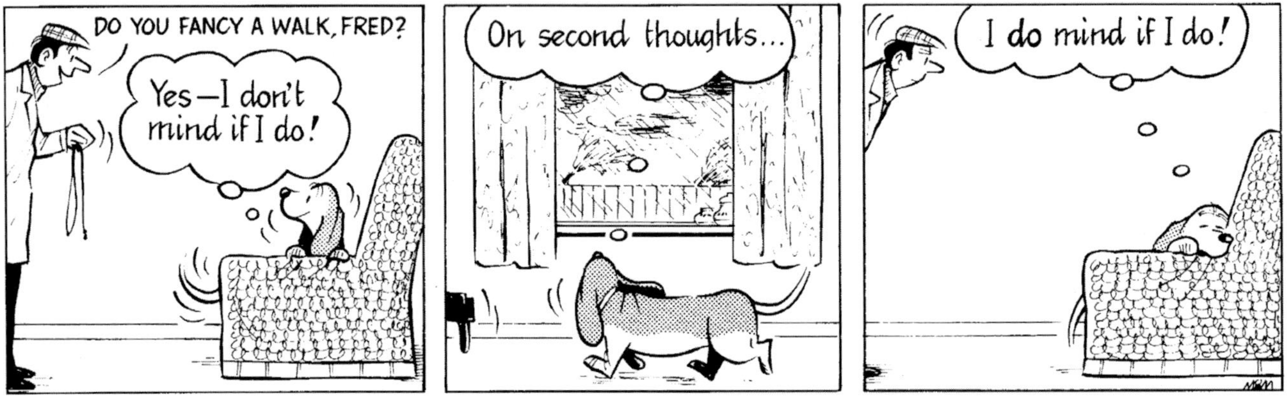
DO YOU FANCY A WALK, FRED?
Yes—I don't mind if I do!
On second thoughts...
I do mind if I do!
MSM

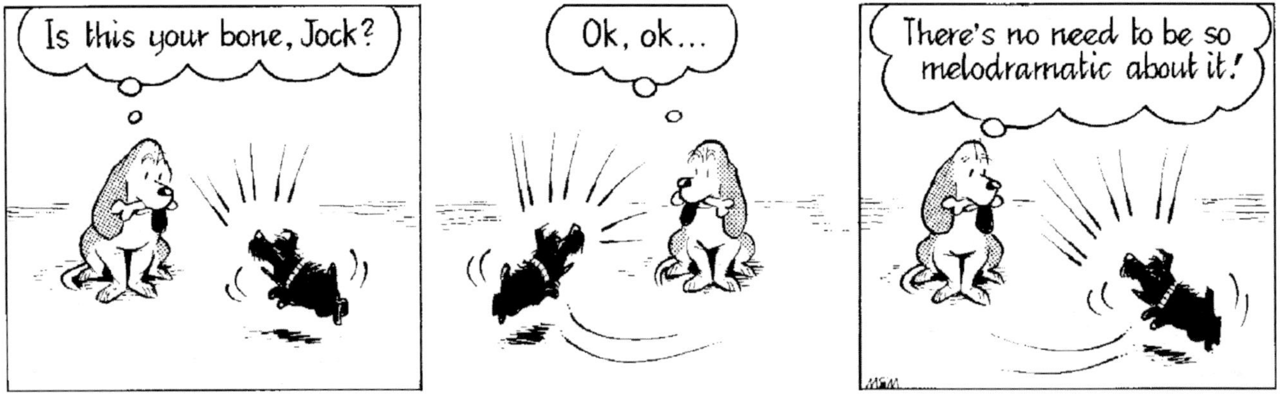
Is this your bone, Jock?
Ok, ok...
There's no need to be so melodramatic about it!
MSM

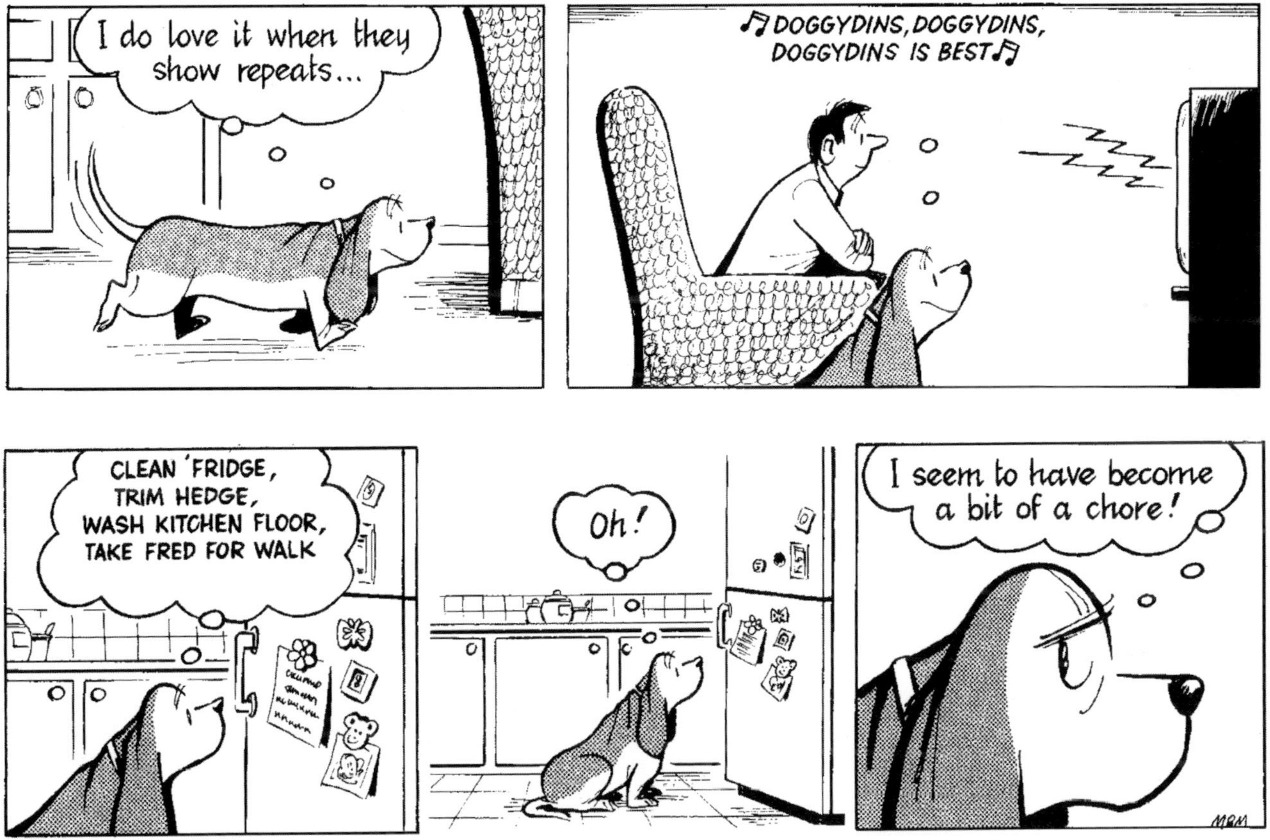
I do love it when they show repeats...
♫ DOGGYDINS, DOGGYDINS, DOGGYDINS IS BEST ♫
CLEAN 'FRIDGE, TRIM HEDGE, WASH KITCHEN FLOOR, TAKE FRED FOR WALK
Oh!
I seem to have become a bit of a chore!
MGM

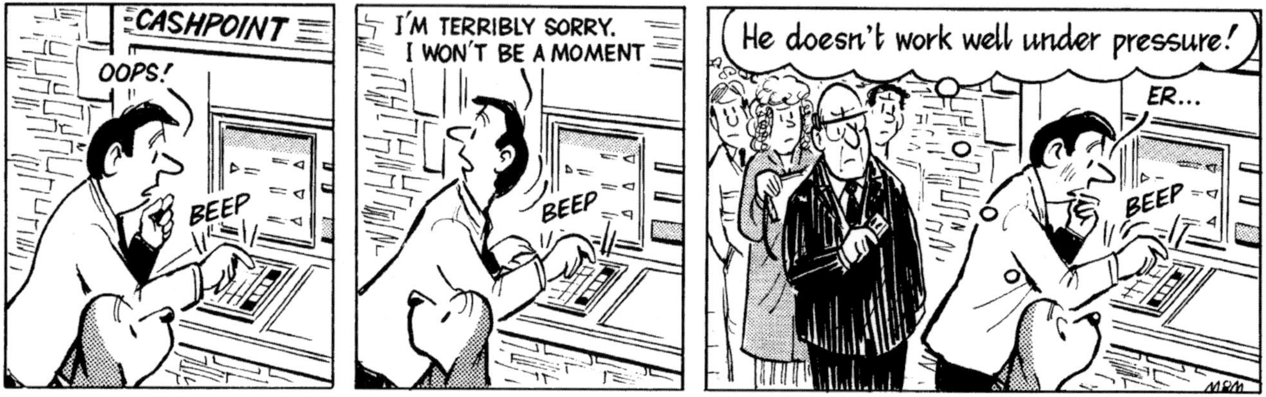
CASHPOINT
OOPS!
BEEP
I'M TERRIBLY SORRY.
I WON'T BE A MOMENT
BEEP
He doesn't work well under pressure!
ER...
BEEP

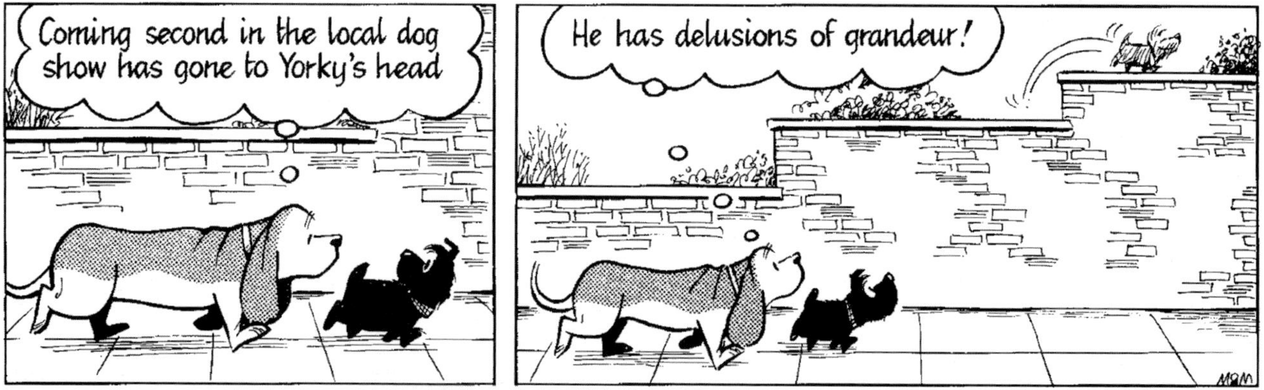
Coming second in the local dog show has gone to Yorky's head
He has delusions of grandeur!

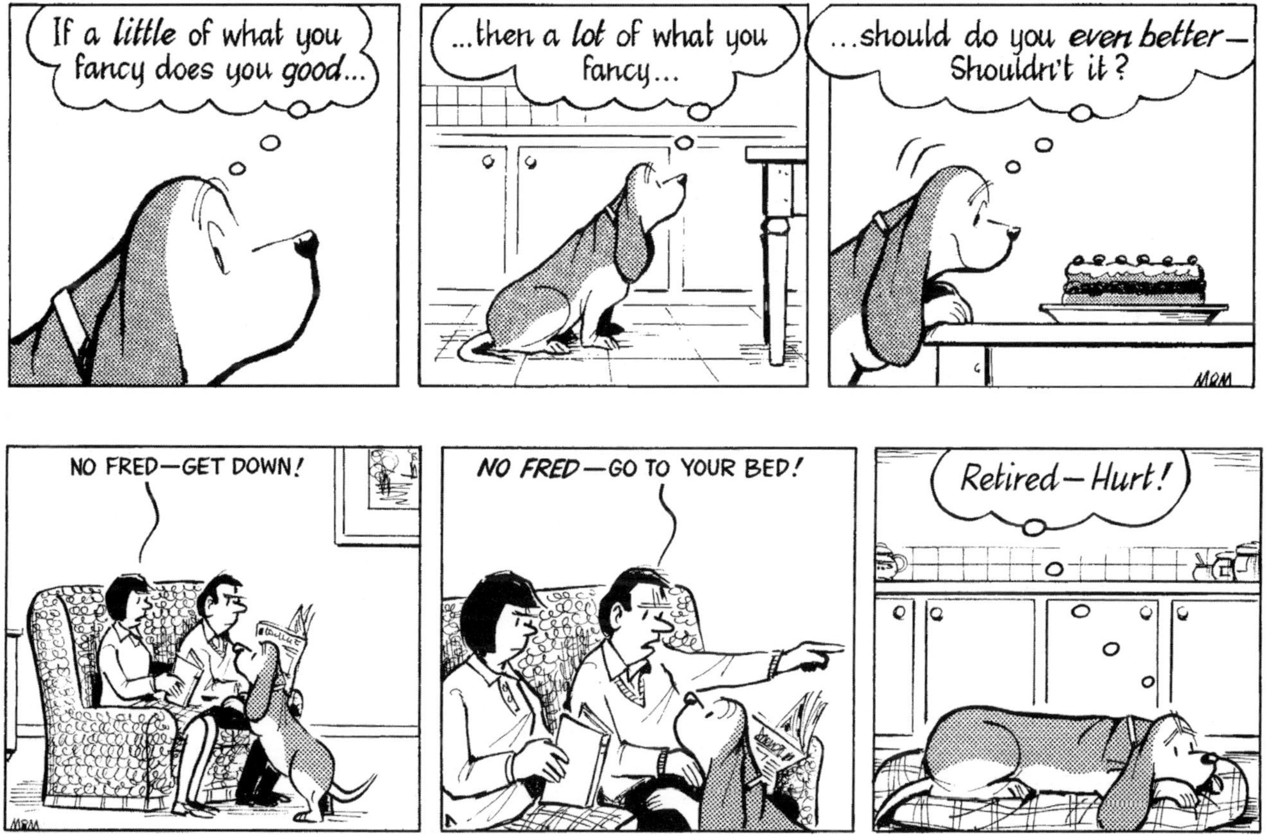
If a *little* of what you fancy does you *good*...
...then a *lot* of what you fancy...
...should do you *even better*—Shouldn't it?
NO FRED—GET DOWN!
NO FRED—GO TO YOUR BED!
Retired—Hurt!

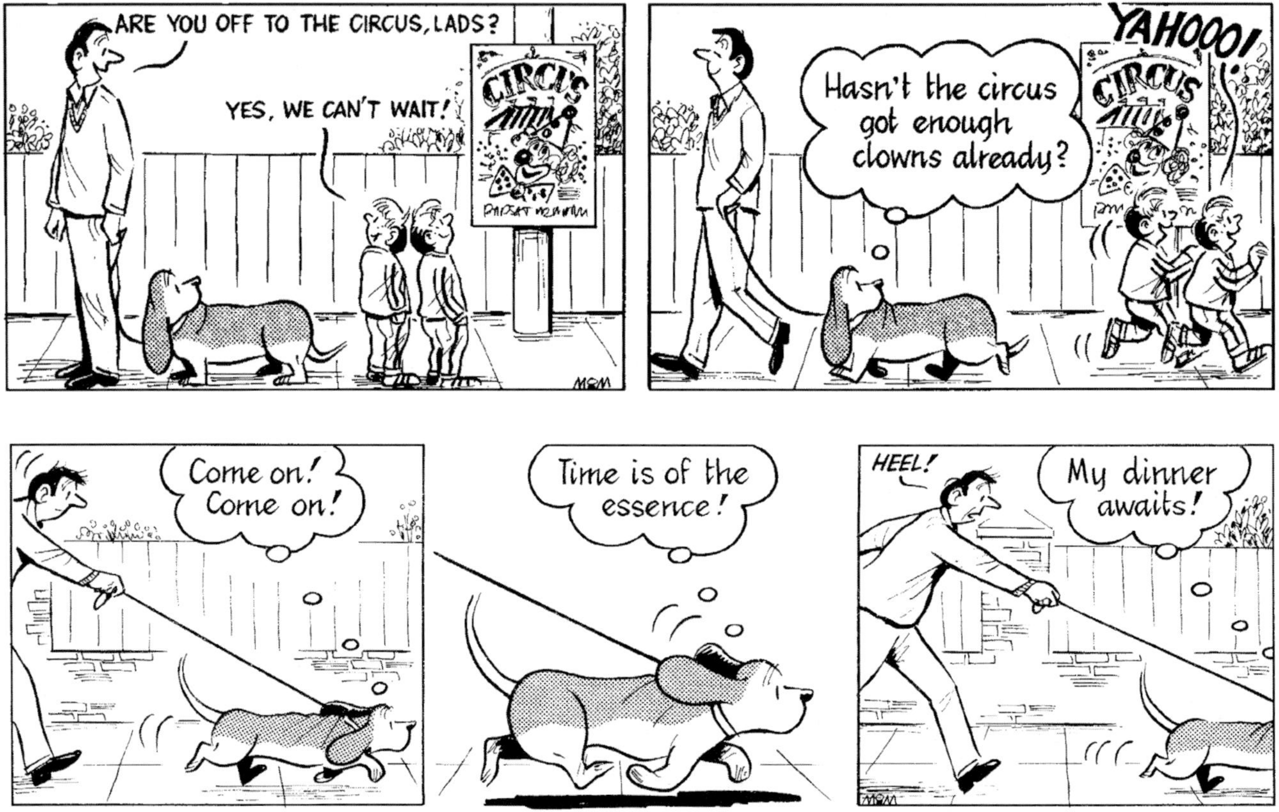
ARE YOU OFF TO THE CIRCUS, LADS?
YES, WE CAN'T WAIT!
CIRCUS
Hasn't the circus got enough clowns already?
YAHOOO!
Come on! Come on!
Time is of the essence!
HEEL!
My dinner awaits!

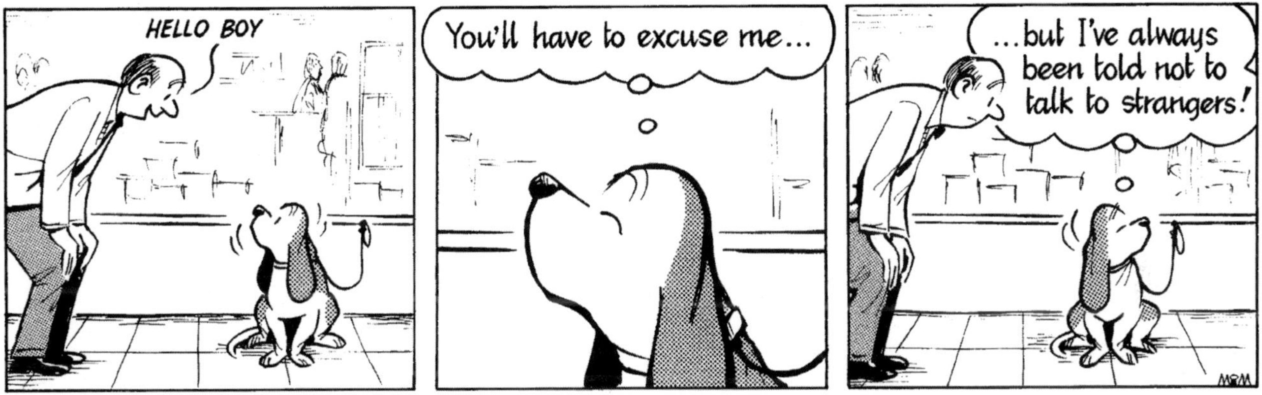
HELLO BOY
You'll have to excuse me...
...but I've always been told not to talk to strangers!

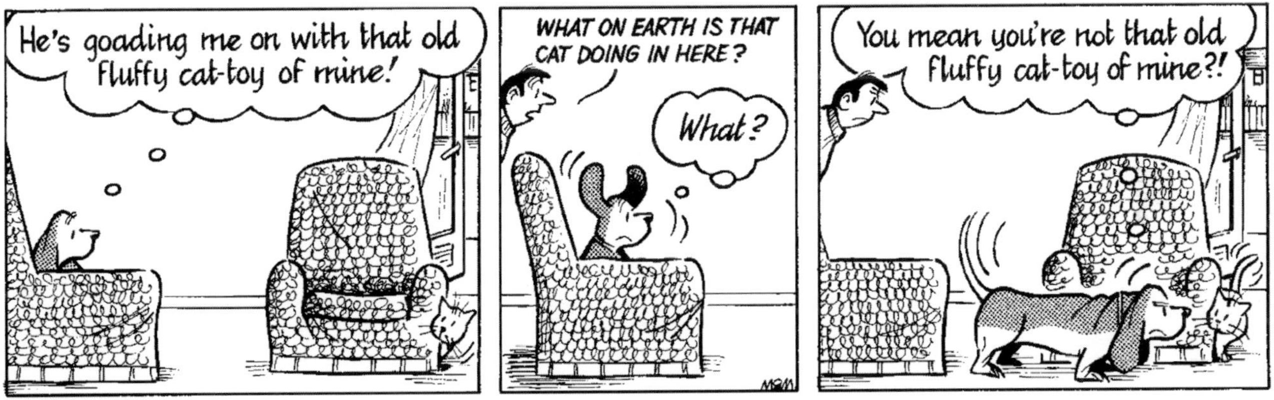
He's goading me on with that old fluffy cat-toy of mine!
WHAT ON EARTH IS THAT CAT DOING IN HERE?
What?
You mean you're not that old fluffy cat-toy of mine?!

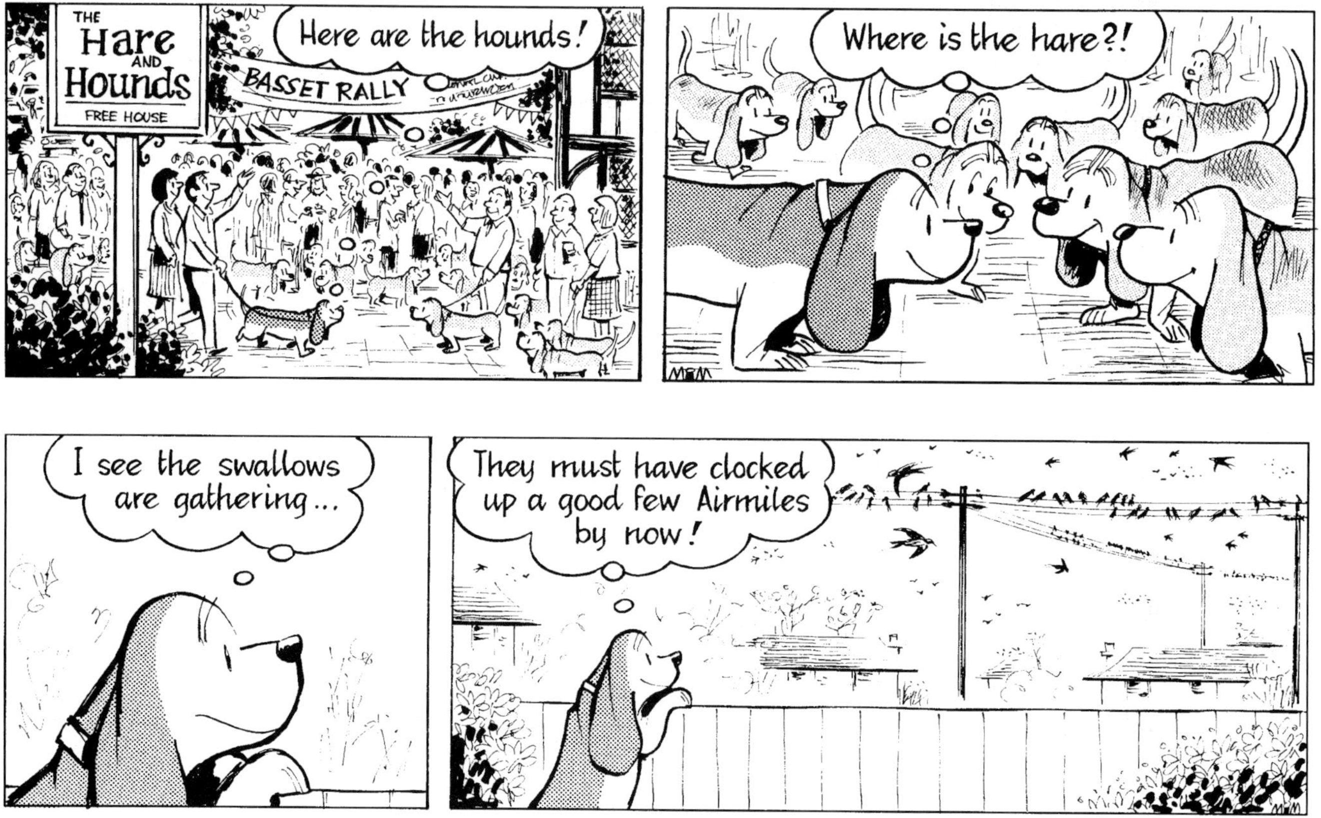
THE Hare AND Hounds
FREE HOUSE
BASSET RALLY
Here are the hounds!
Where is the hare?!
I see the swallows are gathering...
They must have clocked up a good few Airmiles by now!

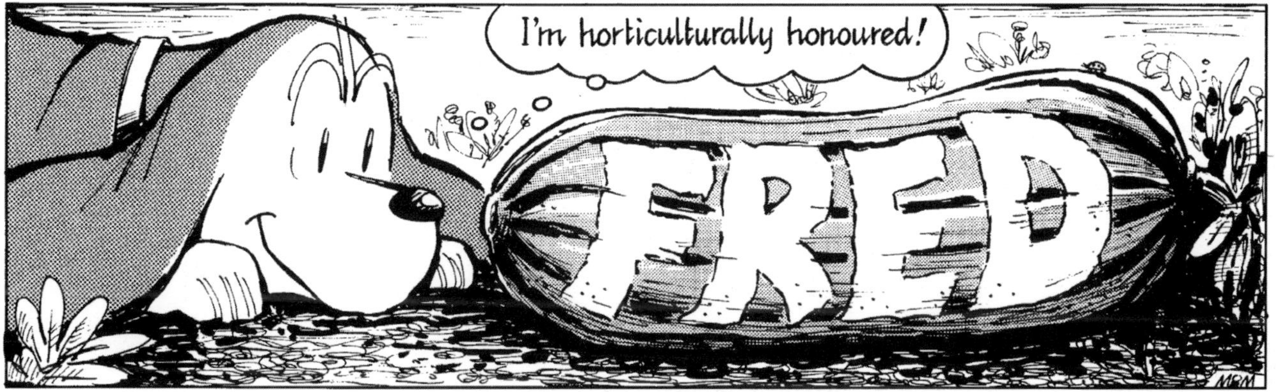
I'm horticulturally honoured!
FRED

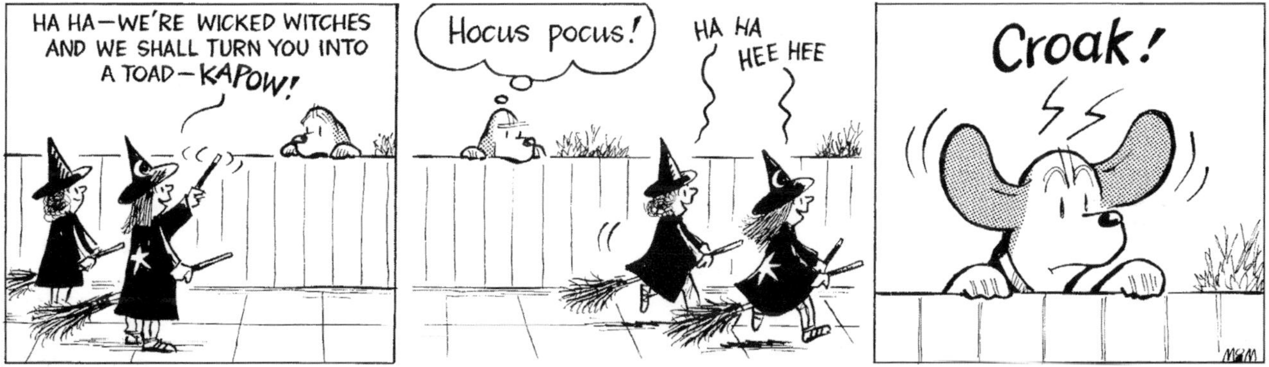
HA HA—WE'RE WICKED WITCHES AND WE SHALL TURN YOU INTO A TOAD—KAPOW!
Hocus pocus!
HA HA
HEE HEE
Croak!

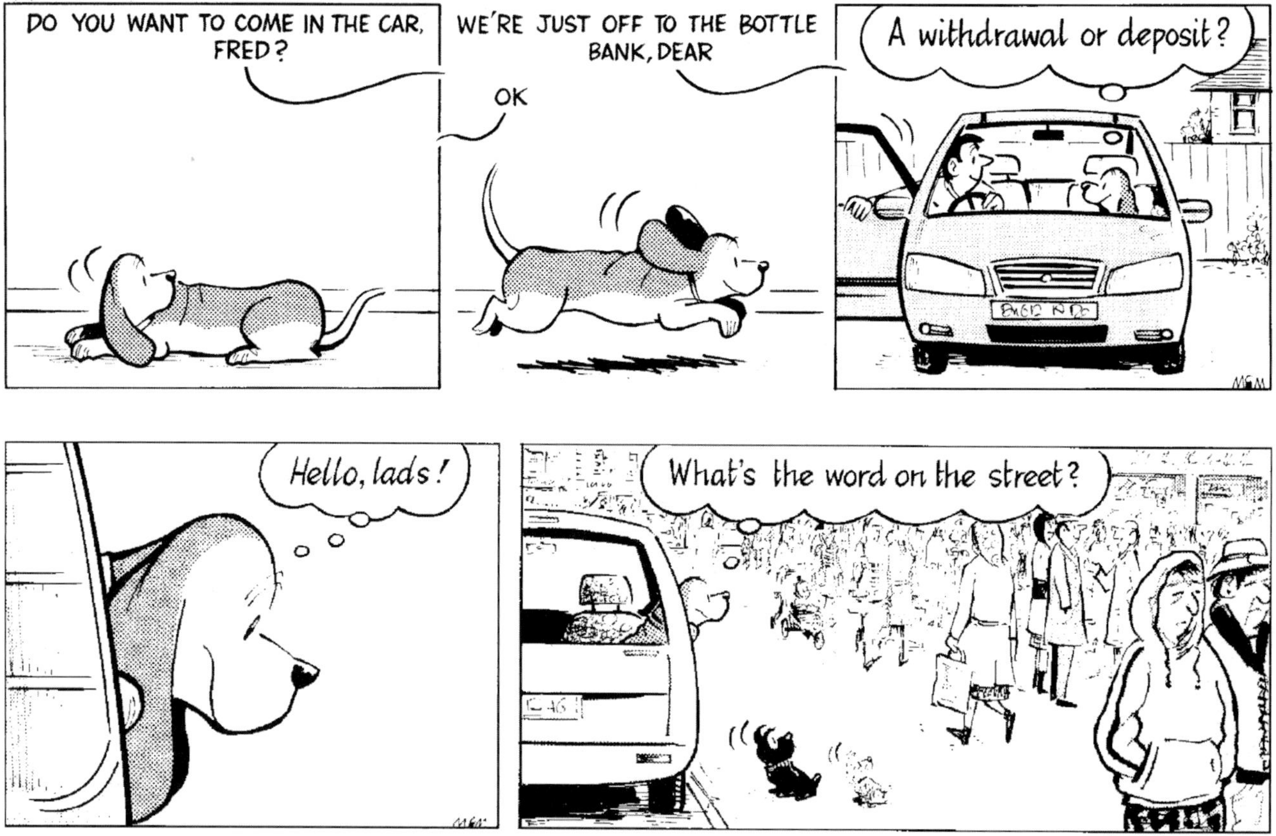
DO YOU WANT TO COME IN THE CAR, FRED?
WE'RE JUST OFF TO THE BOTTLE BANK, DEAR
OK
A withdrawal or deposit?
Hello, lads!
What's the word on the street?

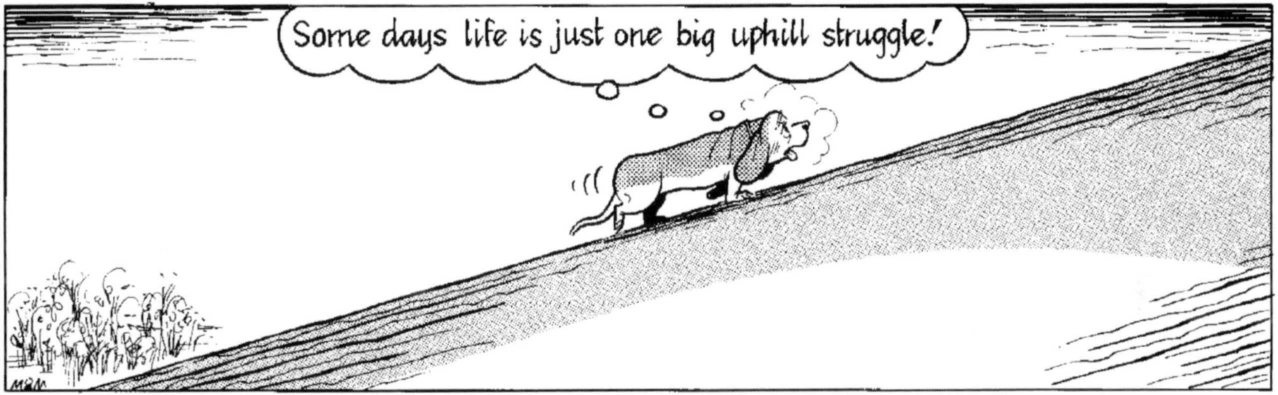
Some days life is just one big uphill struggle!

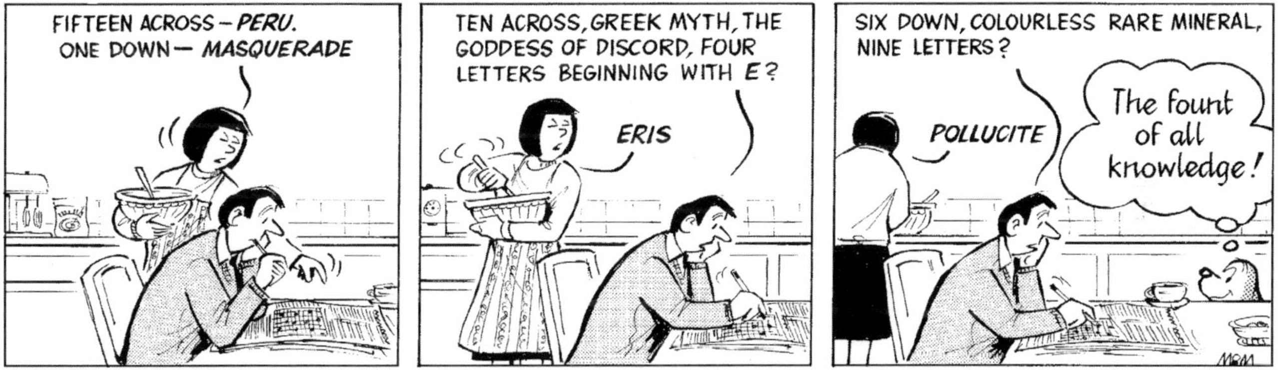
FIFTEEN ACROSS – PERU.
ONE DOWN – MASQUERADE
TEN ACROSS, GREEK MYTH, THE GODDESS OF DISCORD, FOUR LETTERS BEGINNING WITH E?
ERIS
SIX DOWN, COLOURLESS RARE MINERAL, NINE LETTERS?
POLLUCITE
The fount of all knowledge!

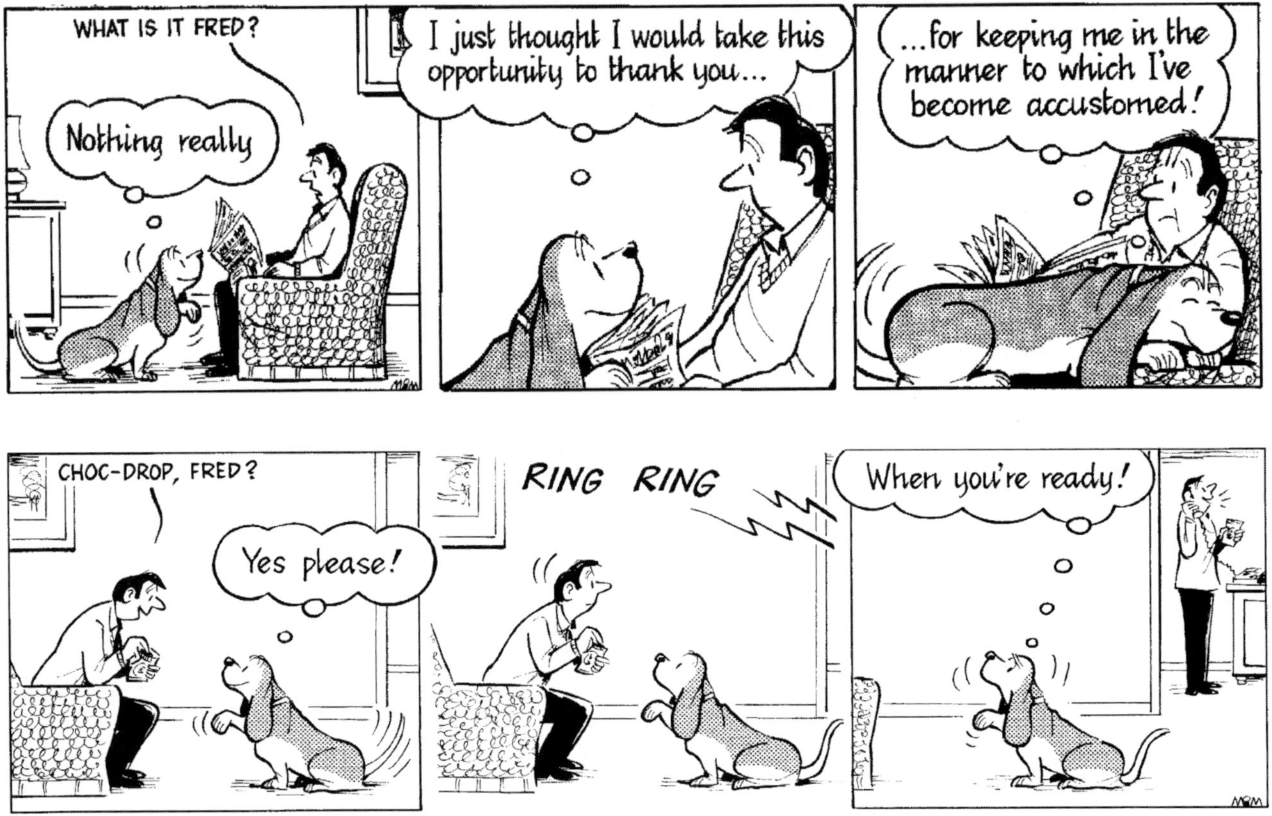
WHAT IS IT FRED?
Nothing really
I just thought I would take this opportunity to thank you...
...for keeping me in the manner to which I've become accustomed!
CHOC-DROP, FRED?
Yes please!
RING RING
When you're ready!

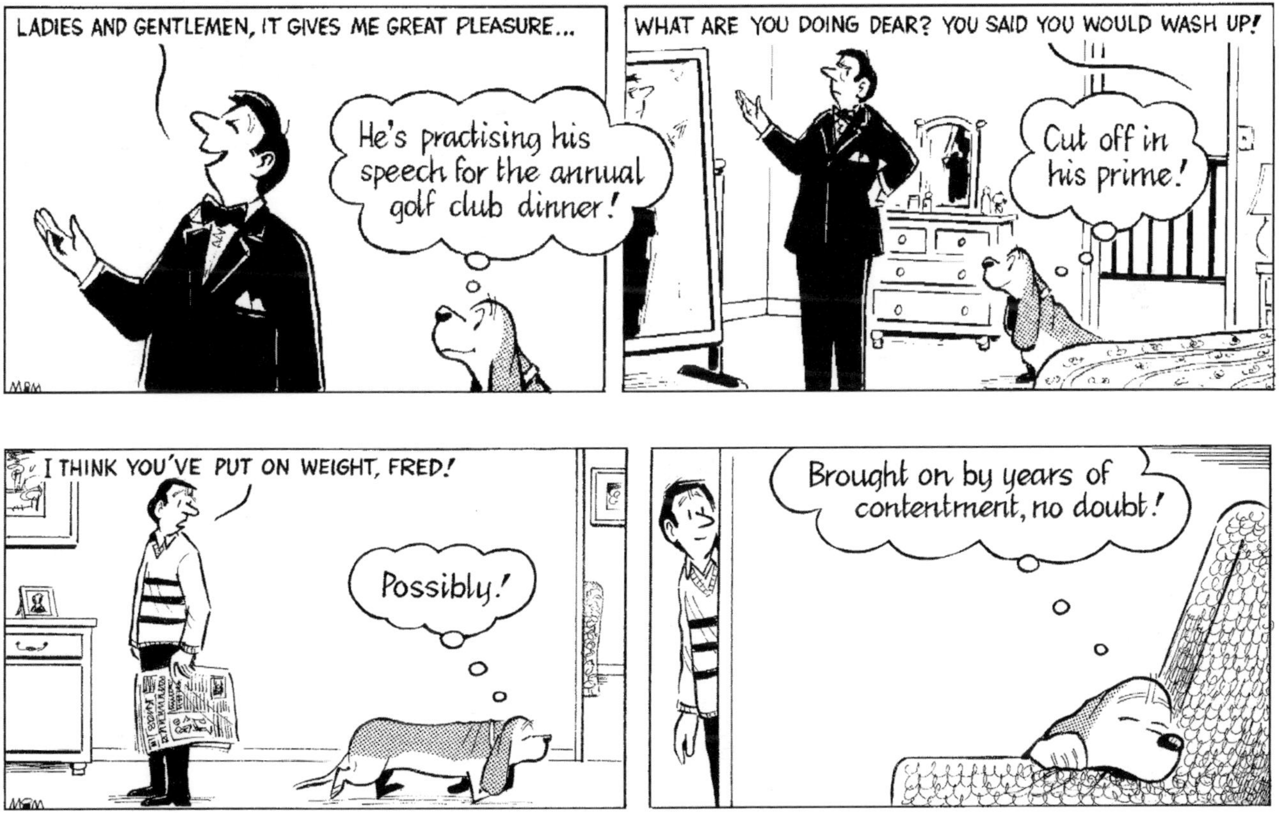
LADIES AND GENTLEMEN, IT GIVES ME GREAT PLEASURE...
He's practising his speech for the annual golf club dinner!
WHAT ARE YOU DOING DEAR? YOU SAID YOU WOULD WASH UP!
Cut off in his prime!
I THINK YOU'VE PUT ON WEIGHT, FRED!
Possibly!
Brought on by years of contentment, no doubt!

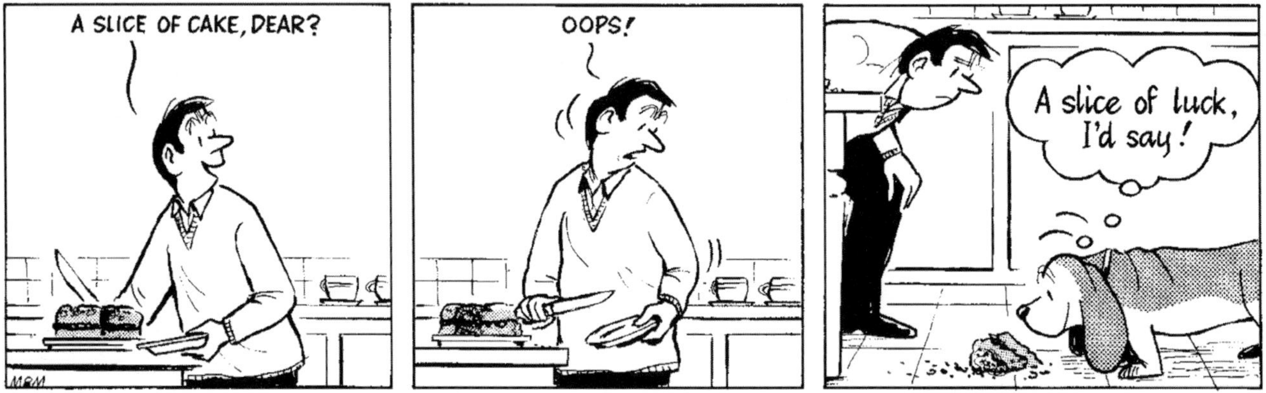
A SLICE OF CAKE, DEAR?
OOPS!
A slice of luck, I'd say!

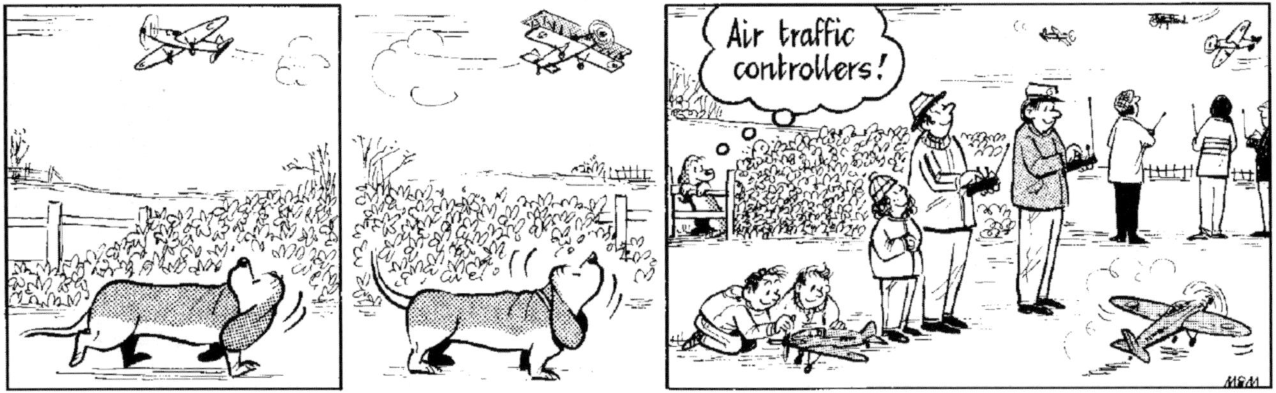
Air traffic controllers!

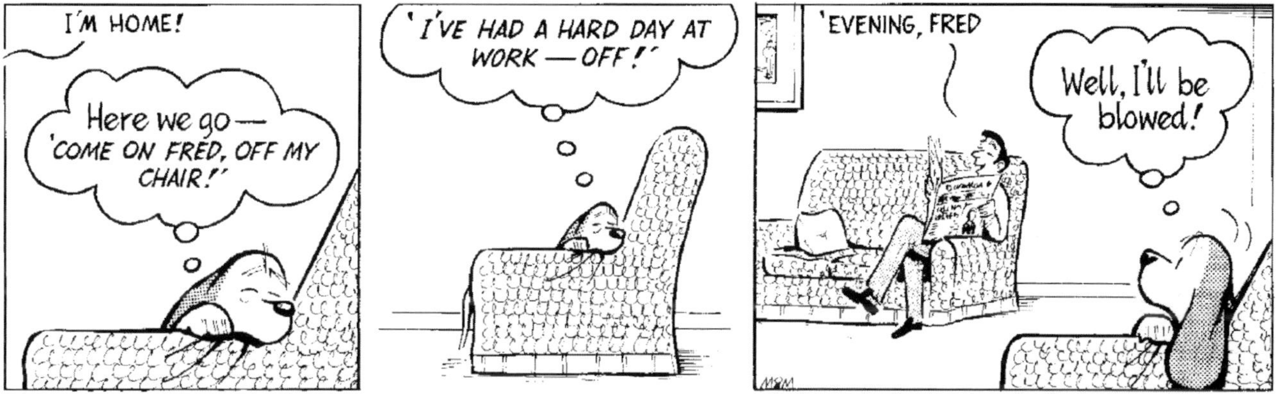
I'M HOME!
Here we go— 'COME ON FRED, OFF MY CHAIR!'
'I'VE HAD A HARD DAY AT WORK — OFF!'
'EVENING, FRED
Well, I'll be blowed!

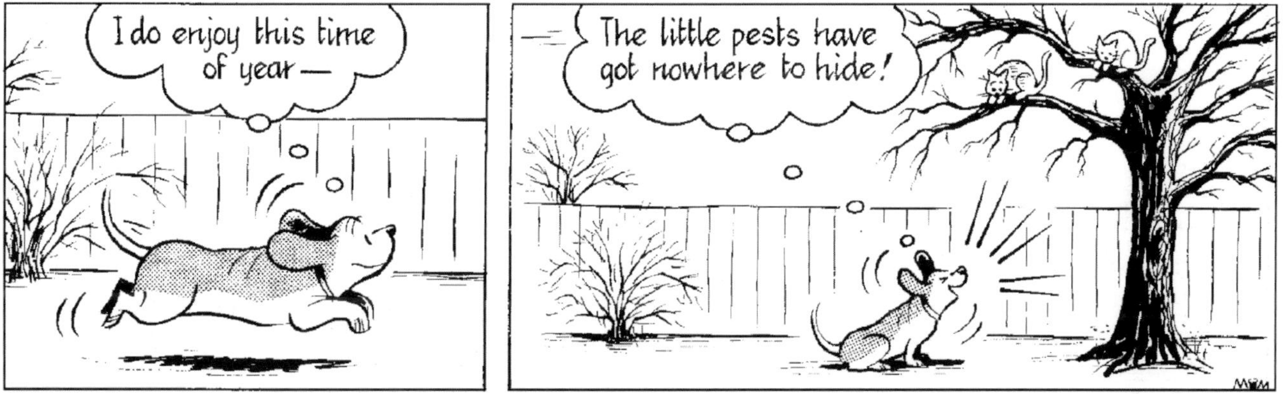
I do enjoy this time of year —
The little pests have got nowhere to hide!

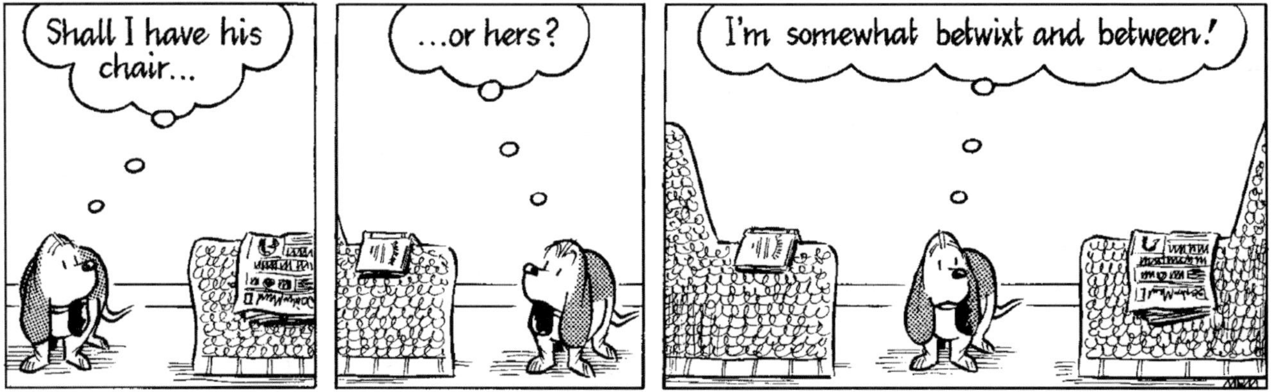
Shall I have his chair...
...or hers?
I'm somewhat betwixt and between!

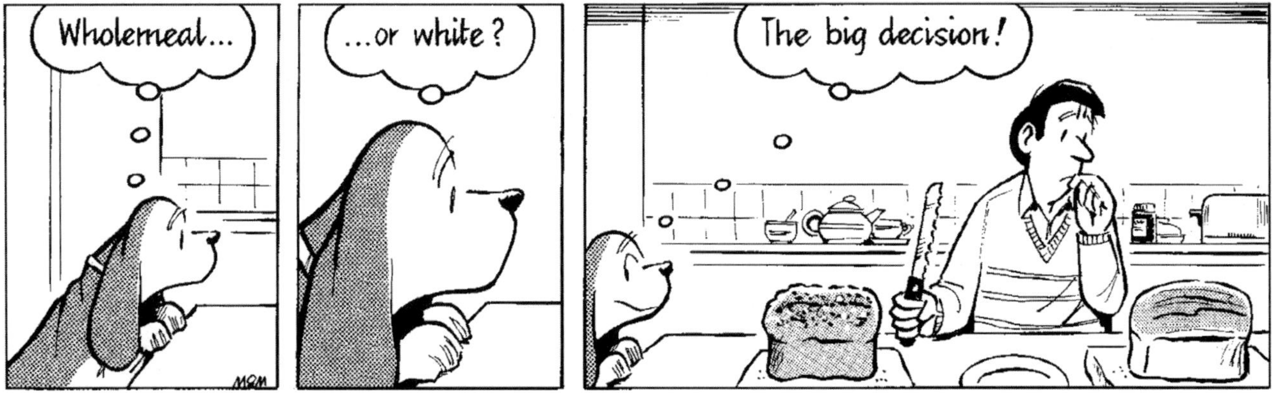
Wholemeal...
...or white?
The big decision!

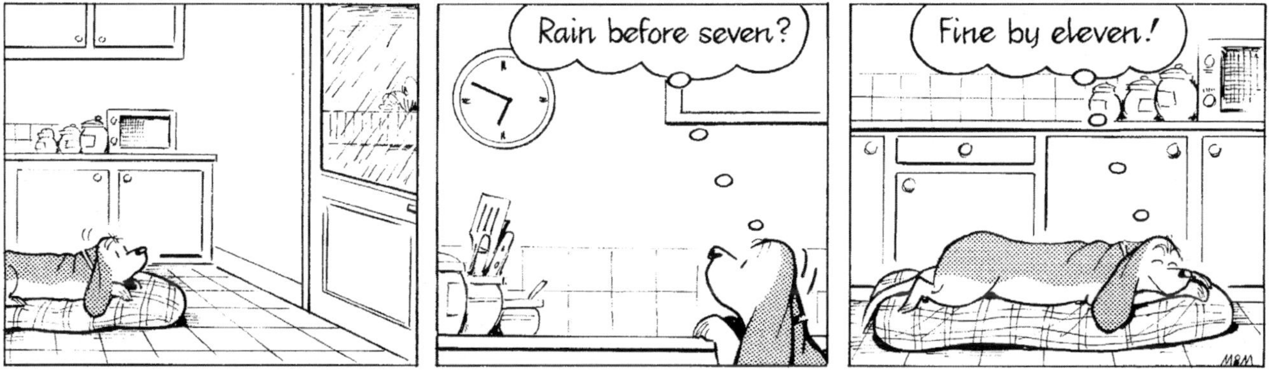
Rain before seven?
Fine by eleven!

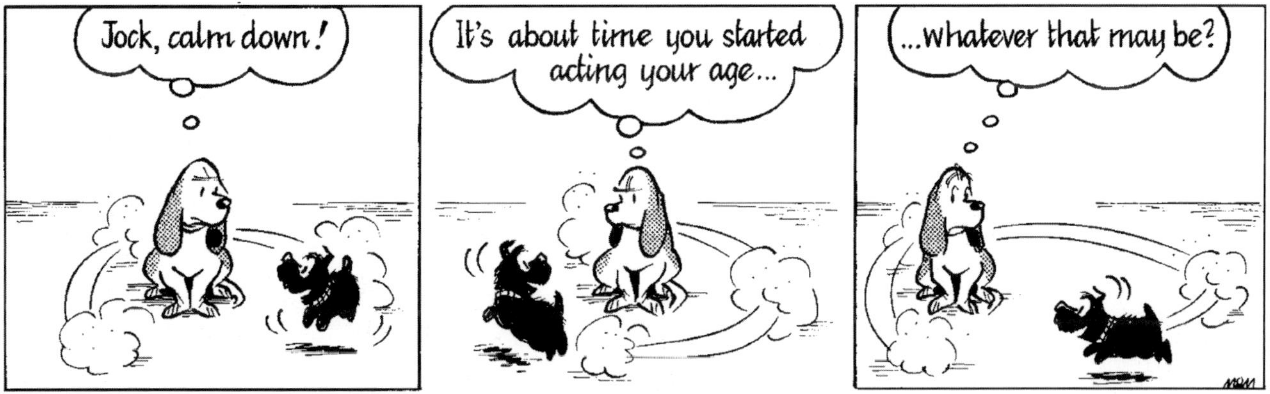
Jock, calm down!
It's about time you started acting your age...
...whatever that may be?

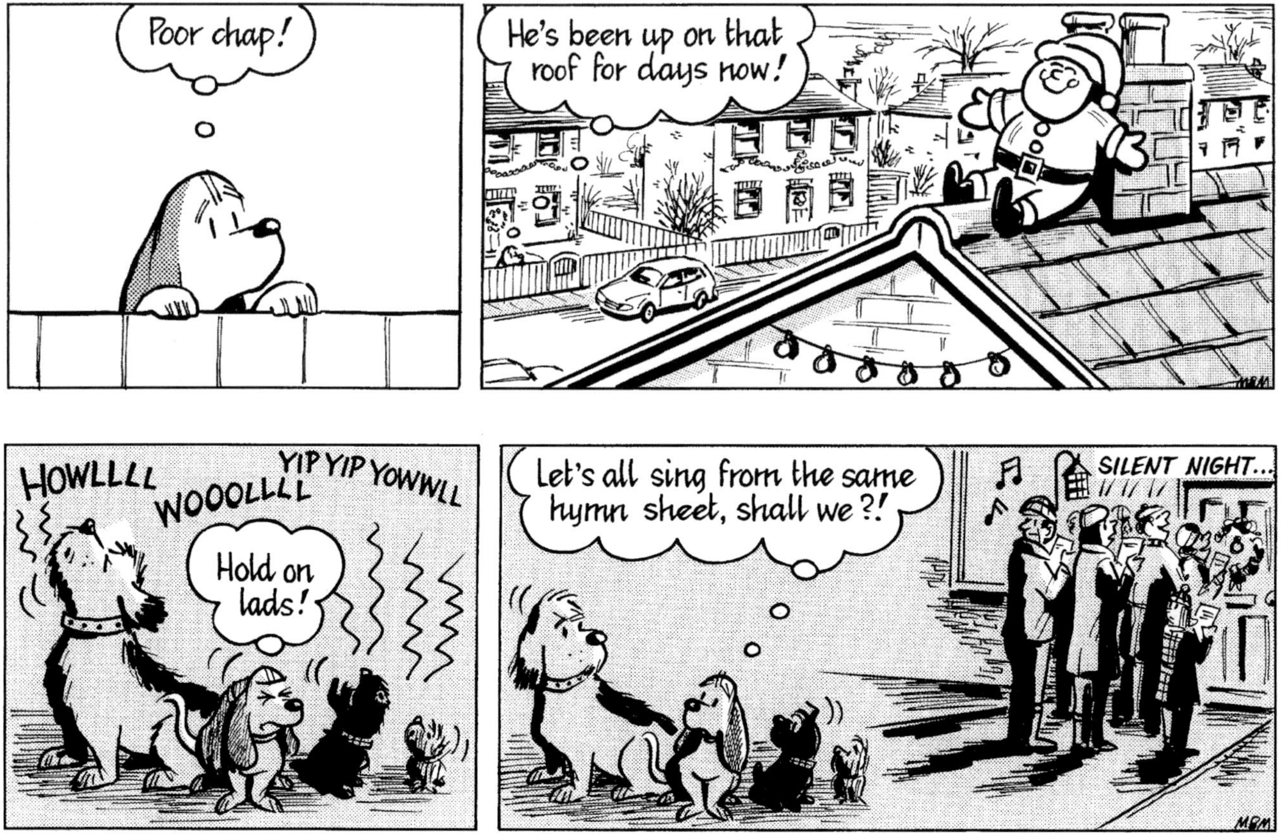
Poor chap!
He's been up on that roof for days now!
MBM
HOWLLLL
WOOOLLLL
YIP YIP YOWWLL
Hold on lads!
Let's all sing from the same hymn sheet, shall we?!
SILENT NIGHT...
MBM

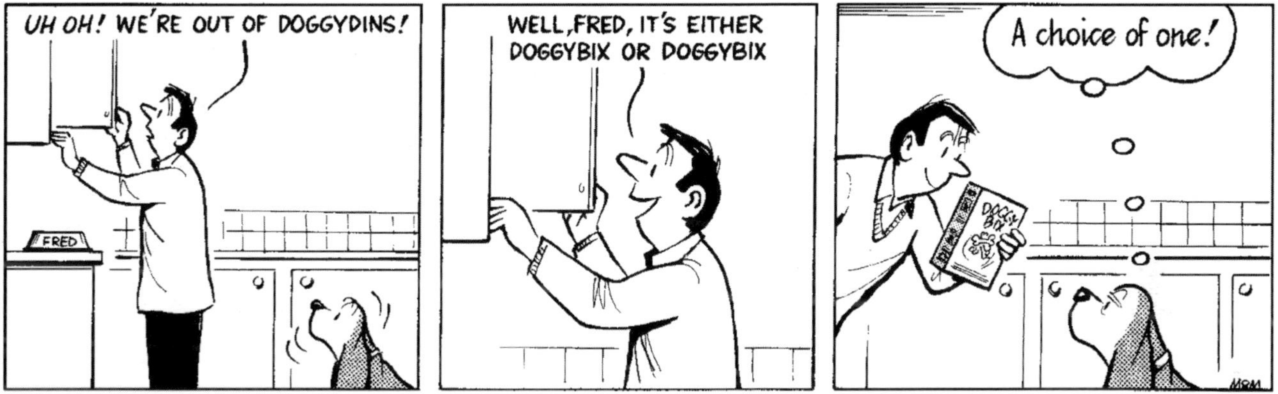
UH OH! WE'RE OUT OF DOGGYDINS!
FRED
WELL, FRED, IT'S EITHER DOGGYBIX OR DOGGYBIX
A choice of one!
DOGGY BIX
M&M

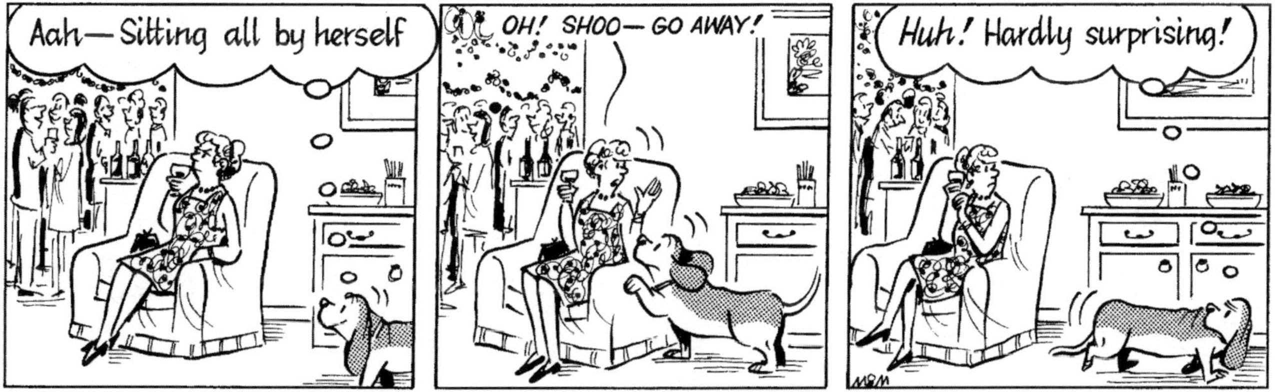
Aah— Sitting all by herself
OH! SHOO— GO AWAY!
Huh! Hardly surprising!
M&M

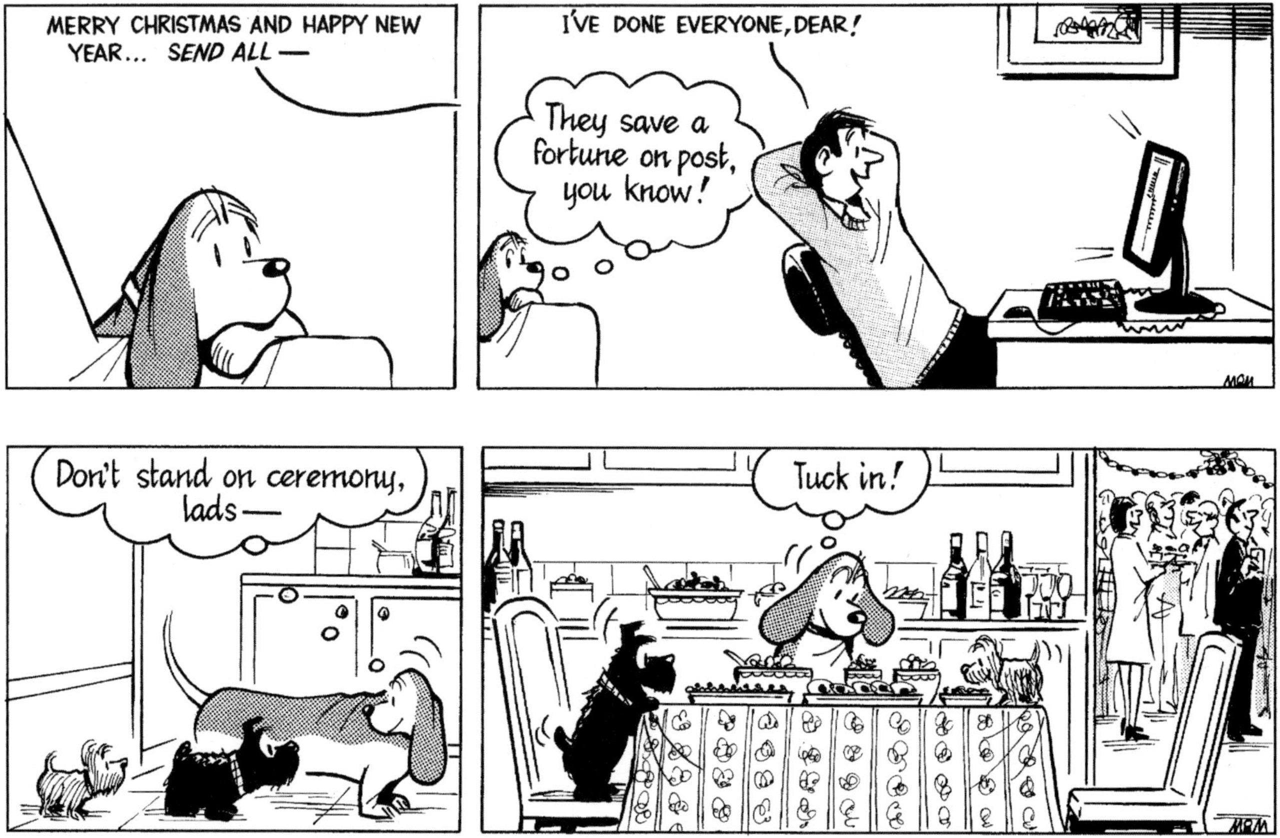
MERRY CHRISTMAS AND HAPPY NEW YEAR... SEND ALL —
I'VE DONE EVERYONE, DEAR!
They save a fortune on post, you know!
Don't stand on ceremony, lads —
Tuck in!

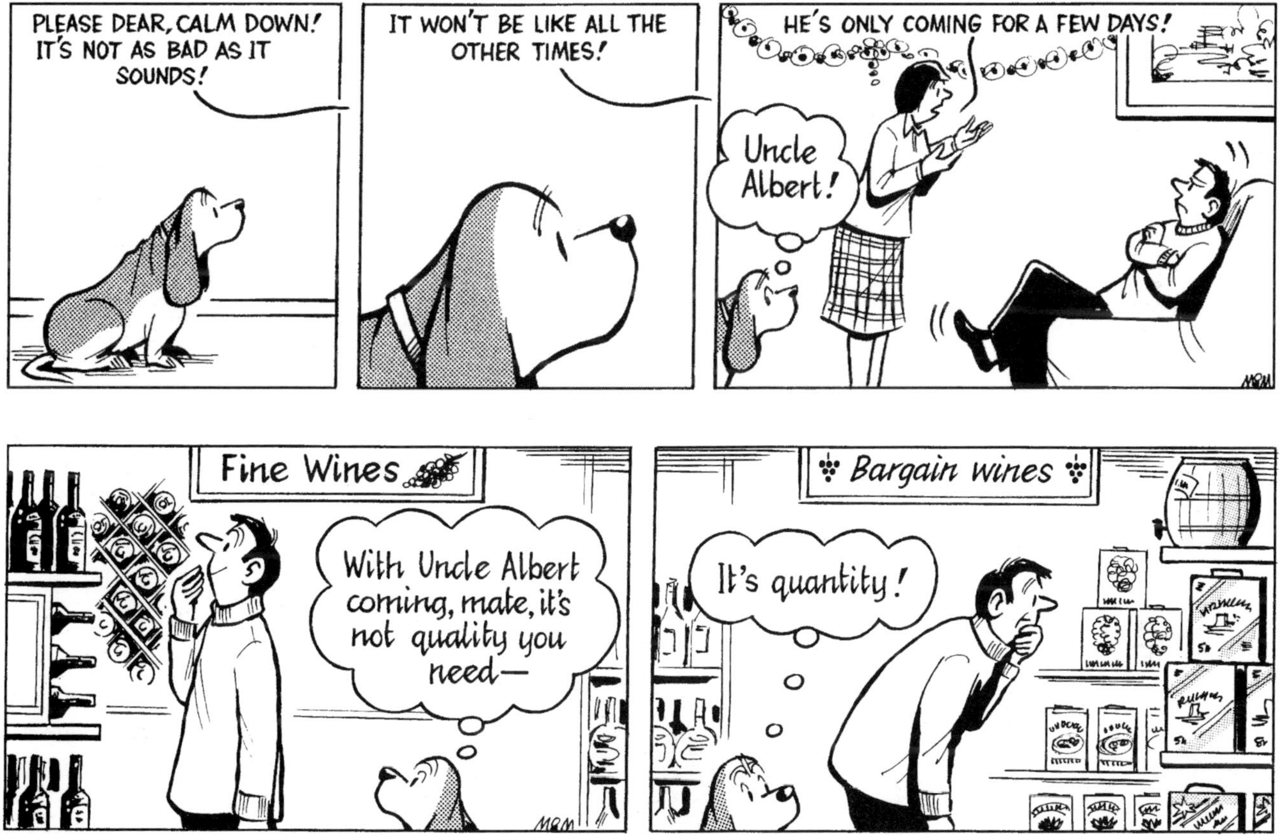
PLEASE DEAR, CALM DOWN! IT'S NOT AS BAD AS IT SOUNDS!
IT WON'T BE LIKE ALL THE OTHER TIMES!
HE'S ONLY COMING FOR A FEW DAYS!
Uncle Albert!
Fine Wines
With Uncle Albert coming, mate, it's not quality you need—
Bargain wines
It's quantity!

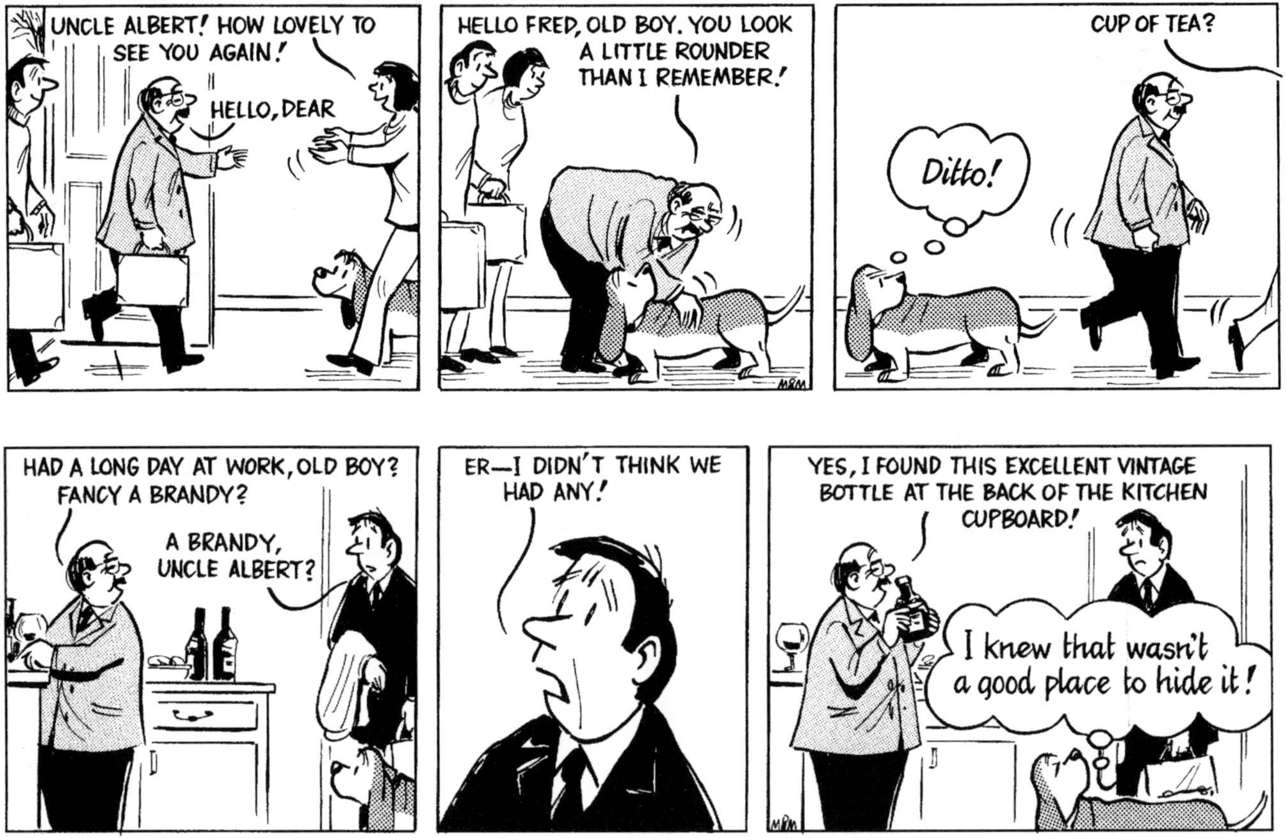
UNCLE ALBERT! HOW LOVELY TO SEE YOU AGAIN!
HELLO, DEAR
HELLO FRED, OLD BOY. YOU LOOK A LITTLE ROUNDER THAN I REMEMBER!
M&M
Ditto!
CUP OF TEA?
HAD A LONG DAY AT WORK, OLD BOY? FANCY A BRANDY?
A BRANDY, UNCLE ALBERT?
ER—I DIDN'T THINK WE HAD ANY!
YES, I FOUND THIS EXCELLENT VINTAGE BOTTLE AT THE BACK OF THE KITCHEN CUPBOARD!
I knew that wasn't a good place to hide it!
M&M

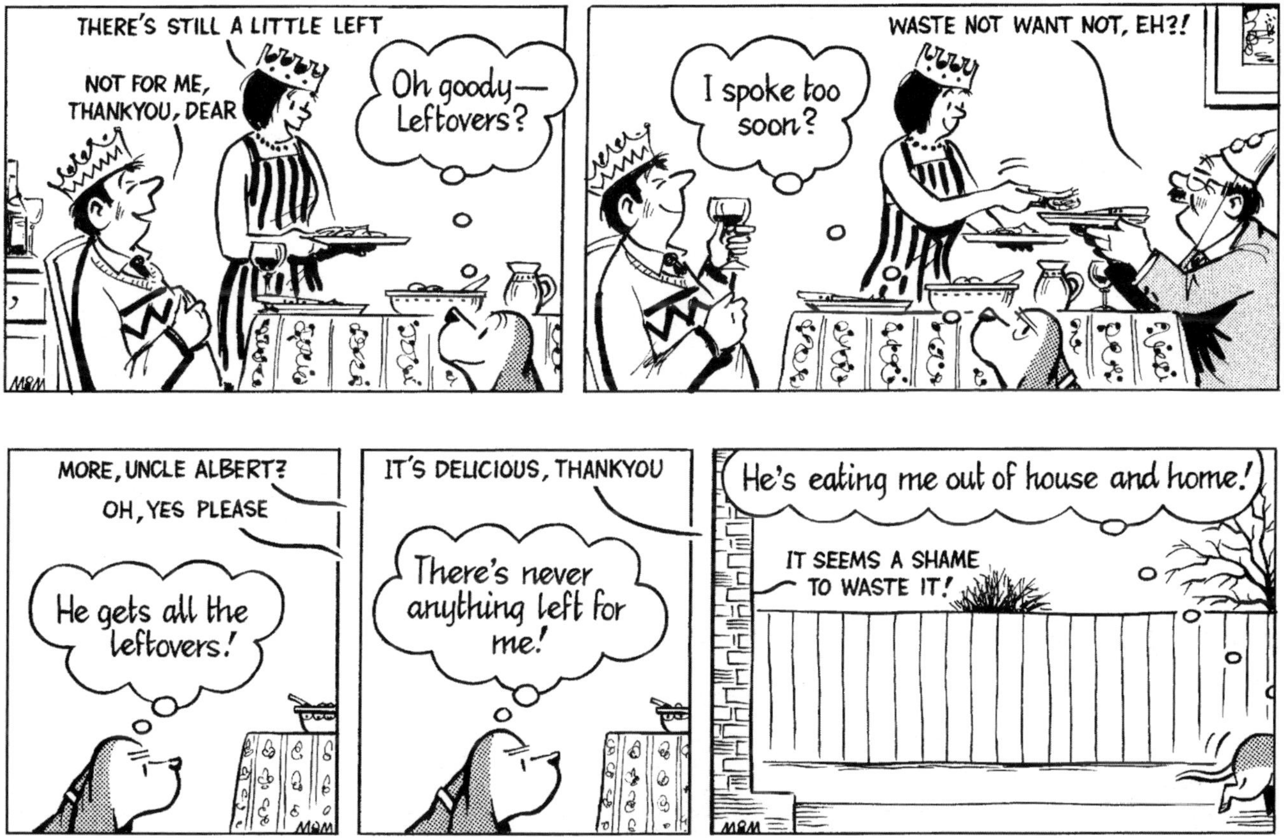
THERE'S STILL A LITTLE LEFT
NOT FOR ME, THANKYOU, DEAR
Oh goody— Leftovers?
WASTE NOT WANT NOT, EH?!
I spoke too soon?
MORE, UNCLE ALBERT?
OH, YES PLEASE
He gets all the leftovers!
IT'S DELICIOUS, THANKYOU
There's never anything left for me!
He's eating me out of house and home!
IT SEEMS A SHAME TO WASTE IT!
M&M

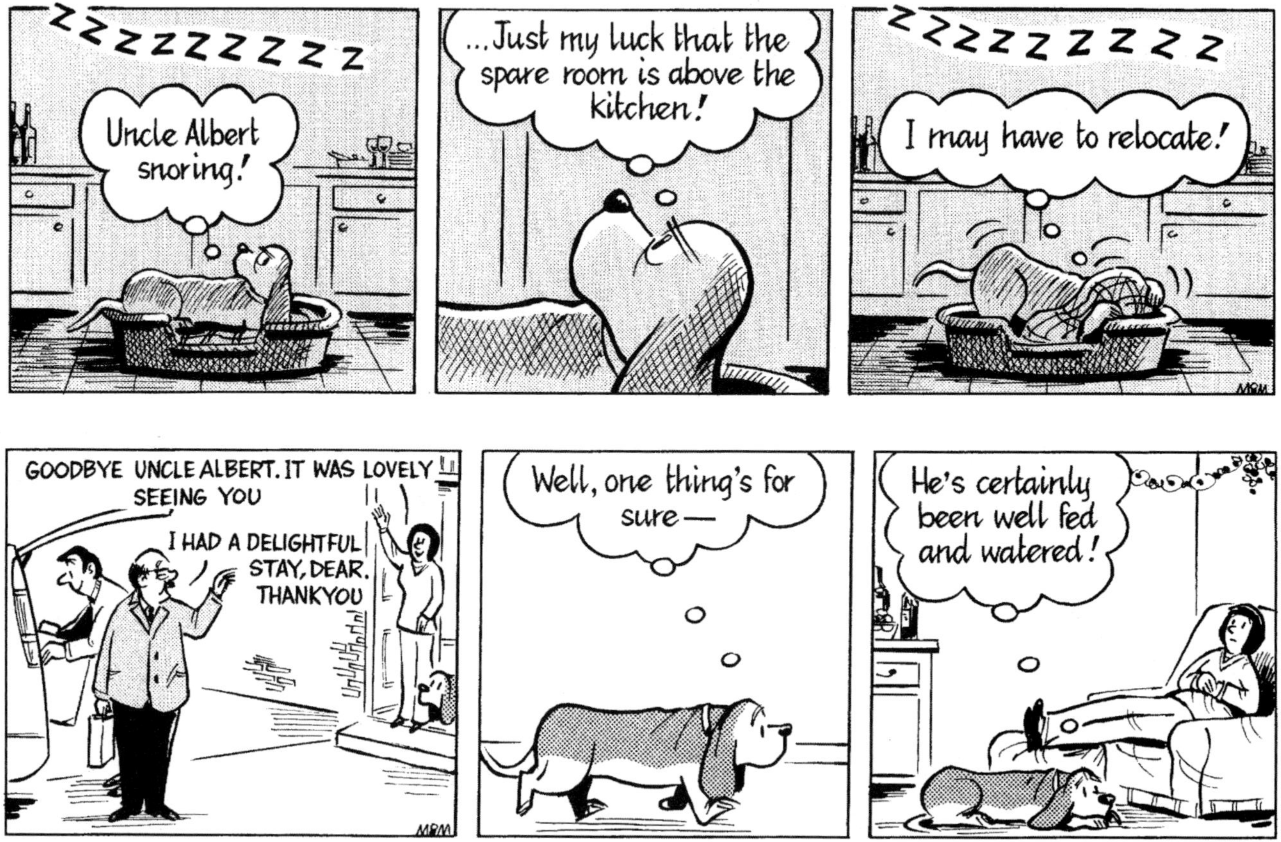
ZZZZZZZZZZZ
Uncle Albert snoring!
...Just my luck that the spare room is above the kitchen!
ZZZZZZZZZZ
I may have to relocate!
MGM
GOODBYE UNCLE ALBERT. IT WAS LOVELY SEEING YOU
I HAD A DELIGHTFUL STAY, DEAR. THANKYOU
MGM
Well, one thing's for sure —
He's certainly been well fed and watered!

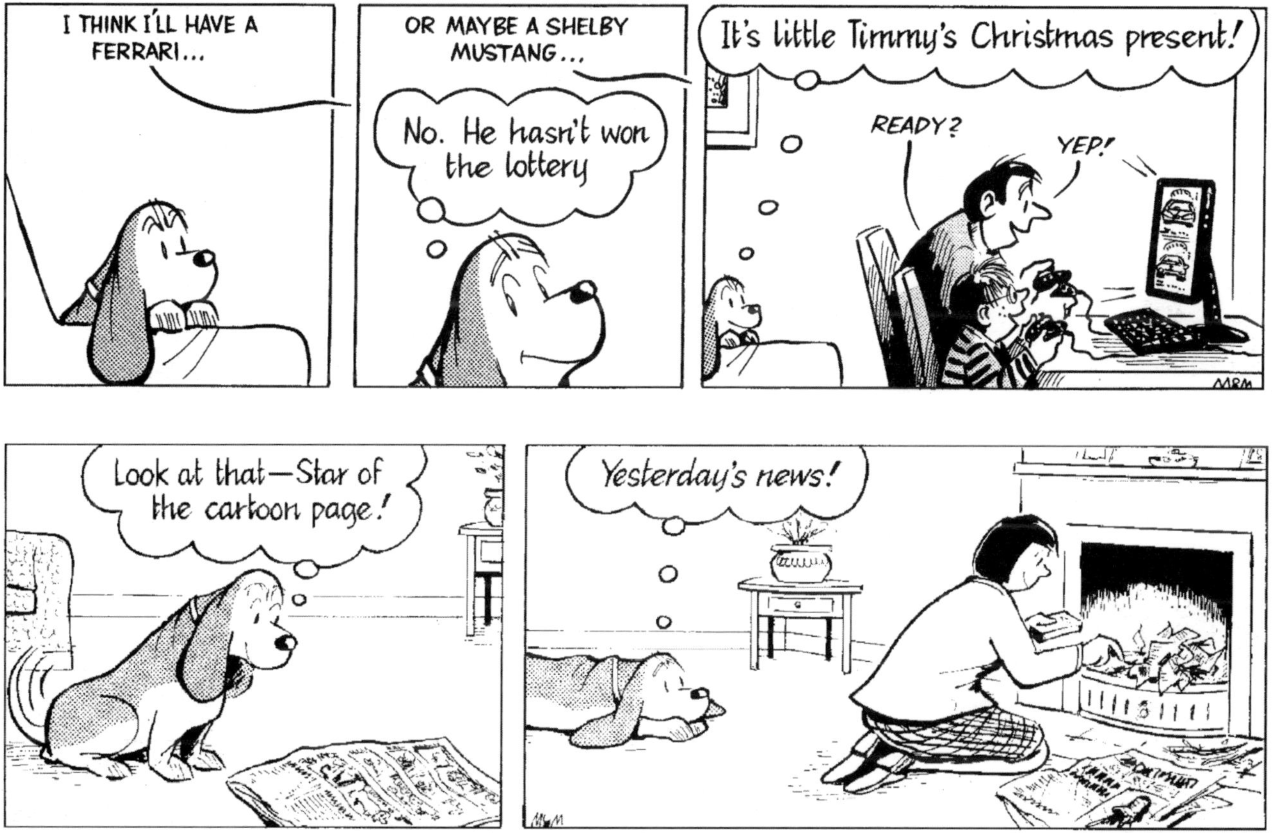
I THINK I'LL HAVE A FERRARI...
OR MAYBE A SHELBY MUSTANG...
No. He hasn't won the lottery
It's little Timmy's Christmas present!
READY?
YEP!
Look at that—Star of the cartoon page!
Yesterday's news!

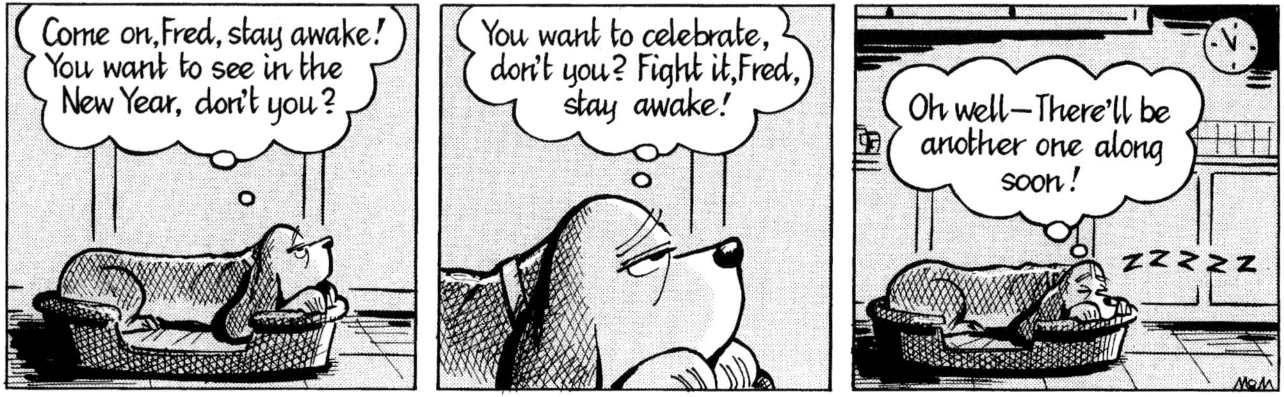
Come on, Fred, stay awake! You want to see in the New Year, don't you?
You want to celebrate, don't you? Fight it, Fred, stay awake!
Oh well—There'll be another one along soon!
ZZZZZ

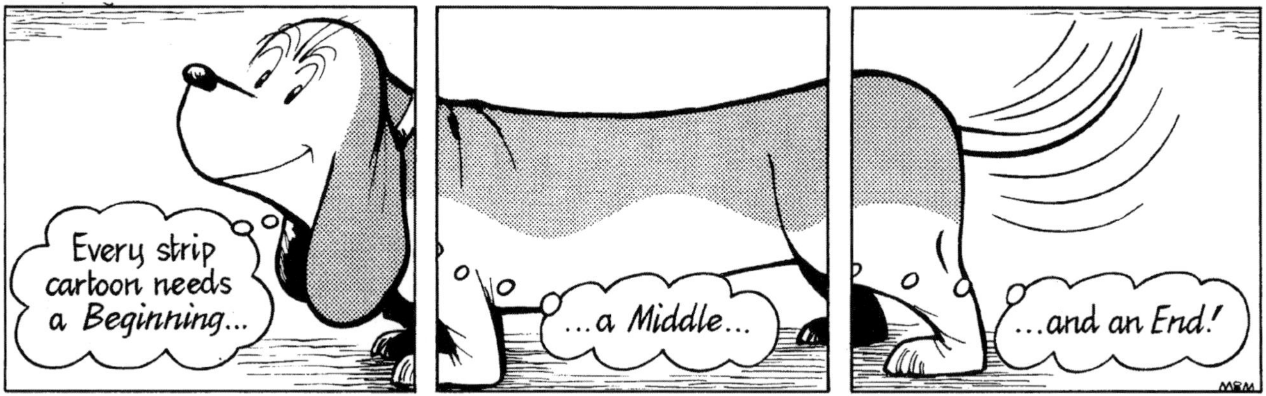
Every strip cartoon needs a *Beginning*...
...a *Middle*...
...and an *End*!